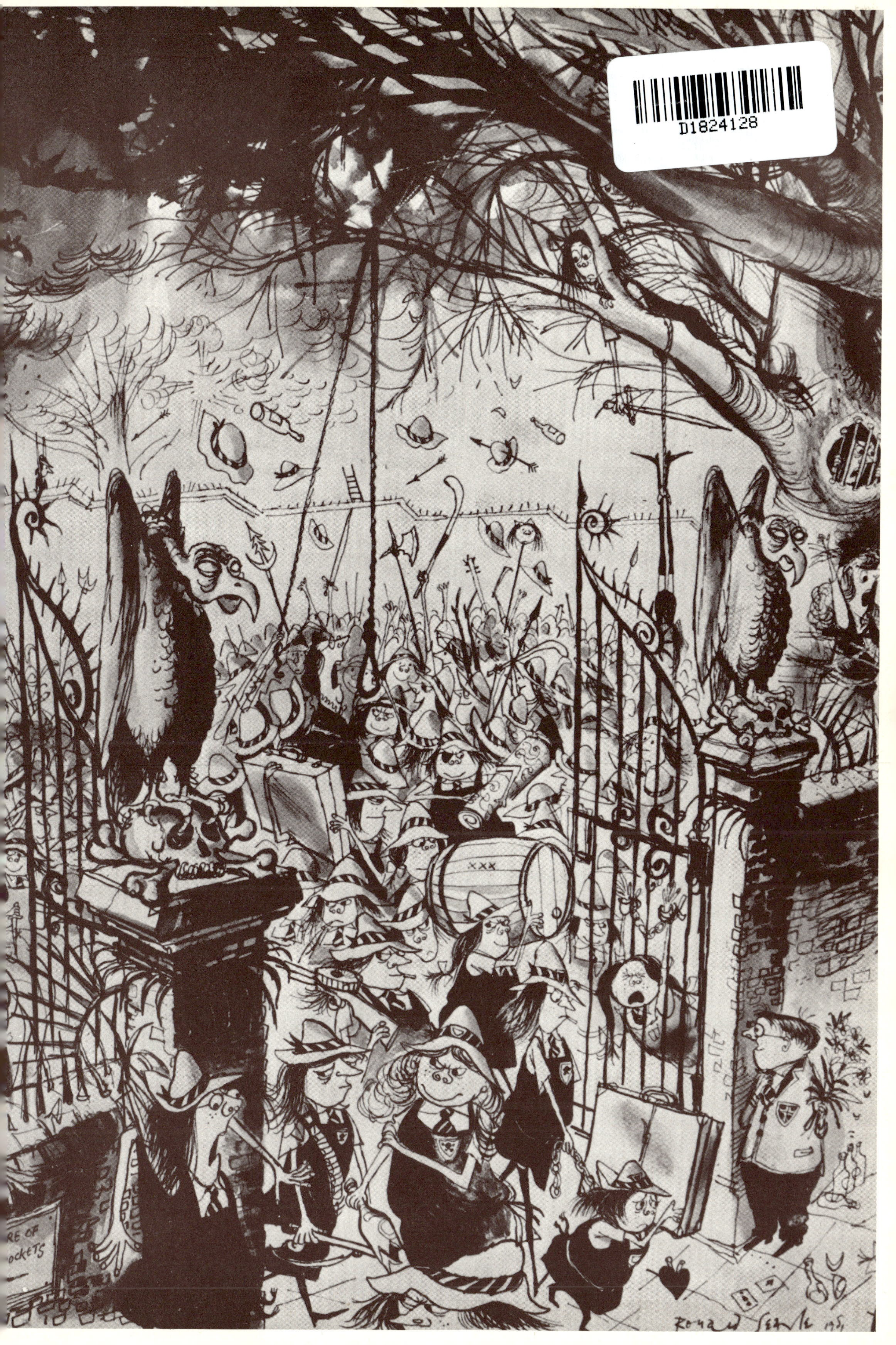
XXX

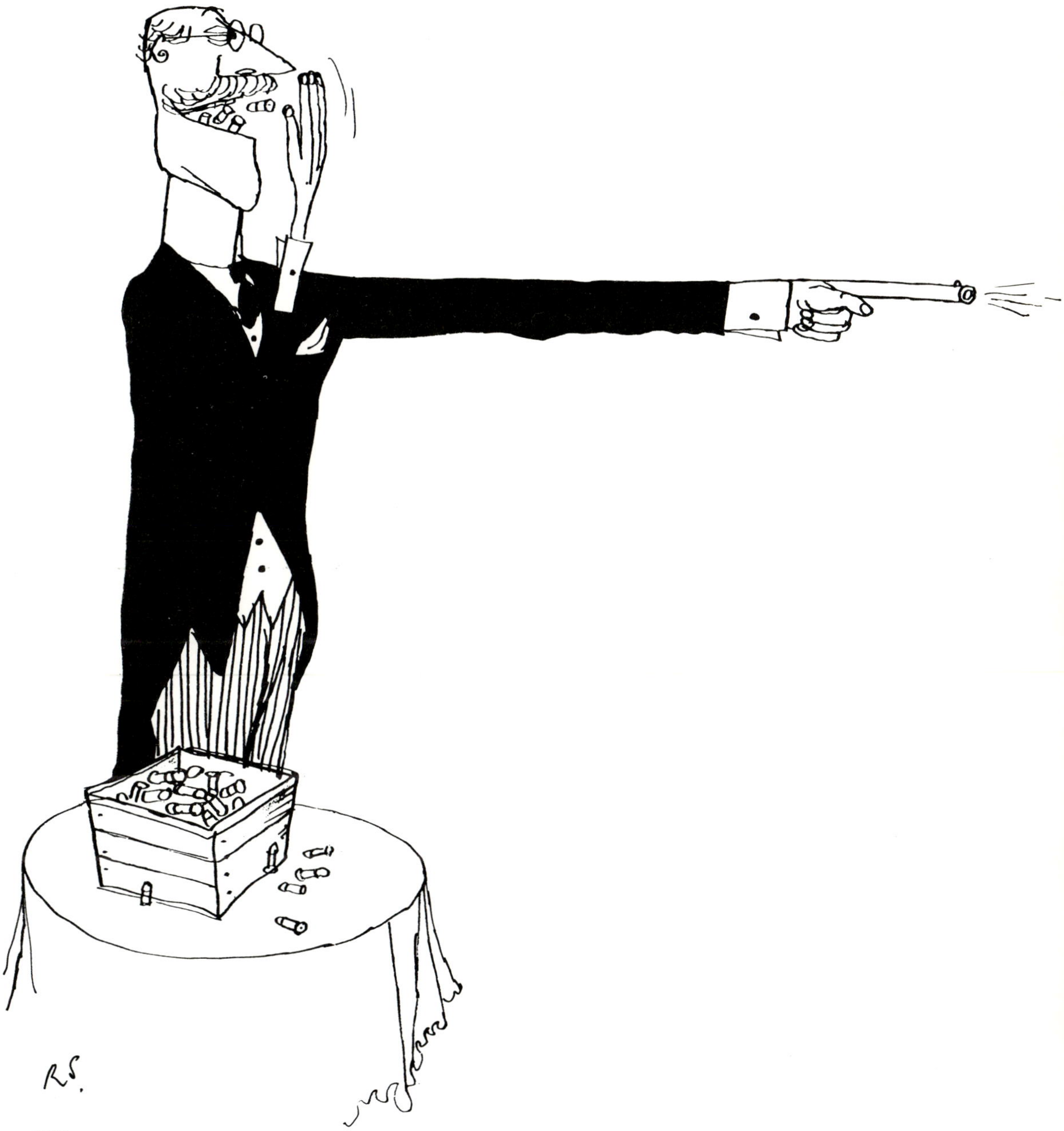
R.S.

[1952]

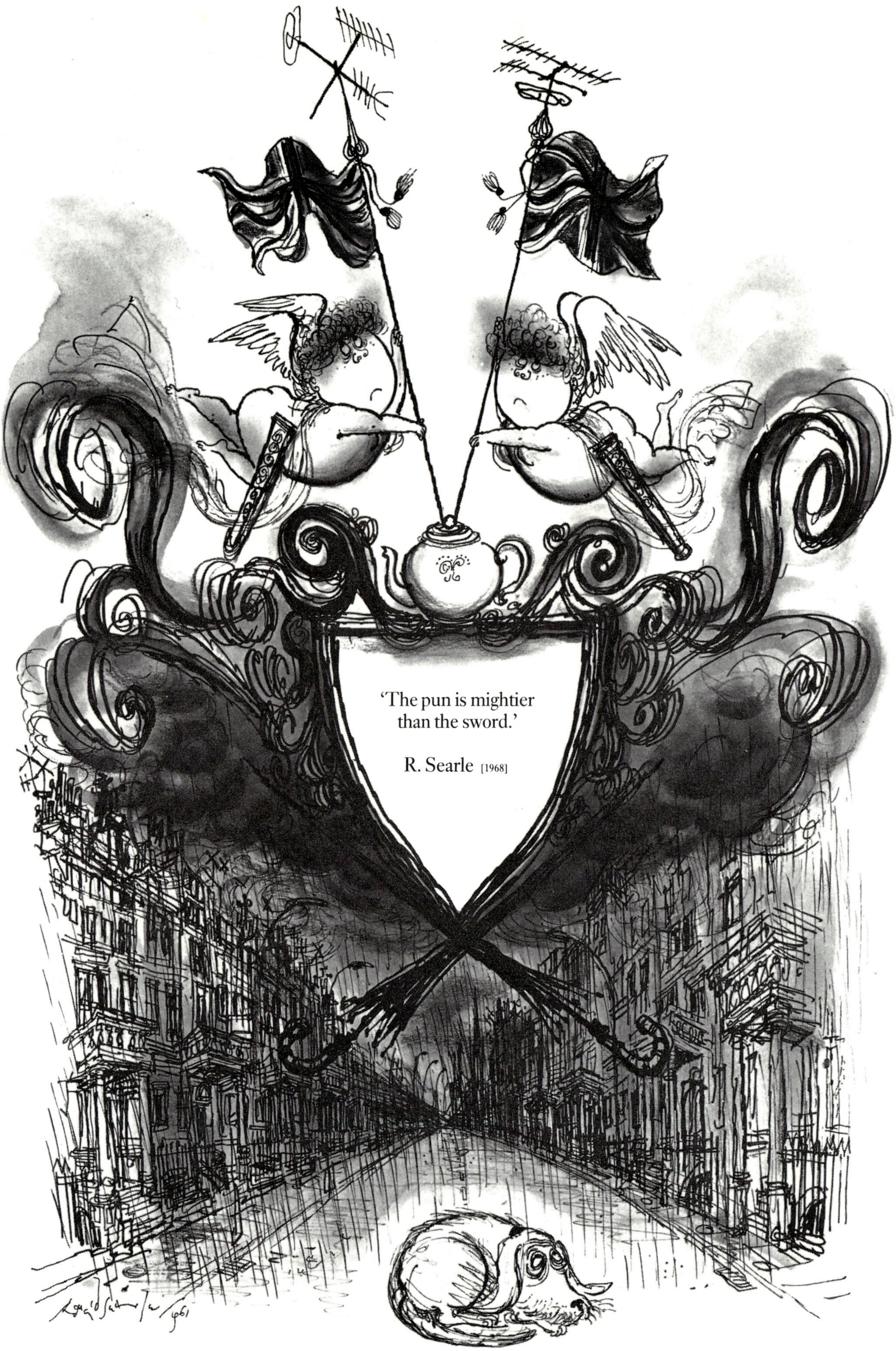
'The pun is mightier
than the sword.'
R. Searle [1968]

RONALD SEARLE'S

GOLDEN OLDIES

1941–1961

PAVILION
MICHAEL JOSEPH

This anthology has been selected from drawings
originally published under the following titles:

Hurrah for St Trinian's!, London 1948
The Female Approach, London 1949
Back to the Slaughterhouse, London 1951
The Terror of St Trinian's, London 1952
Souls in Torment, London 1953.
The Female Approach, New York 1954
Merry England, etc., London 1956
The St Trinian's Story, London 1959
Which Way Did He Go? London 1961
and *Pardong m'sieur*, Paris 1965

This selection
first published in Great Britain in 1985
by Pavilion Books Limited
196 Shaftesbury Avenue, London WC2H 8JL
in association with Michael Joseph Limited
44 Bedford Square, London WC1B 3DU

British Library Cataloguing in Publication Data

Searle, Ronald
    Ronald Searle's golden oldies: 1941-1961.
    I. Title
    741.5'942   PN6737.S4

ISBN 1-85145-102-1

Printed in Great Britain by
Butler & Tanner Ltd, Frome and London

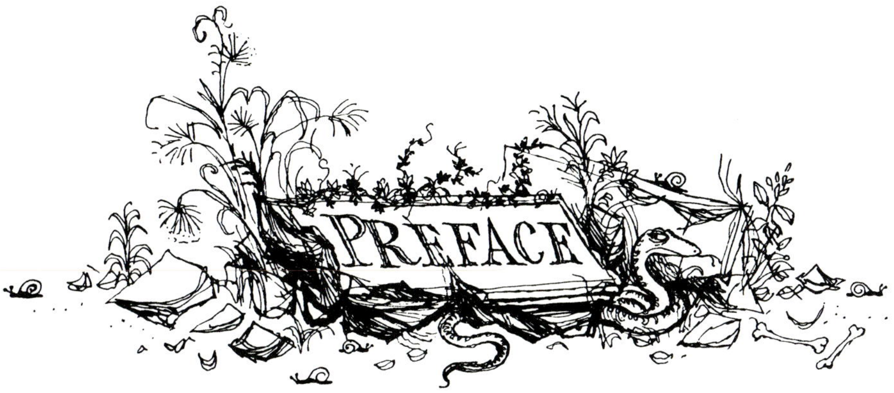
PREFACE

ALTHOUGH I had been trained from an early age to draw in the laudably (some would say laughably) solemn tradition of Ingres and Tonks so as to be capable, at the worst, of illustrating *Gray's Anatomy* with one hand tied behind my back, the moment came when the academic flesh weakened and the eye began to glue itself on passing venison. Finally it was no struggle to succumb to producing comic drawings and from the age of fifteen or so, I was being published at least once a week. At art school in Cambridge this was considered interesting, but only marginally short of prostitution and, later, in the 'fifties, when I went so far as to accept briefly the fetters of regular employment, from the *Tribune*, *Sunday Express* and the tottering *News Chronicle*, my already shady reputation was irrevocably smirched in the tighter-lipped circles of the Cambridge Drawing Society.

This does not lead me directly to St. Trinian's which occupies the second half of this album, but it will do.

The first isolated St. Trinian's cartoon was published by *Lilliput* in October 1941 when I was twenty-one, the series actually got going with drawing number two, published by the same pocket magazine in April 1946. Six years later I contributed the last St. Trinian's joke ('Bloody sportsdays!') to its pages and conveniently announced the demise of the school when my book, *Souls in Torment*, was published and needed something to attract the attention of the media. Although this thin slice of gory folklore lasted barely seven years, it seemed interminable to me. Only those colleagues who have experienced several years of wringing the nuances out of one single idea, will appreciate the burden of trying to appease the insatiable public appetite for repetition of the familiar.

In the 'forties and 'fifties most graphic humour was still dragging its feet through the dregs of Victorian and between-wars banality and, if one hoped to ensnare popular favour (e.g. earning enough to get by as a freelance and hopefully selling a few extra albums at Christmas), it did not pay to flutter about in an unidentifiable manner. Instant recognition was necessary, everything in its place – and no surprises, please! There was a need to be comforted and comfortable. Hence the cartoon world of that time, with its eccentric trains, talking doggies, titillating t&b, comical ponies, sexless children, exploding colonels, its 'Molesworths' and its 'Moles'.

When I joined this motley throng through having plucked the magical (until then relatively unheard) chord of black humour, my juvenile originality was accepted by editors and public alike only because, however outrageously sick or gruesome, it was always safely and cozily British. None of your Transylvanian rubbish, but good, heroic stuff carried back by one of our boys from a Jap prison camp, bless him.

Eventually heroism reached its limits and St. Trinian's had to go when the search for yet another variation on an over-familar theme began to keep me awake at night. Only those preferring punishment to crime would choose to suffer thus day by day, or week by week, in order to amuse.

I am no longer around to savour the workings of this exotic scene, but news has filtered to me down here in France, of cases where Her Majesty has been so upset by the sight of elderly cartoonists being forced to repeat the same tragic gestures in a cruelly confined space for a quarter of a century or more, that she has ennobled them. I bow to no man in my admiration for our Royal Family. But I do feel that under the circumstances even ennoblement may not be enough. Perhaps something unique, like the rare papal blessing normally reserved for examples of extreme mortification of the flesh in the bars of outer Cork, could possibly be a small compensation for such appalling suffering merely in order to keep the populace cheerful.

I also gather from *France Dimanche* that there exist horrifying cases which are beyond help from even the royal touch or a papal blessing. It is perhaps not generally known that the hypnotic effect of black on white, combined with daily Indian Ink sniffing, can lead the unwary artist not only to total addiction, but also to a state of folly almost too sickening to describe as he becomes irrevocably confused with Leonardo, D. Hockney, or some equally godlike figure. There is little to be done, beyond wringing the hands in a tragic manner and trying to persuade the tainted one to accept confinement in a clinic attractively camouflaged as a glossy Noah's Ark, in which he can pass his final days exchanging pleasantries with witty beautiful people, until that day when he is put ashore on the farthest bank of the bourne from which no traveller returns – or whatever it is.

Nevertheless, even in the face of such risk the show must go on, for the cartoonist, however infected, inflated, or addicted, remains perfectly aware that he or she is nothing more than this week's stand-up comic battling as always for attention, just reward, a better place on the playbill, full copyright, and the hearts of a public who have paid to be diverted in the old music-hall tradition in which comic drawing was born.

Of course there are the clever ones who manage to do it only on Sunday. There are others who modestly and steadily plod on, to suffer the whips and the chip-wrapping. There are some, like me, who mingle it with illustration and call it satirical drawing for, like eccentricity, the British cartoon formula comes in many attractive flavours.

But to get to the reason for this foreword. Without trying to be all that meaningful I would say that close study of the following pages reveal what can happen to an innocent boy between the ages of twenty-one and thirty-one when he is encouraged to do it in print. What is here has been carefully skimmed from a dozen long out-of-print albums, that enjoyed considerable popular success in the 'forties and 'fifties. Now they are archive material.

And yet…the shock of recognition…can these wrinkled oldies be those I once loved? But, of course! Those hysterical visual acrobatics, the witty anachromisms and the delicate literary nuances, the talking dogs, a desert island scene…

Obviously there are bound to be insensitive ones for who such graphic originality is mere dross. This collection, then, is not for them. Preferring to place my faith in those multitudes who still remain addicted to the sparkling cliché and the polished pun, I reach for my daily half-bottle of champagne *blanc de blanc perlant* and toast them for their discrimination in acquiring a treasury of Golden Oldies that will, hopefully, keep me in socialist bubbly next year as well.

Ronald Searle

March 1985

6

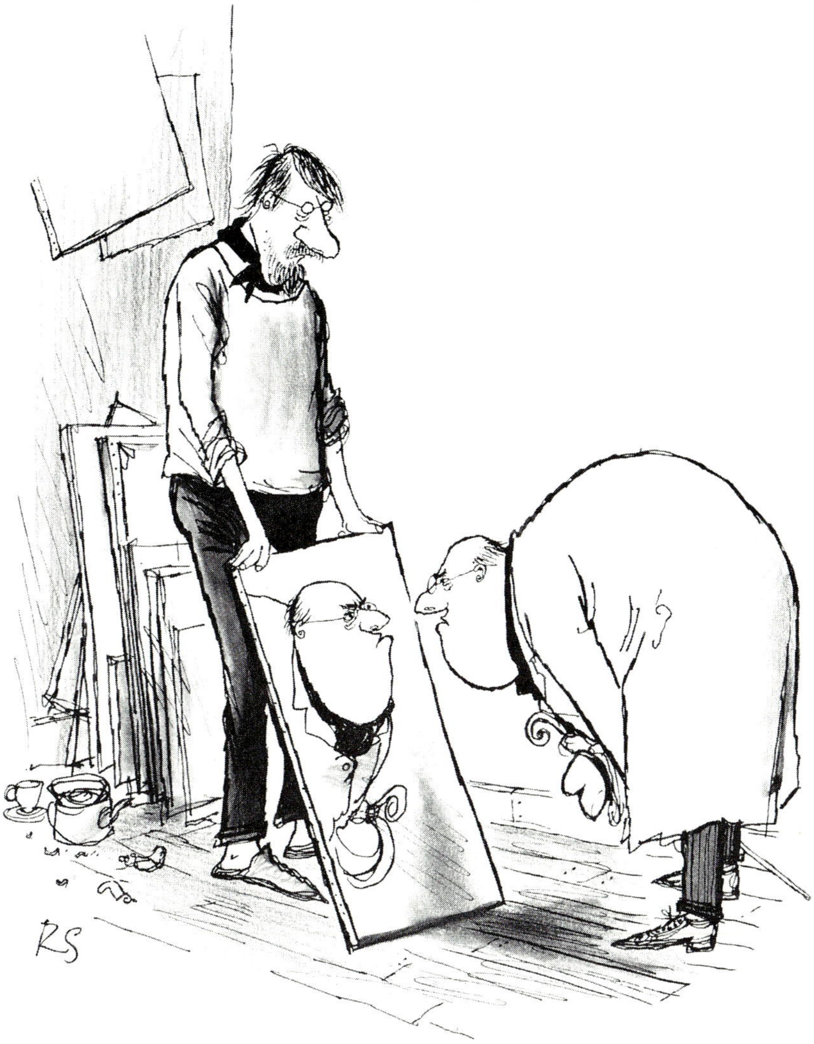
RS

[1955]

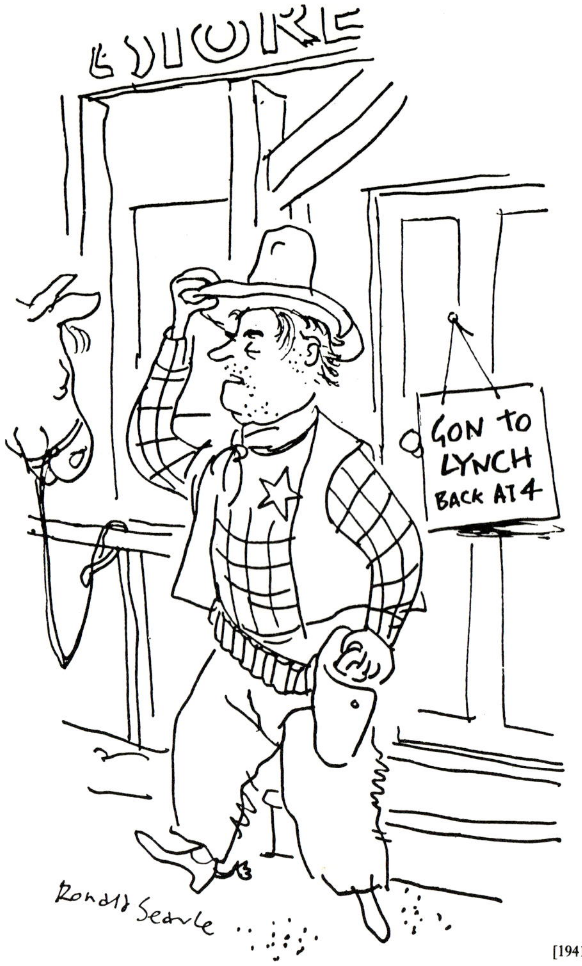
GON TO
LYNCH
BACK AT 4
Ronald Searle

[1941]

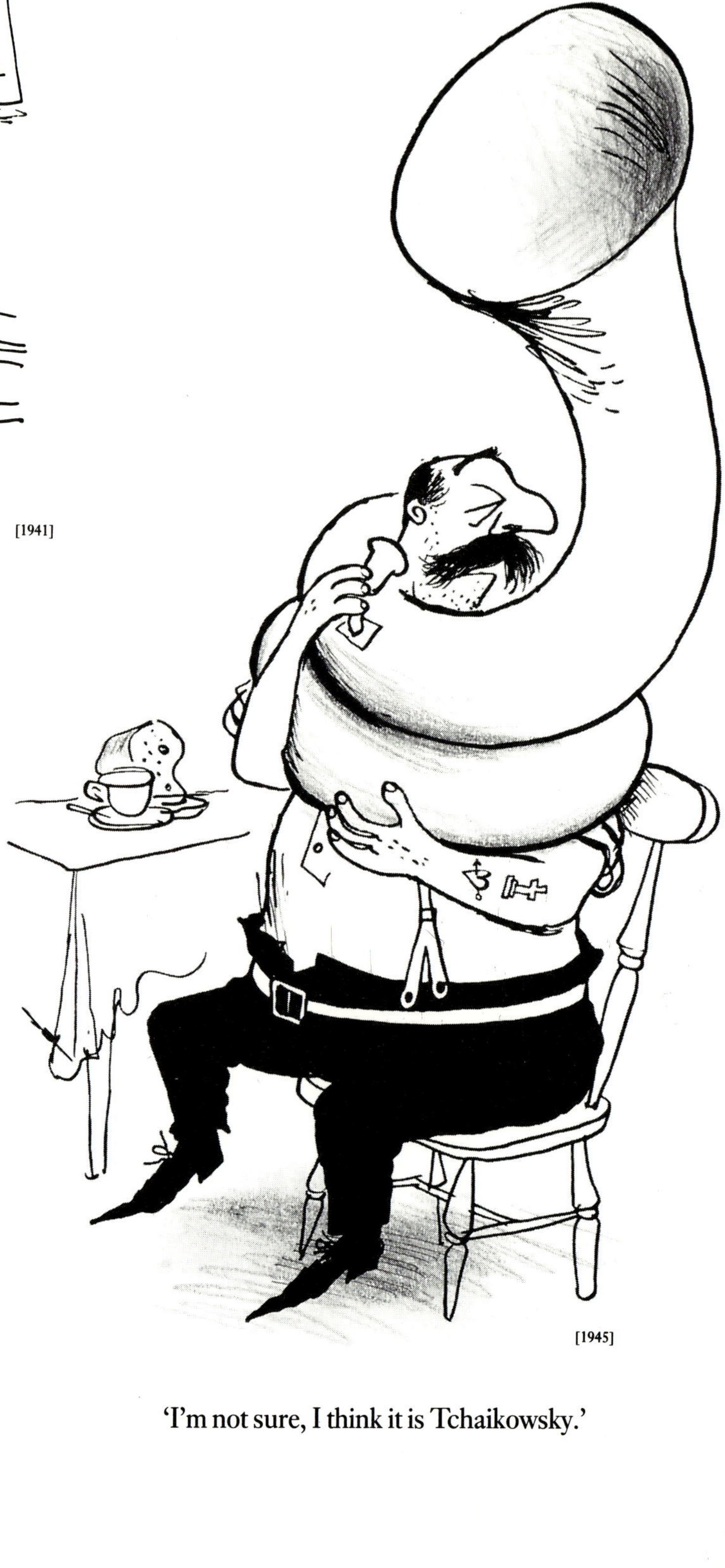

[1945]

'I'm not sure, I think it is Tchaikowsky.'

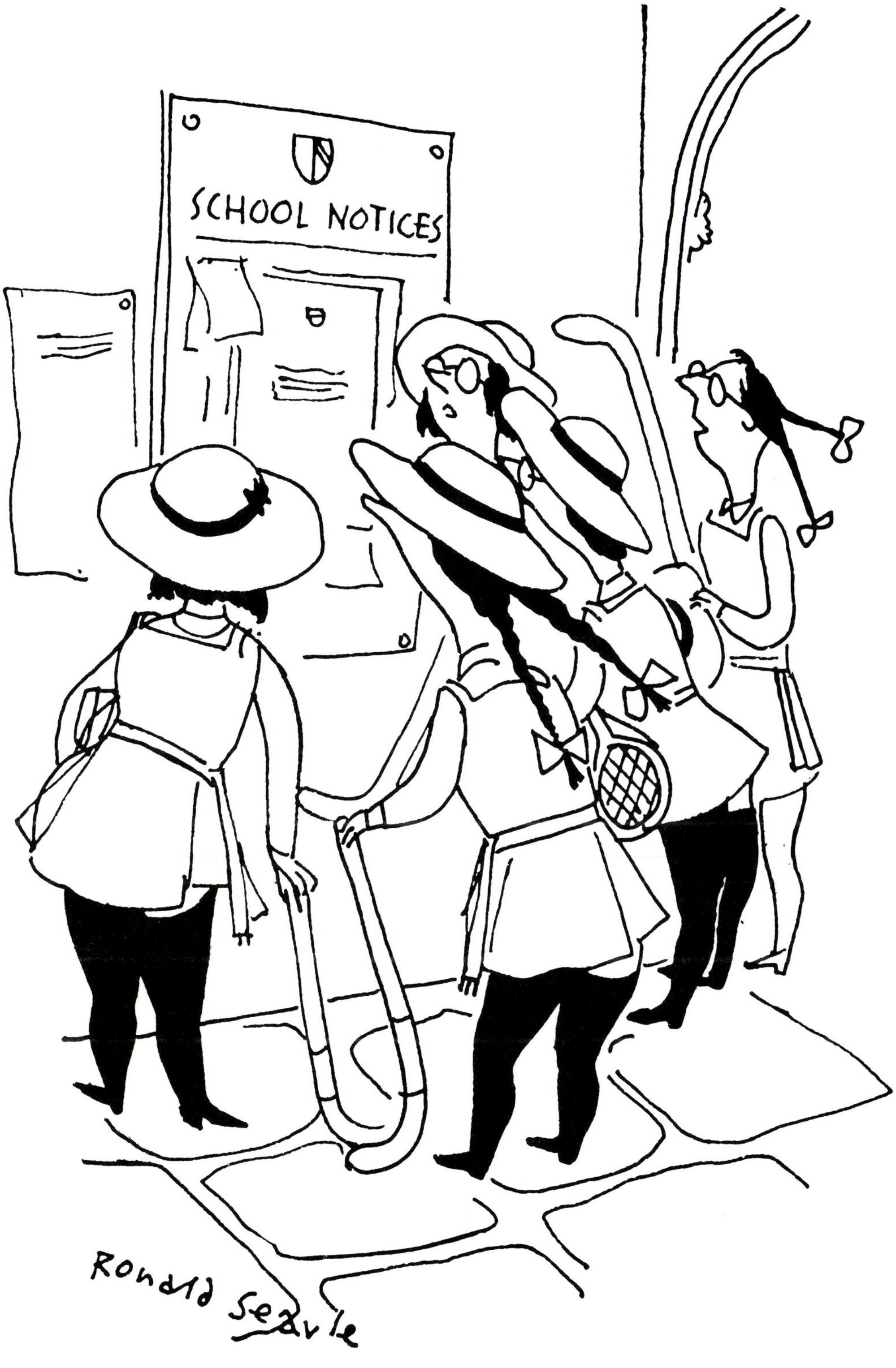
SCHOOL NOTICES
Ronald Searle

[1941]

'Owing to the international situation the match with St. Trinian's has been postponed.'

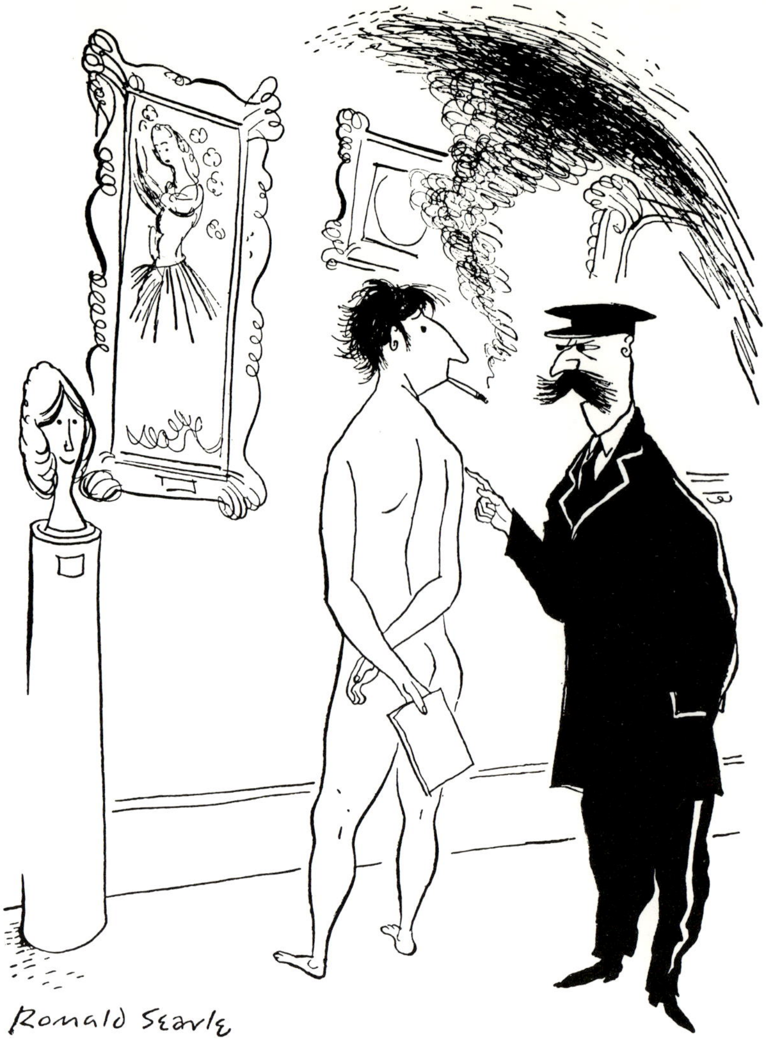
Ronald Searle

[1944]

'Sorry sir, no smoking in the museum.'

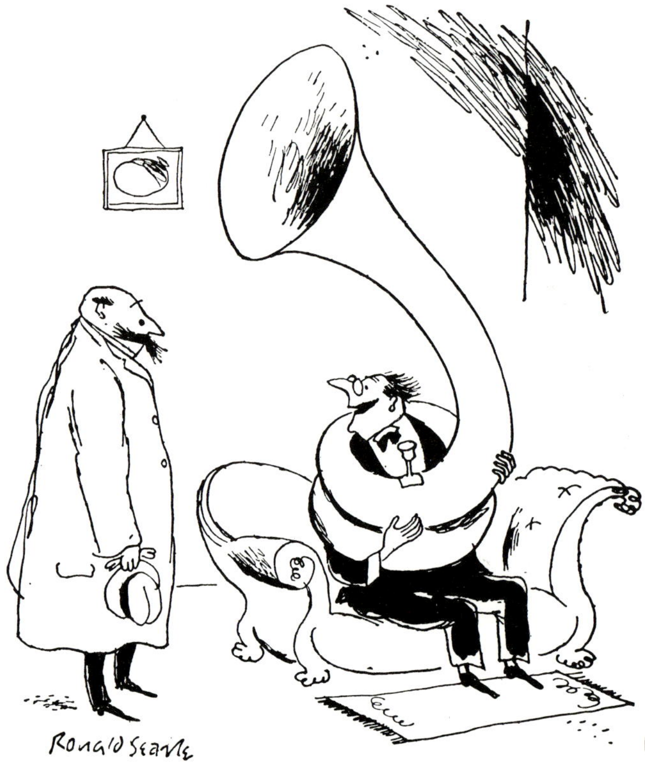
Ronald Searle

[1946]

'No, I can't play it, but it keeps me warm.'

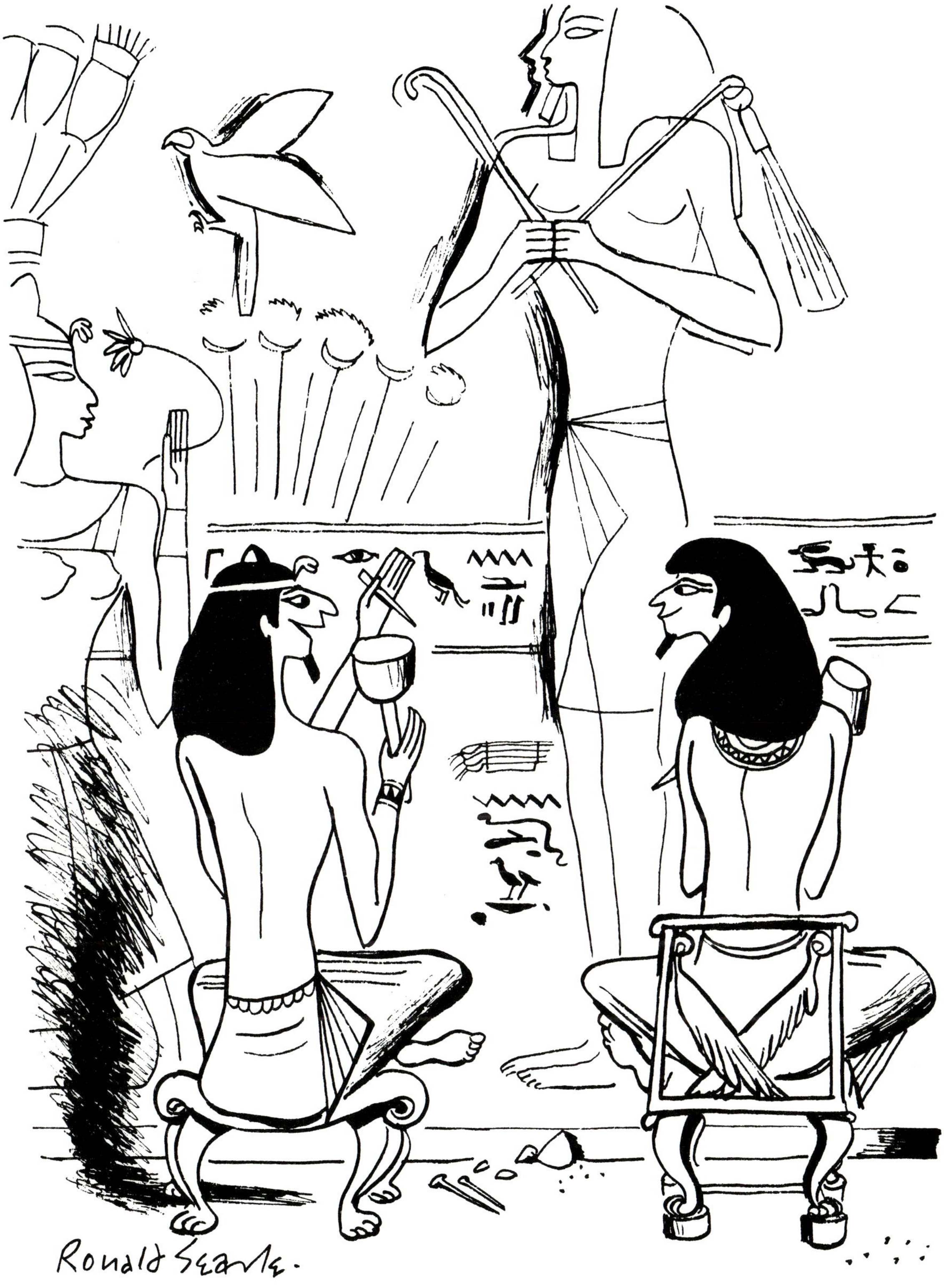
Ronald Searle.

[1945]

'Do you know, I can never remember whether to spell with an or an .'

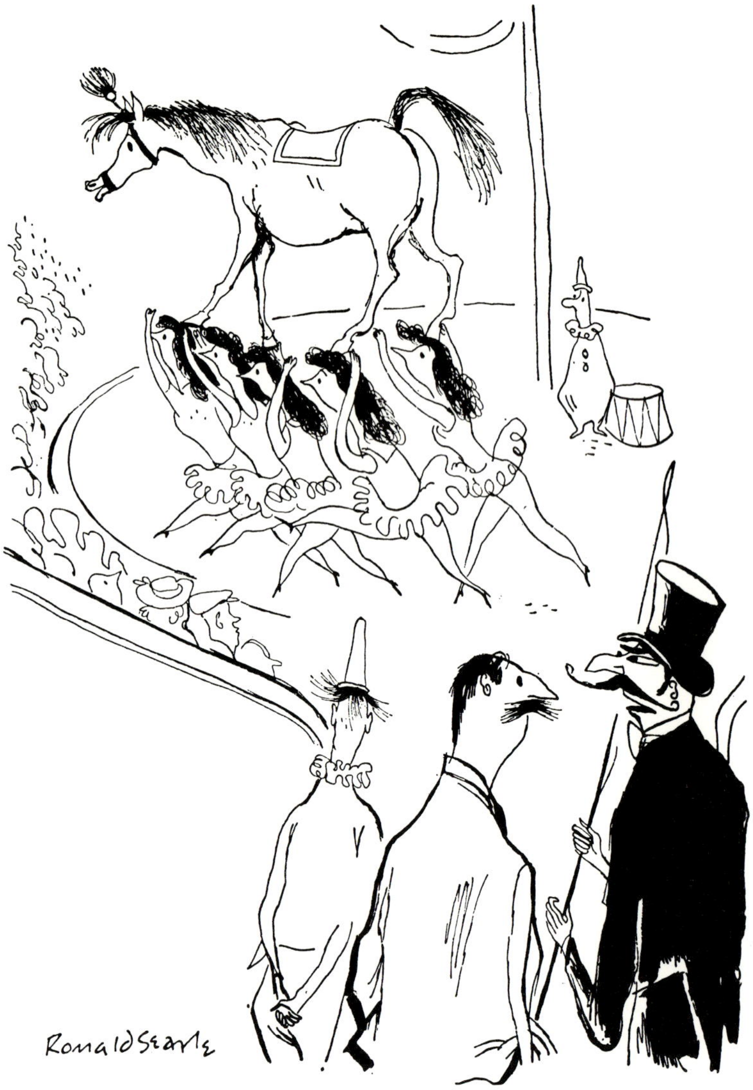
Ronald Searle

[1947]

'I've got a feeling that there's something bizarre about this act...'

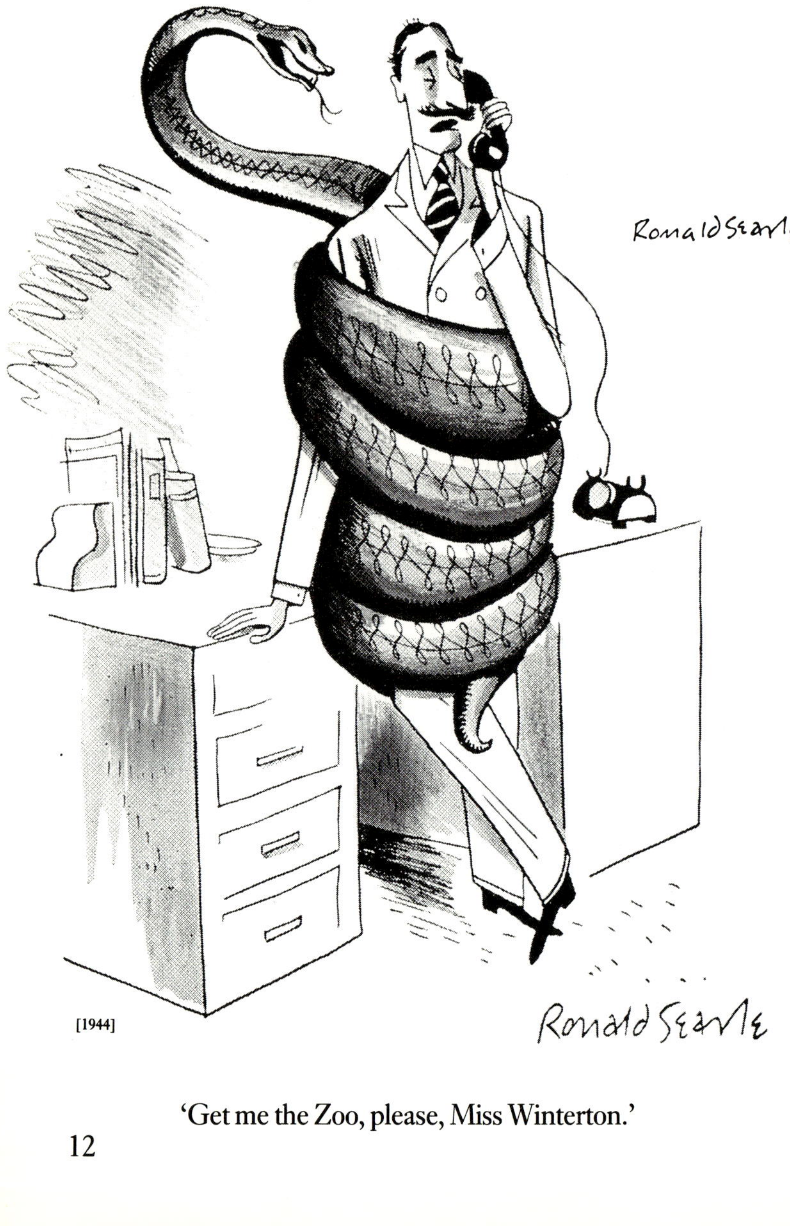
Ronald Searle

[1944]

'Get me the Zoo, please, Miss Winterton.'

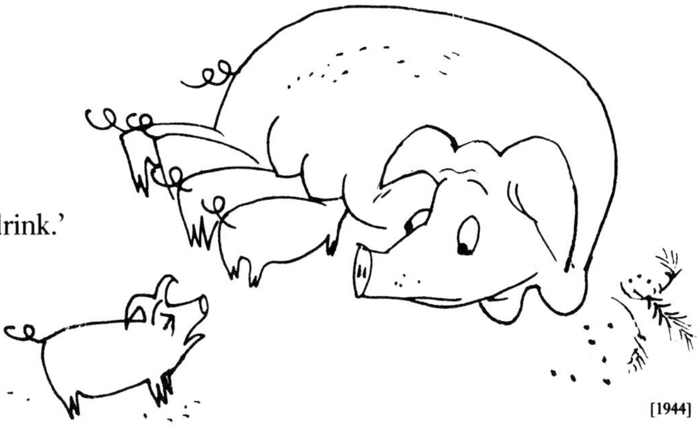

‘No thanks, I don’t drink.’

[1944]

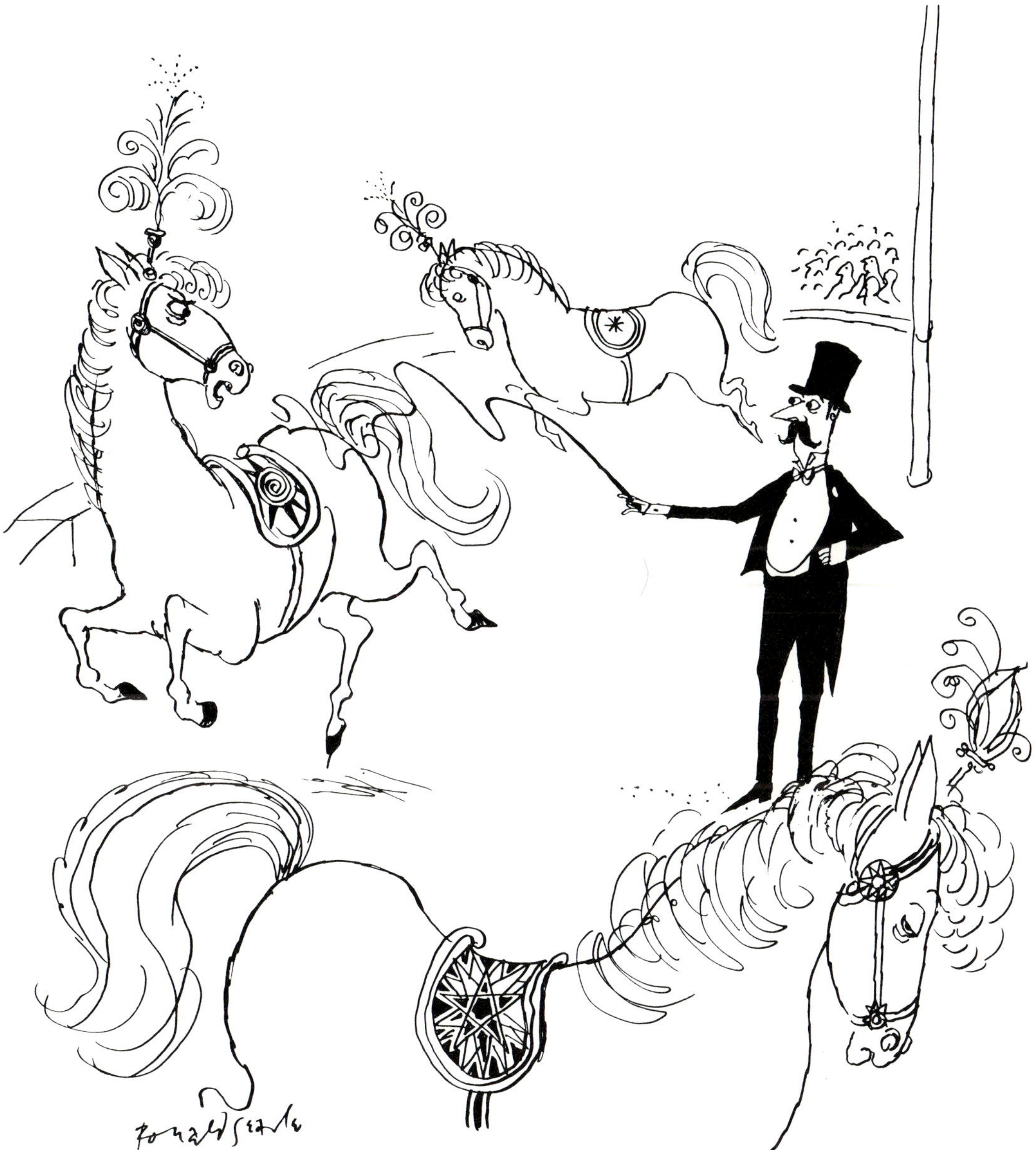

[1947]

‘Careful – that stung.’

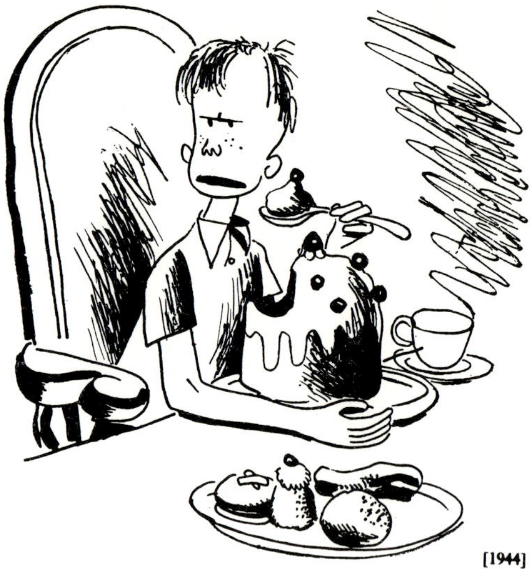

[1944]

Ronald Searle

'But I don't *feel* sick yet.'

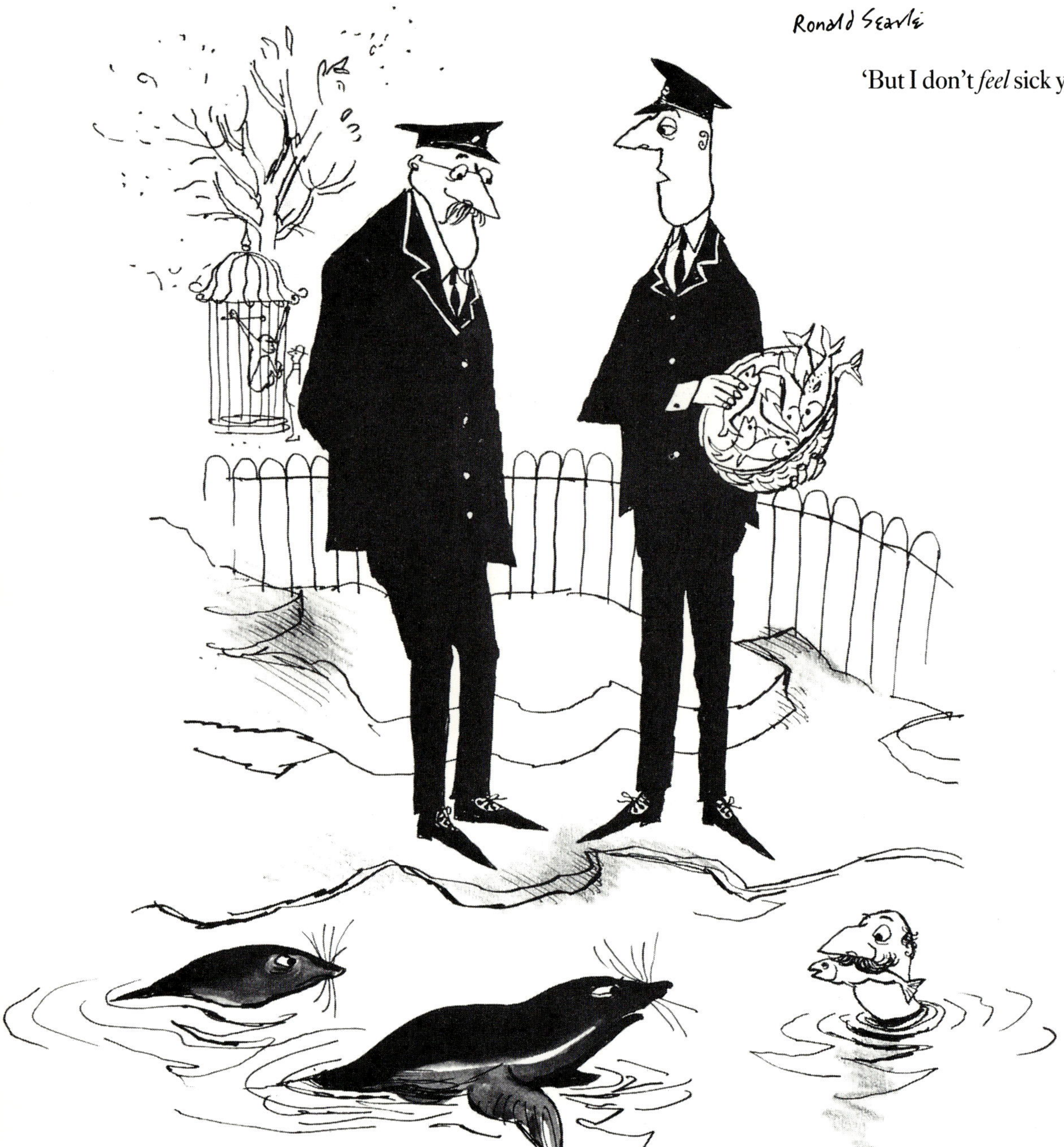

[1942]

'I think he must be catholic – he turns up every Friday.'

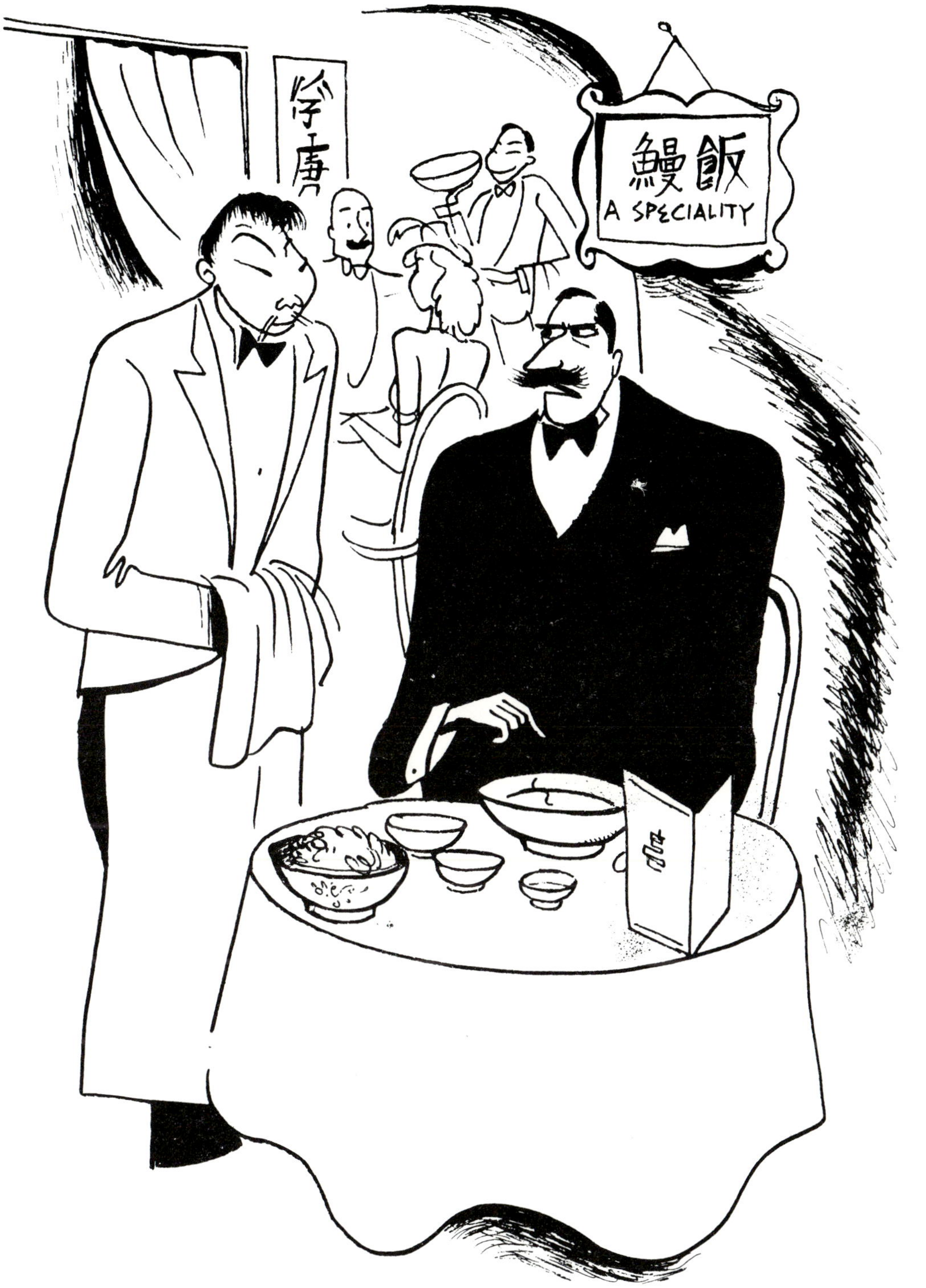

鰻飯
A SPECIALITY

[1944]

‘Waiter, there’s a 毛 in my 饂飩汁.’

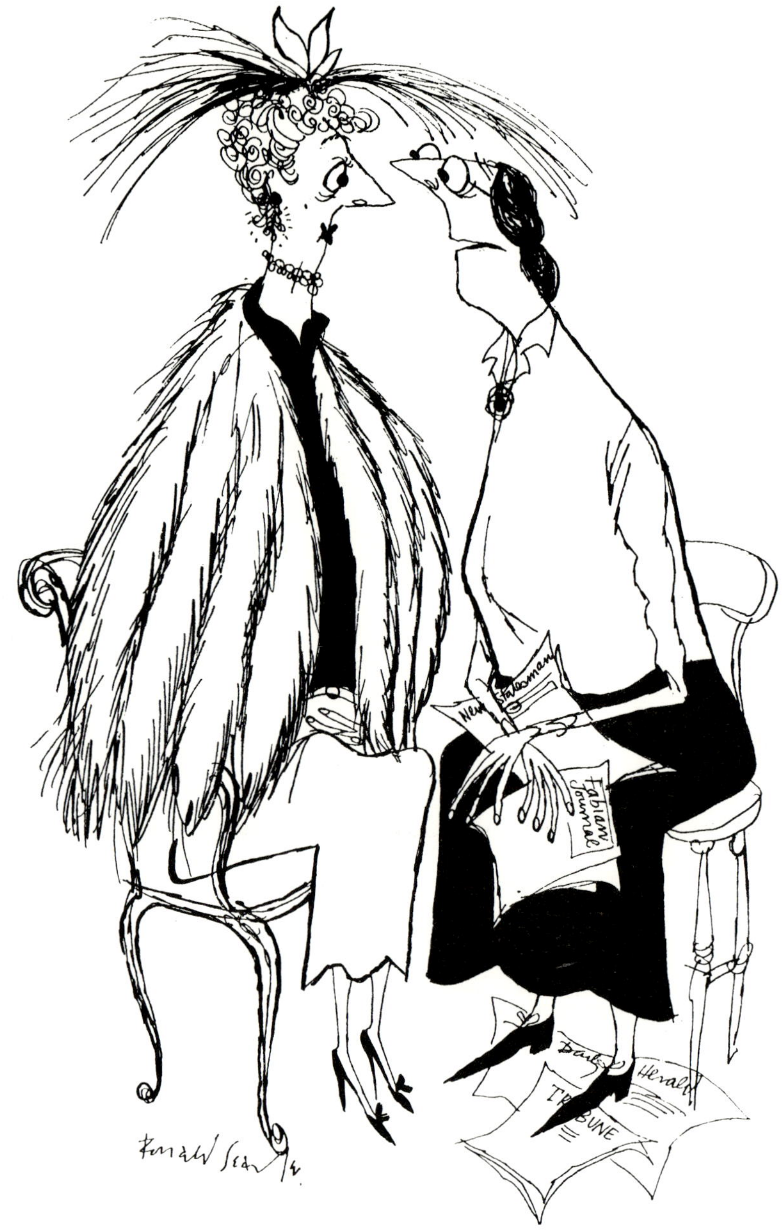
New Statesman
Fabian Journal

[1948]

'Of course, it is not you personally I am against, Agnes, it's the capitalist system as a whole...'

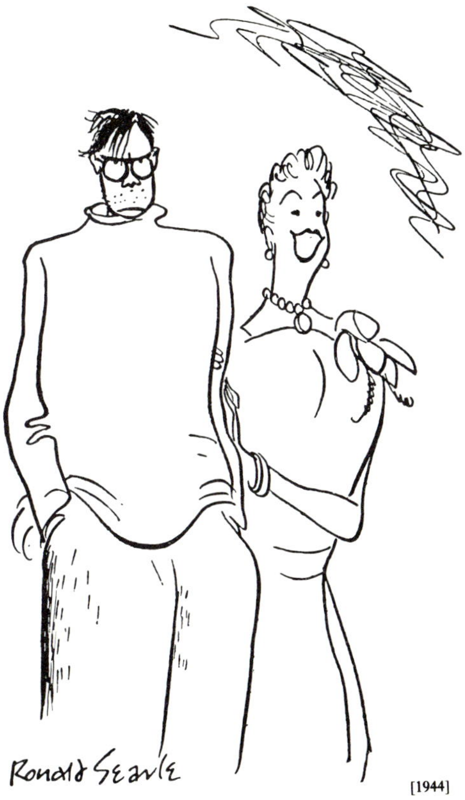
Ronald Searle

[1944]

'And this is Mr. Eccleshare. He wants a bloody revolution.'

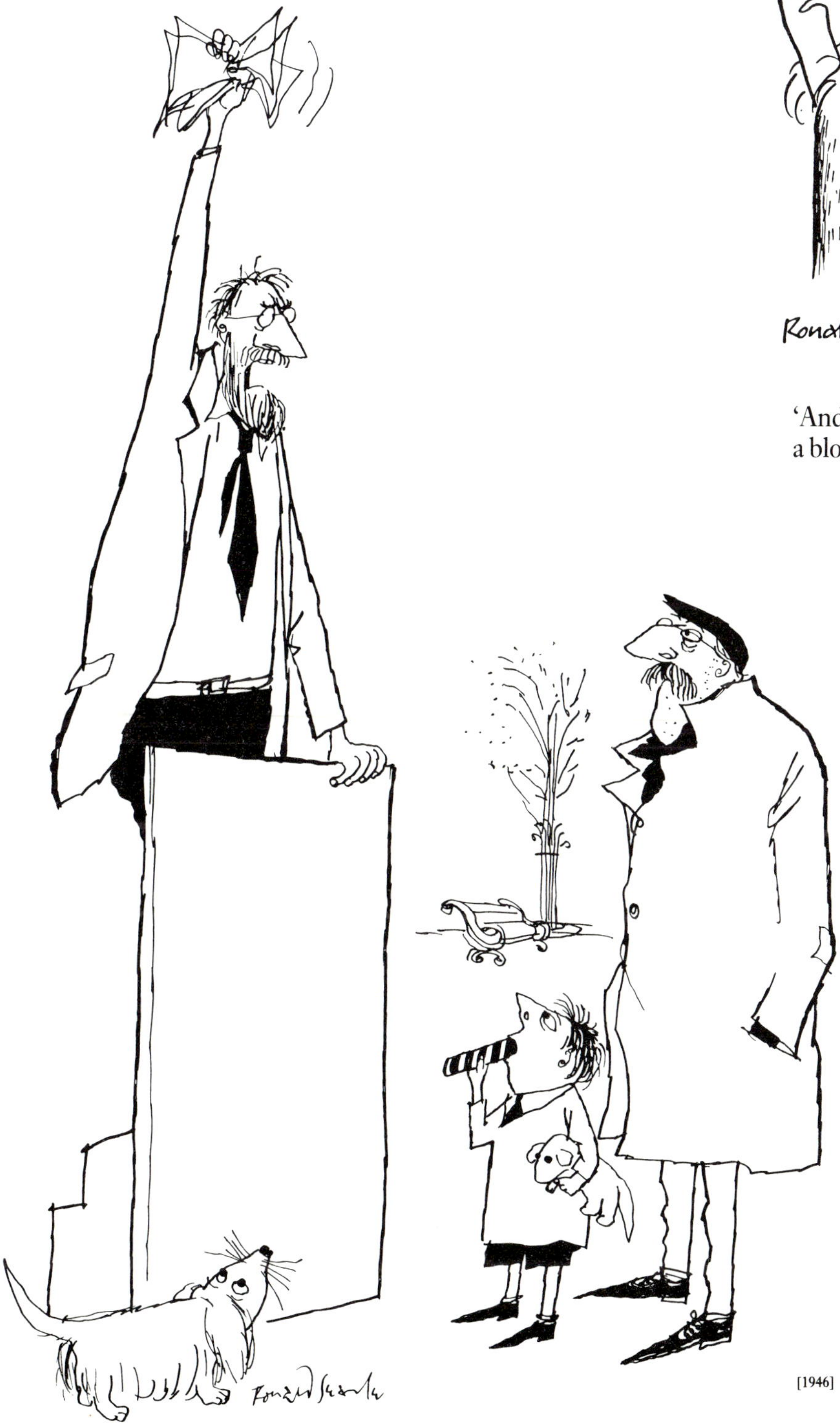

[1946]

'It is not my intention to work you up into a state of mass hysteria...'

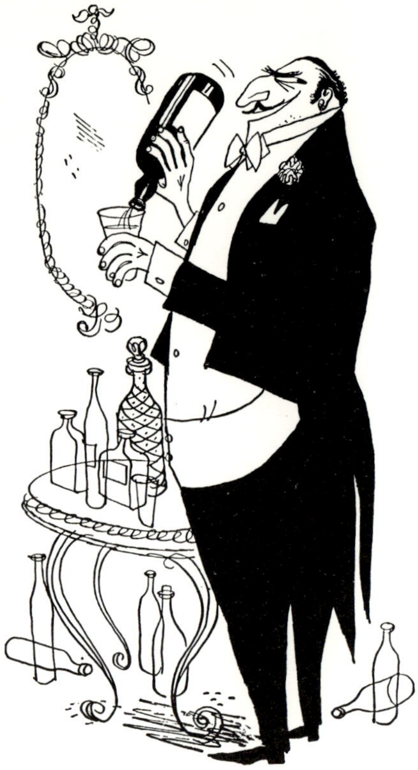

'This? Sparklin' lemonade, my dear.'

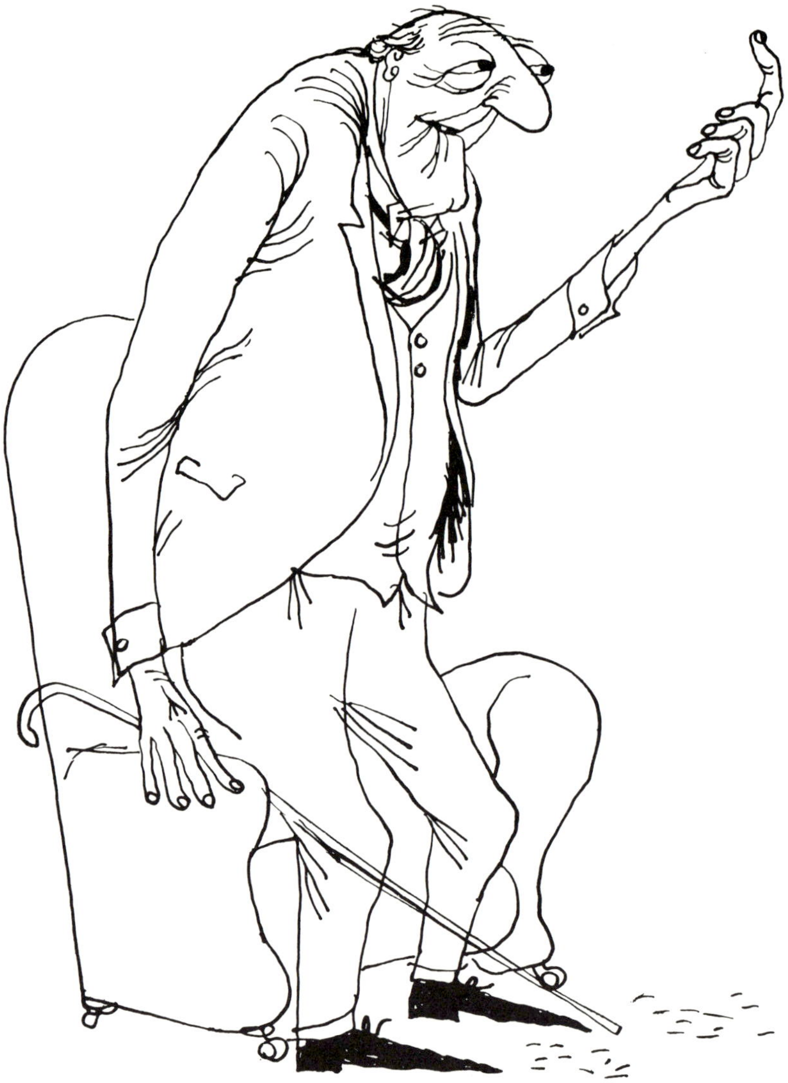

'Show me that pretty necklace, child.'

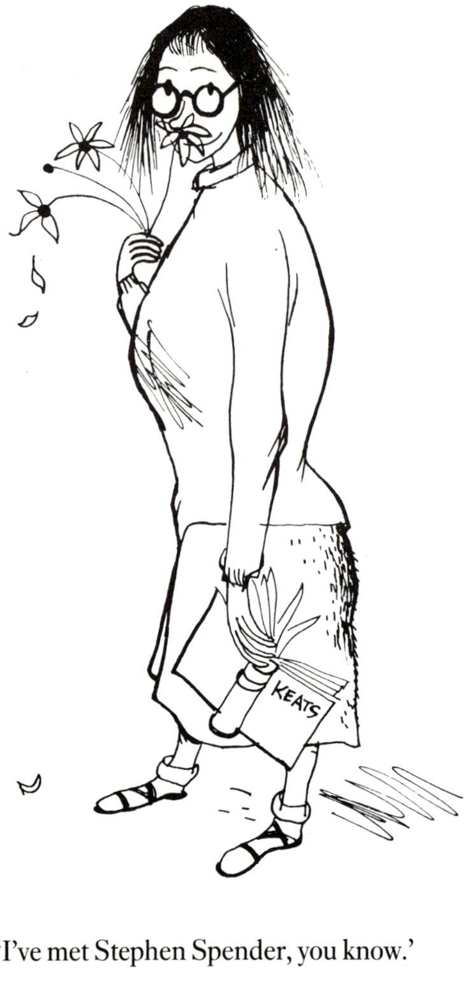
KEATS

[1947]

'I've met Stephen Spender, you know.'

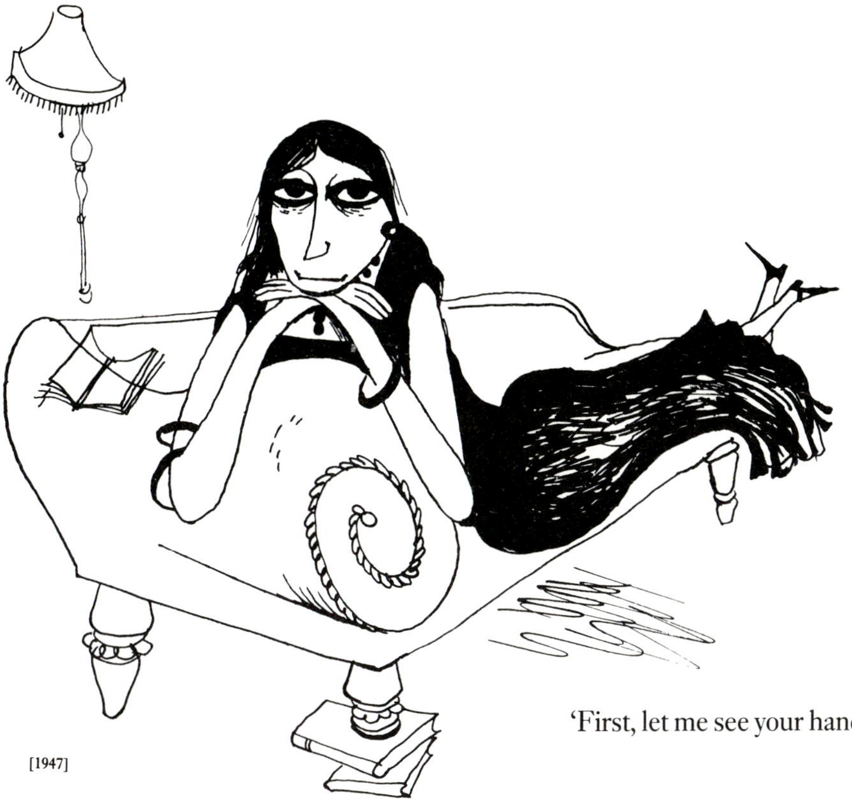

'First, let me see your handwriting.'

[1947]

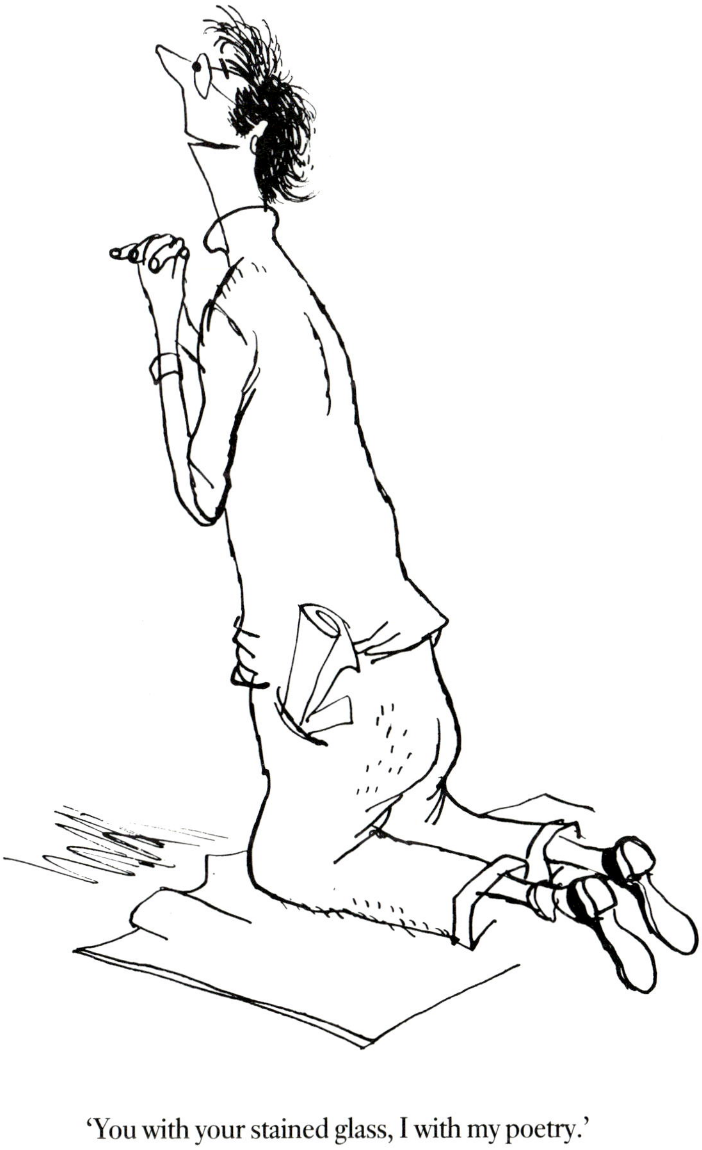

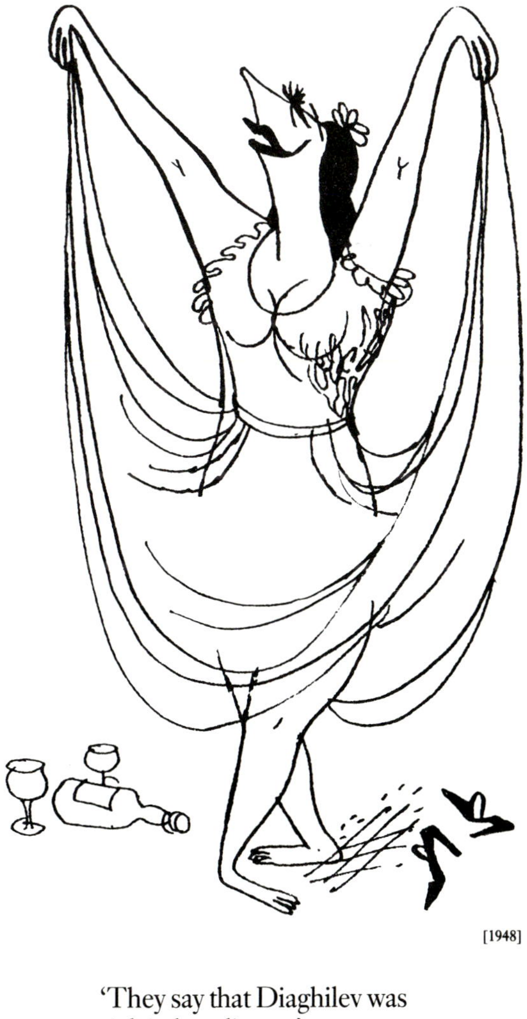

[1948]

'They say that Diaghilev was sick in her slipper.'

'You with your stained glass, I with my poetry.'

LEASE EXPIRING

EVER... MUST...

MUST CLOSE

...NG GO

PRICES SLASHED!

Ronald Searle

[1948]

[1949]

[1951]

'I hear the cost of living is still rising.'

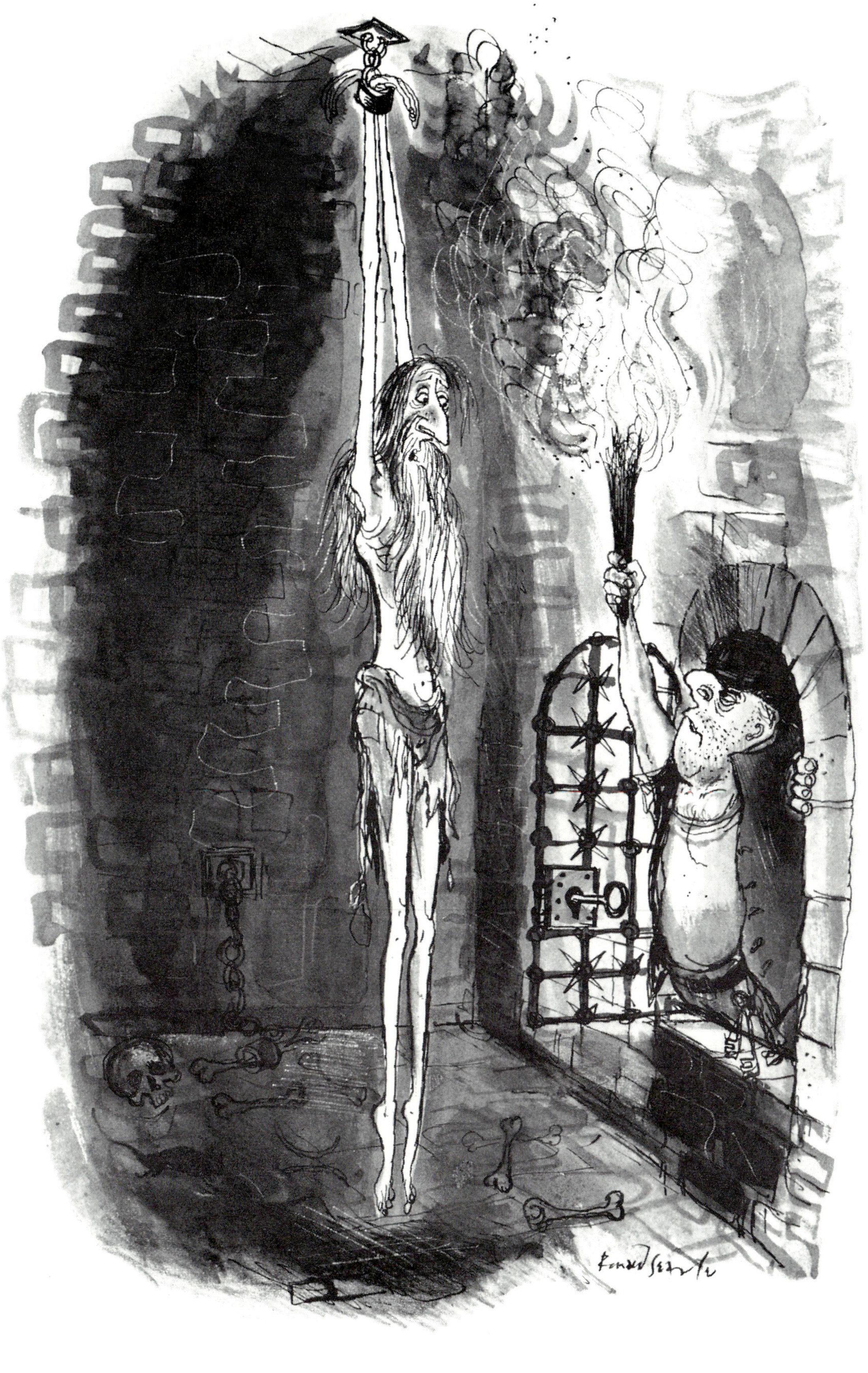

[1945]

'Could you tell me the time, please?'

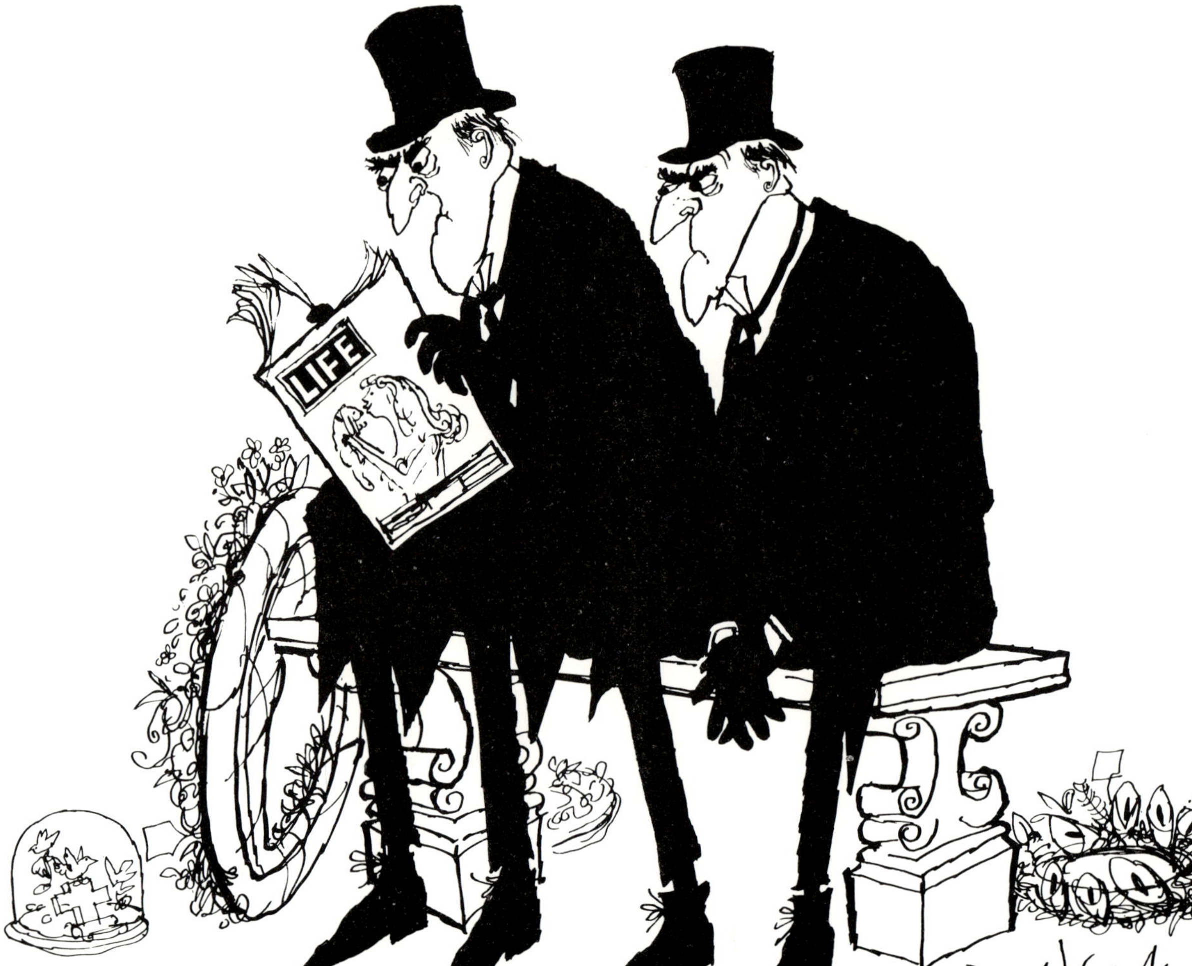
LIFE
Ronald Searle

[1955]

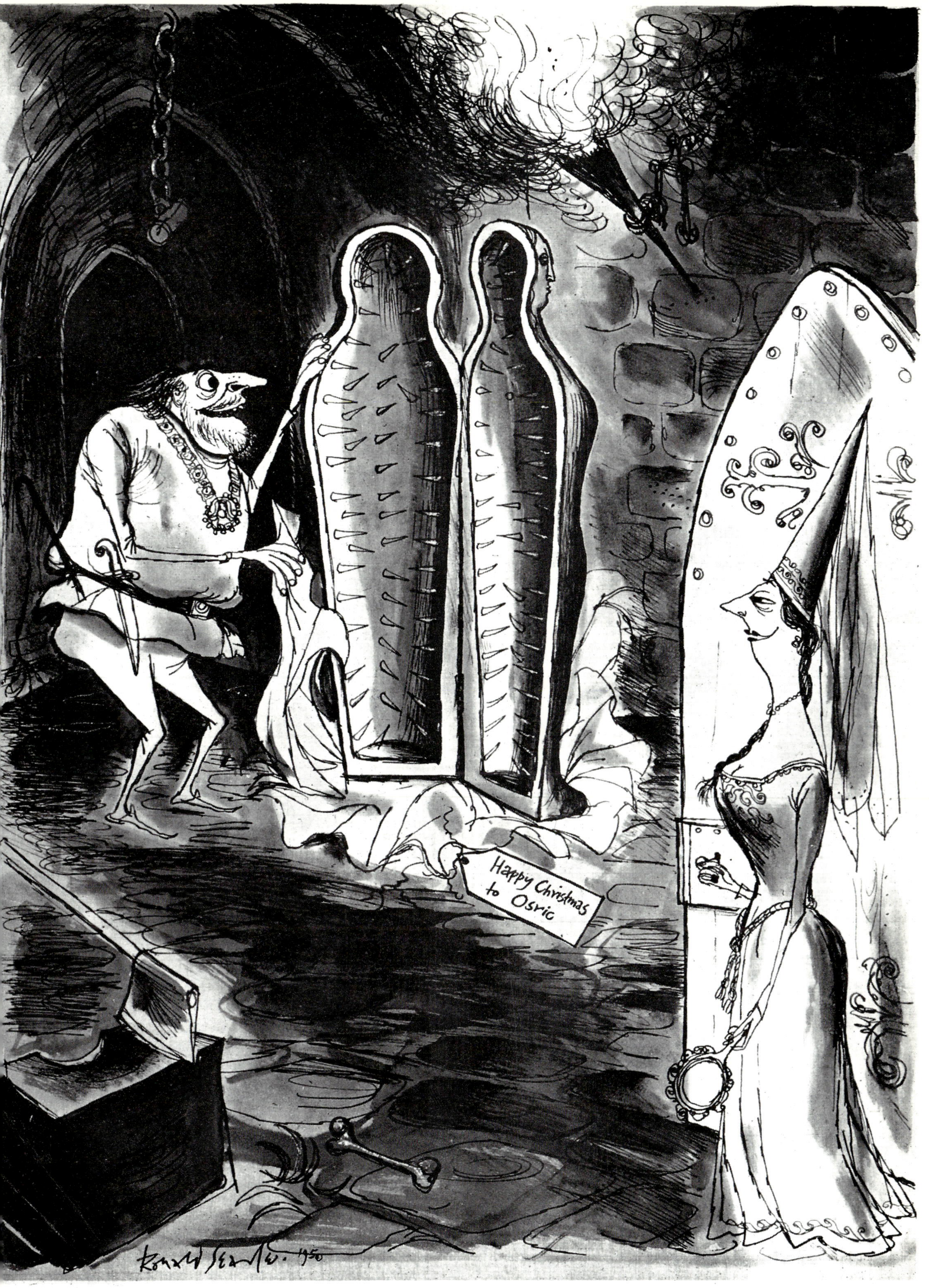
Happy Christmas to Osric
Ronald Searle. 1950

'Darling! Just what I wanted.'

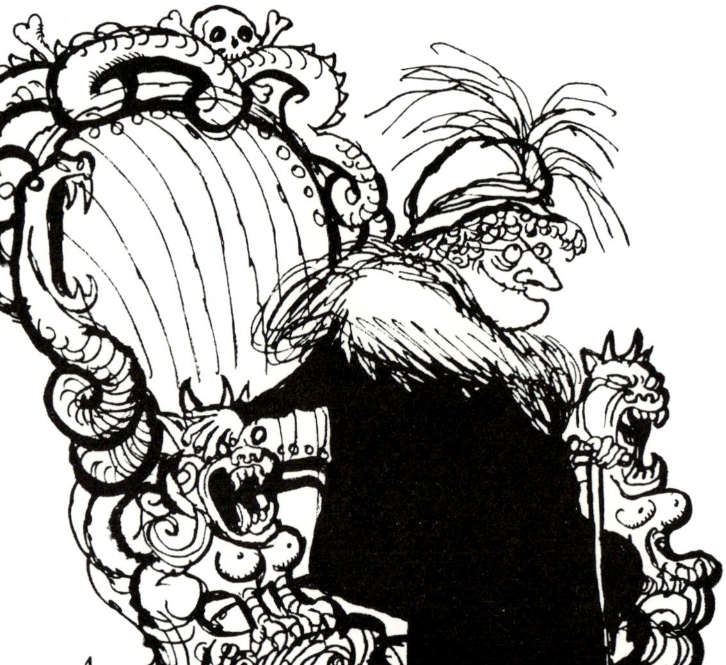
RS

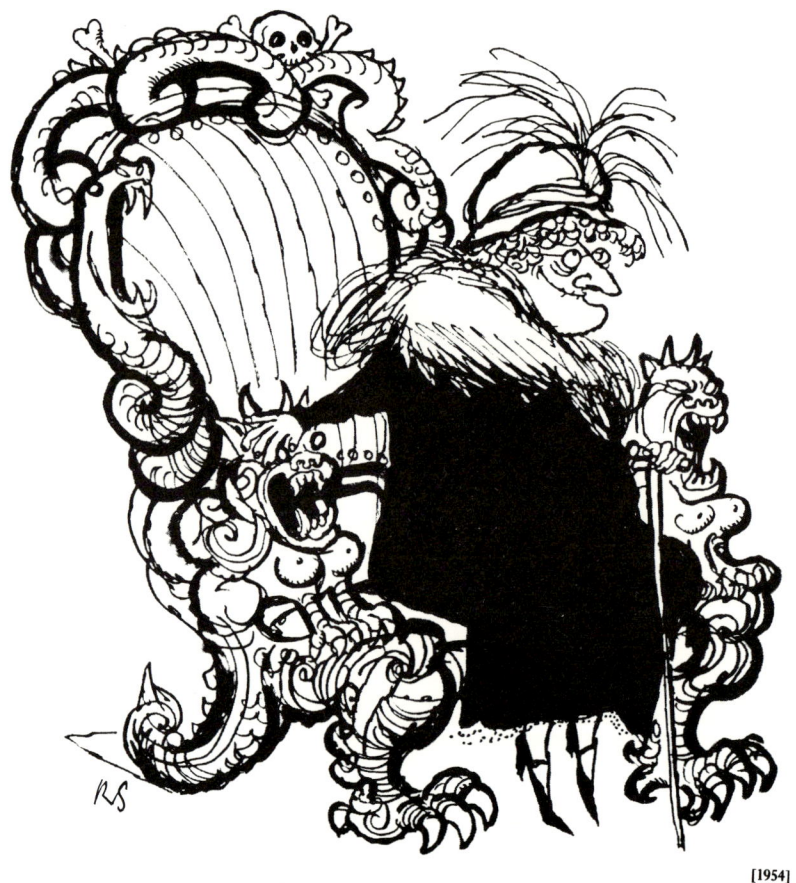

[1954]

'How much is this one?'

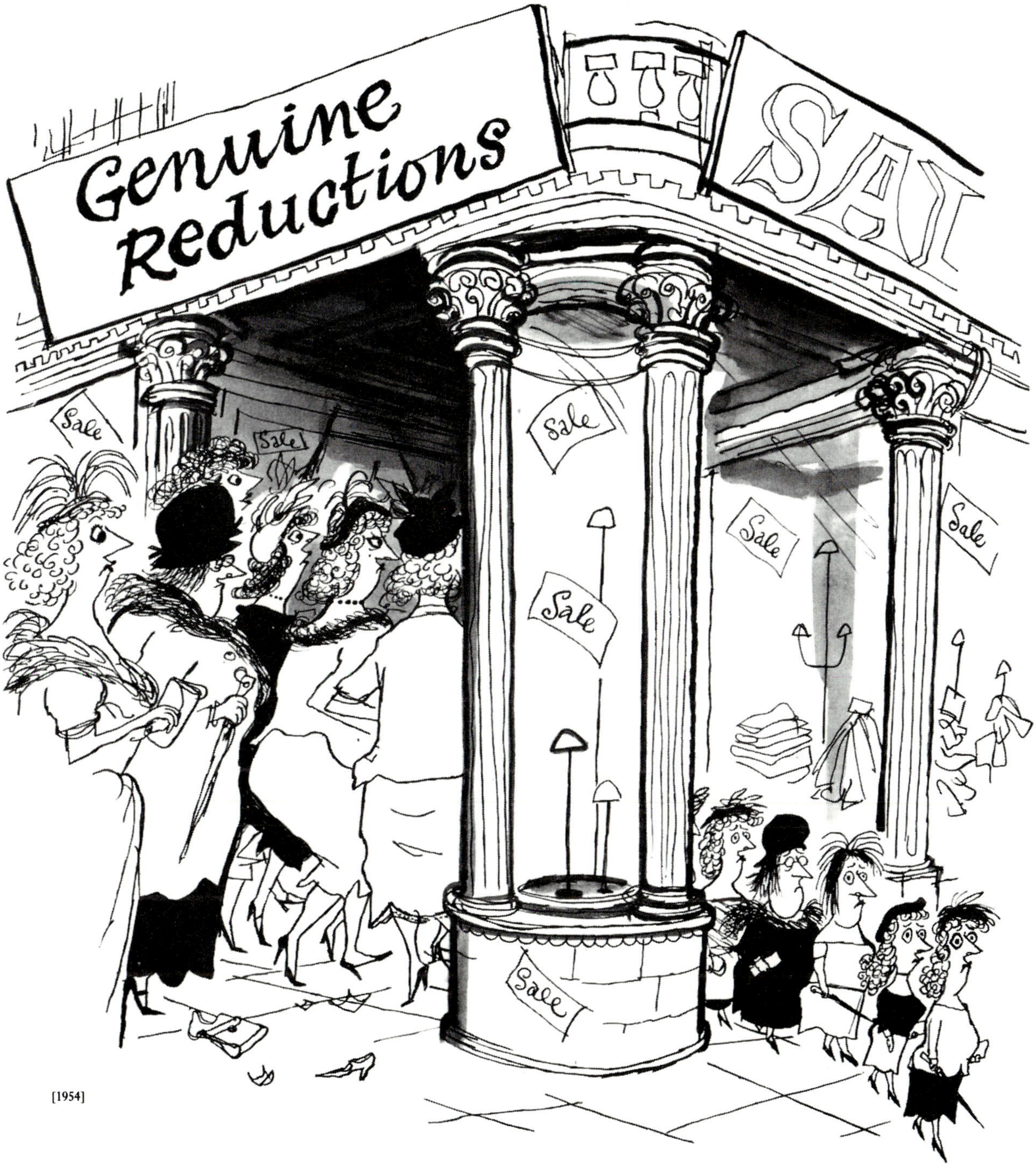
Genuine Reductions
Sale
Sale
Sale
Sale
Sale
Sale
Sale
[1954]

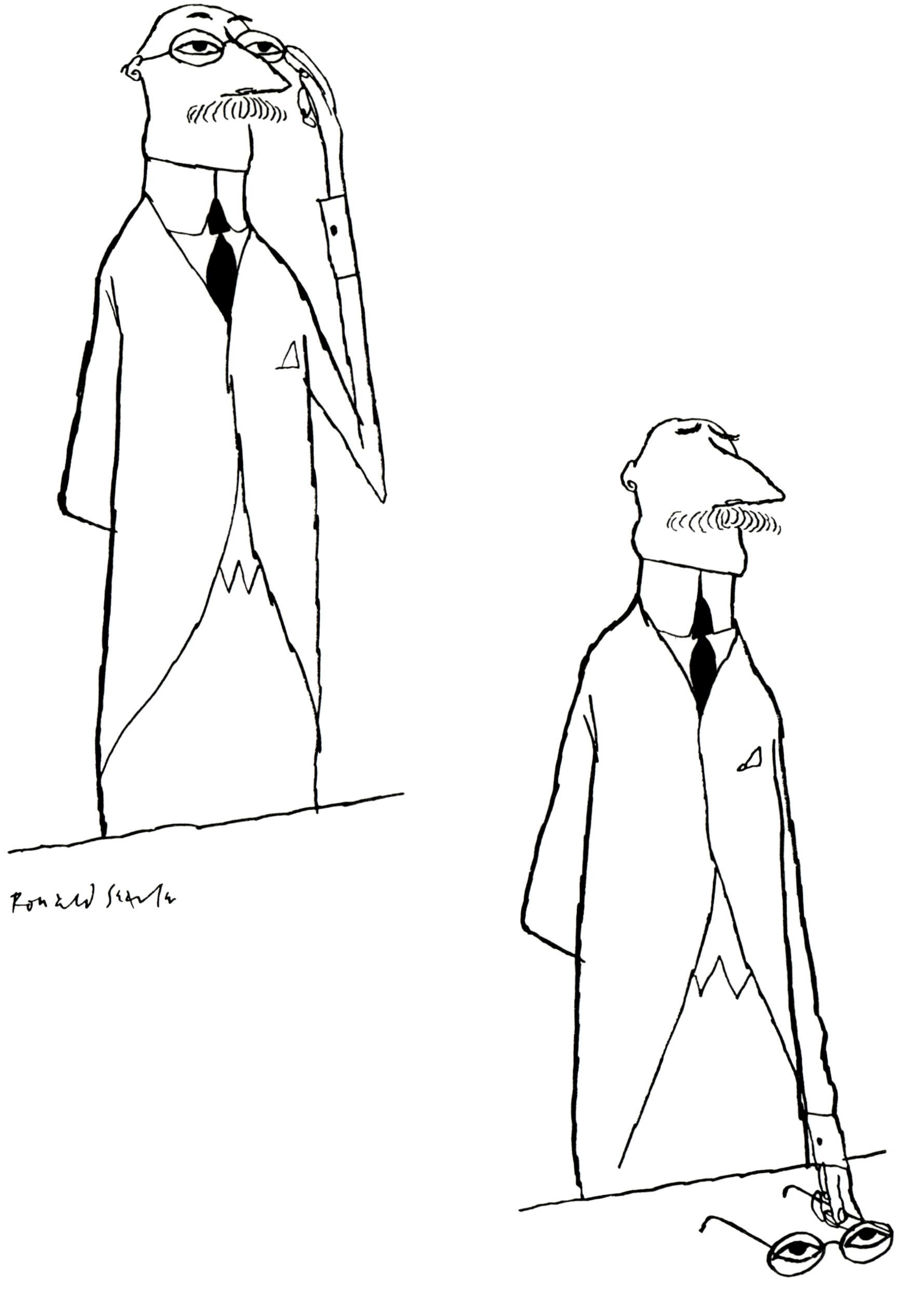
Ronald Searle

[1952]

[1954]

'Her rock cakes are marvellous.'

[1954]

[1954]

'Oh, please, not yet, not yet…'

[1952]

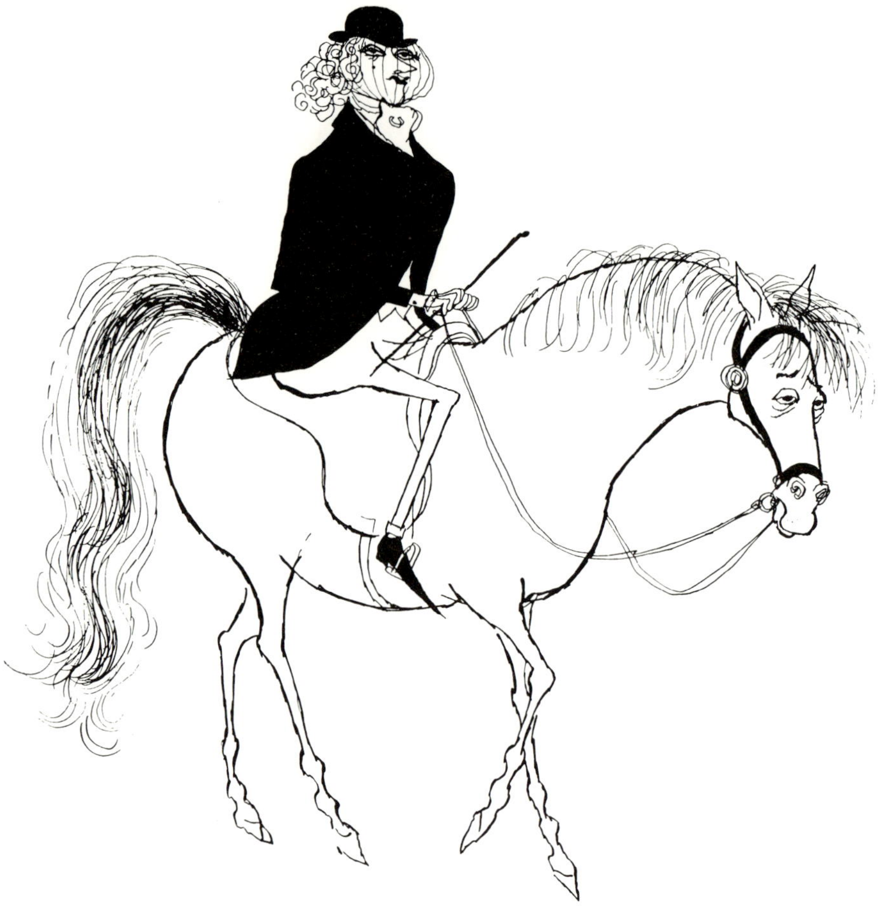

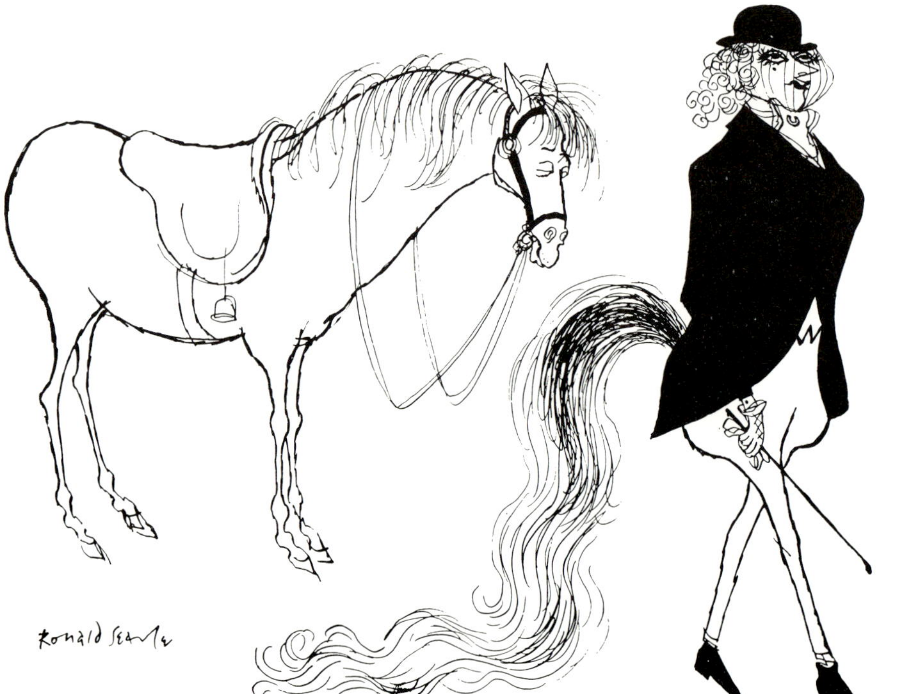
Ronald Searle

[1952]

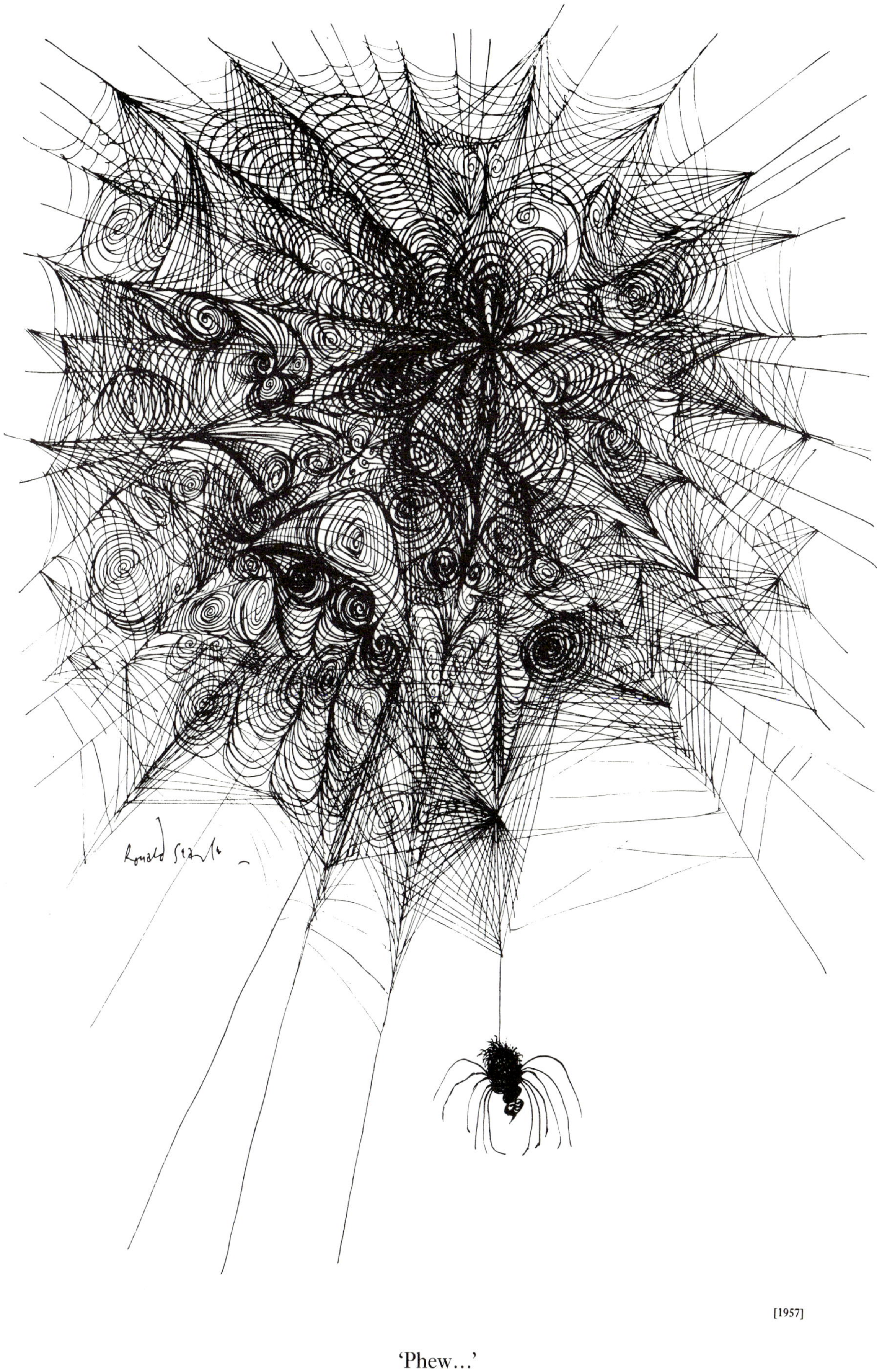

[1957]

'Phew...'

[1952]

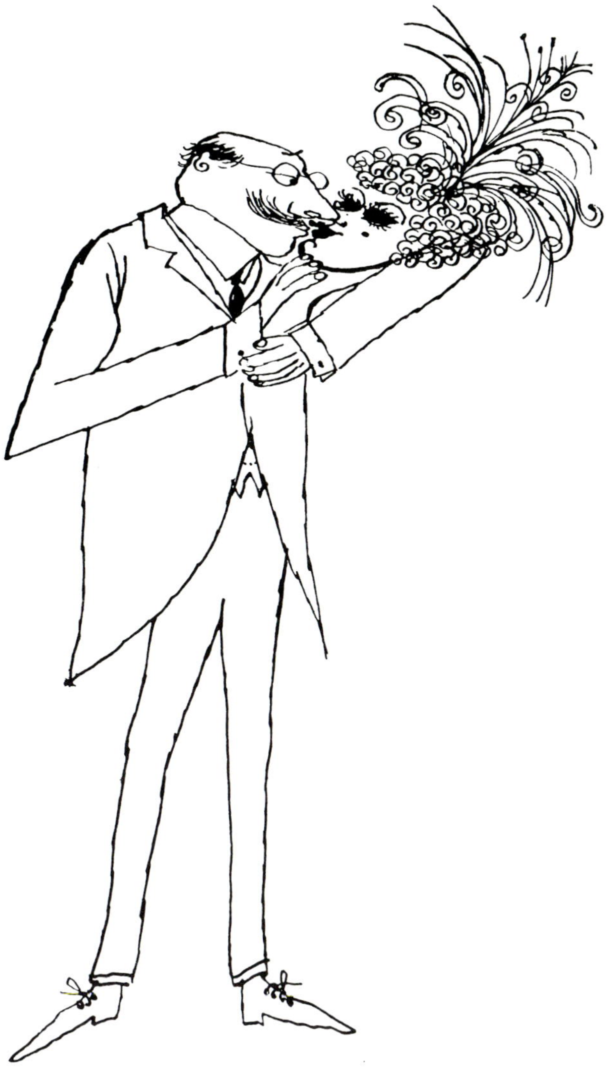

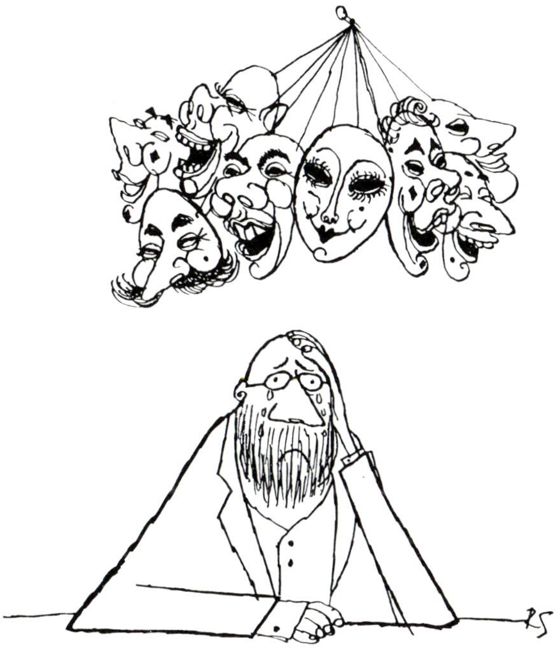

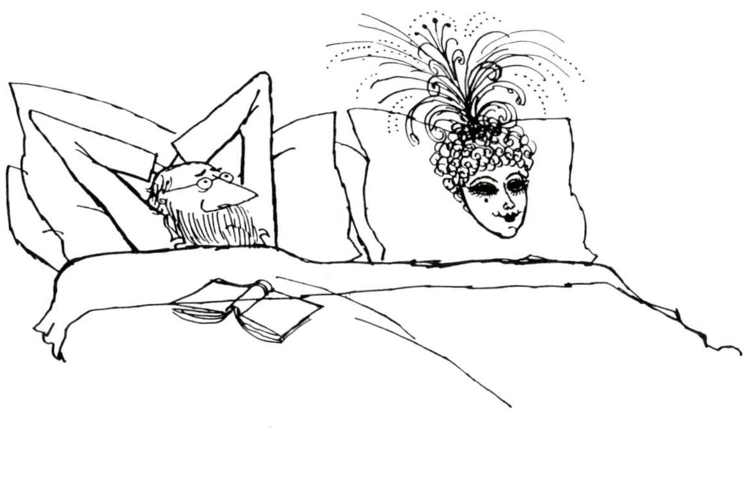

[1952]

[1954]

'Unaccountable thing, heredity…'

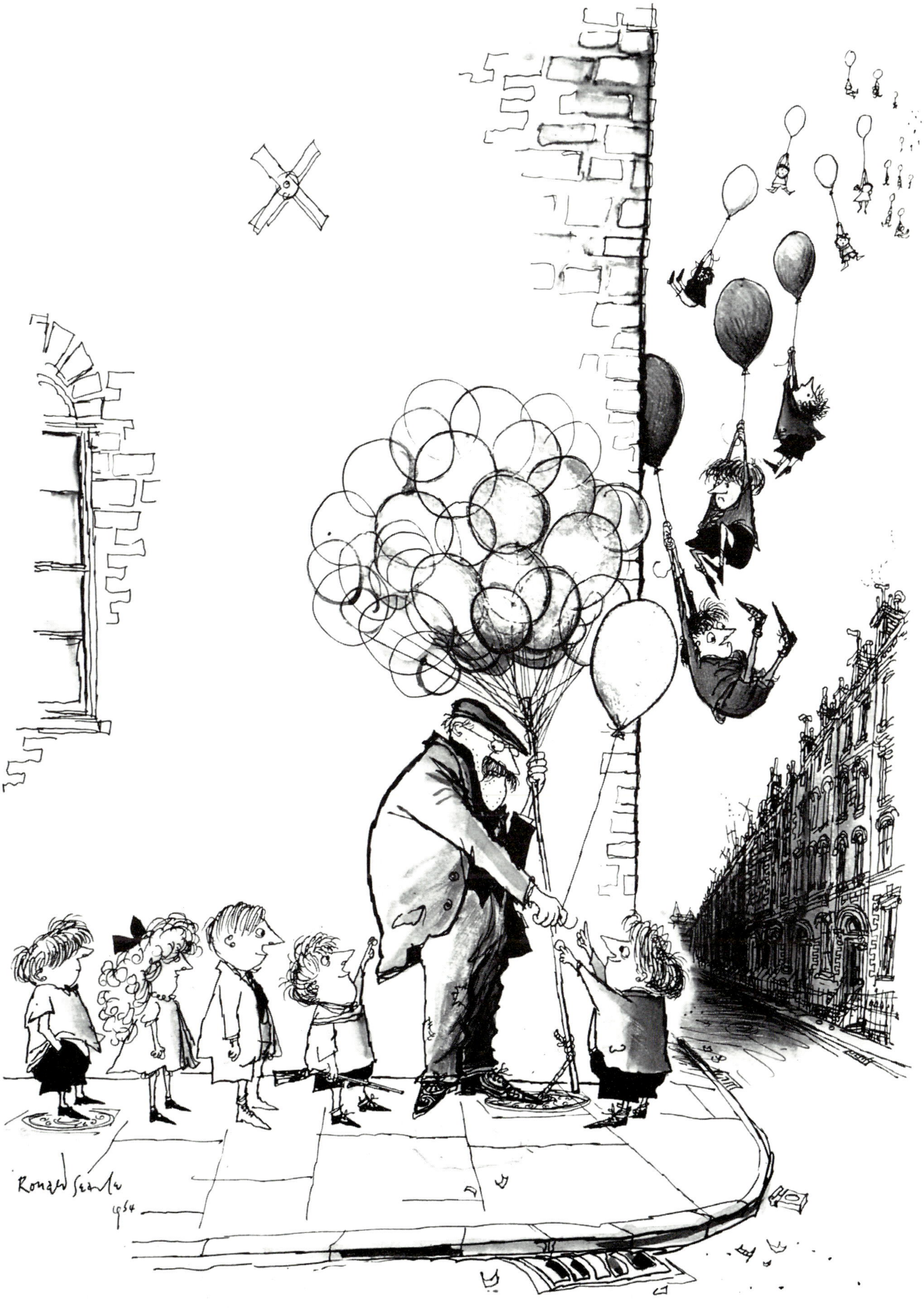
Ronald Searle
1954

Child-hater

[1957]

[1957]

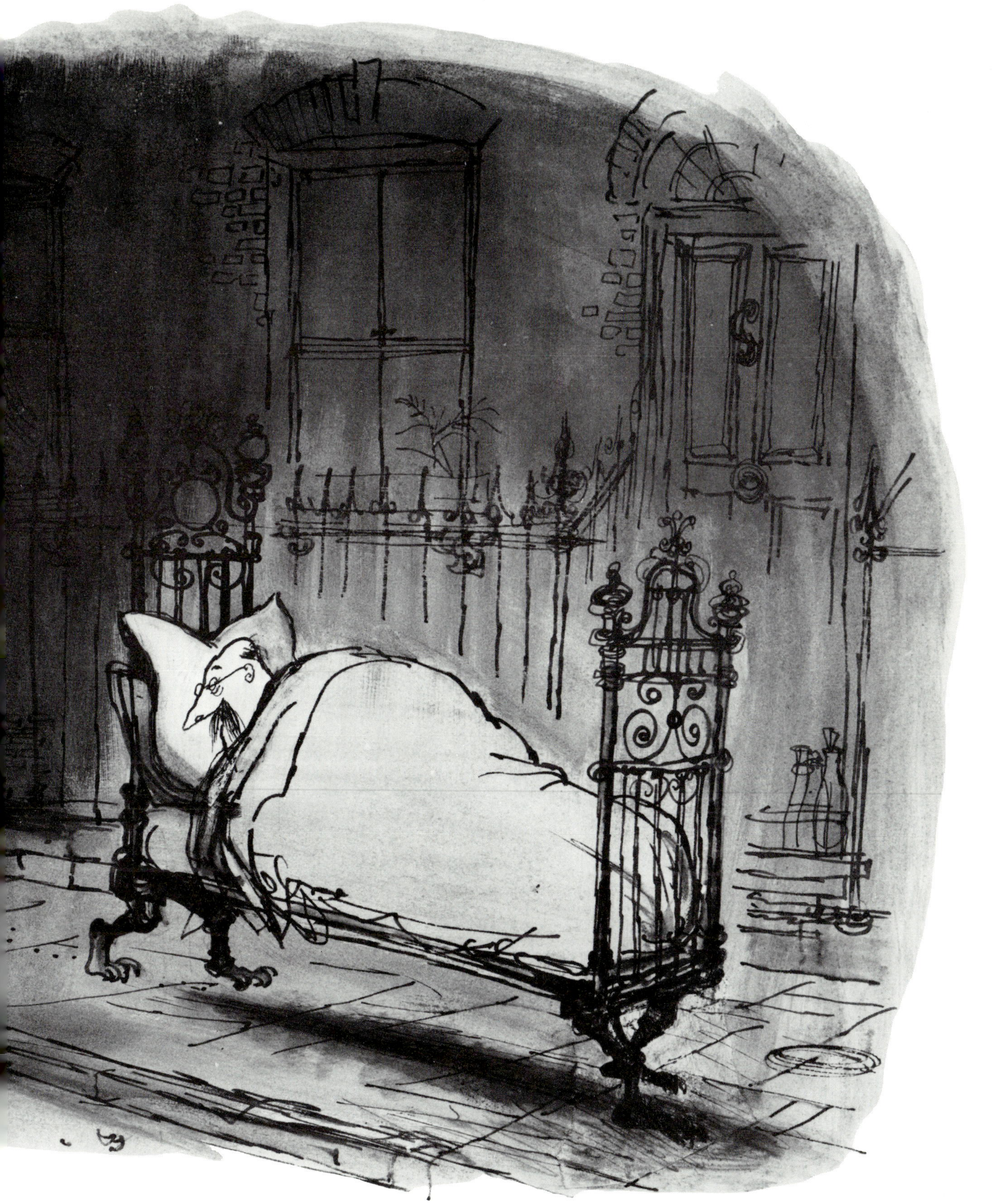

[1957]

Ronald Searle

[1957]

[1952]

'You've trapped me in music's lair, Miss Filby.'

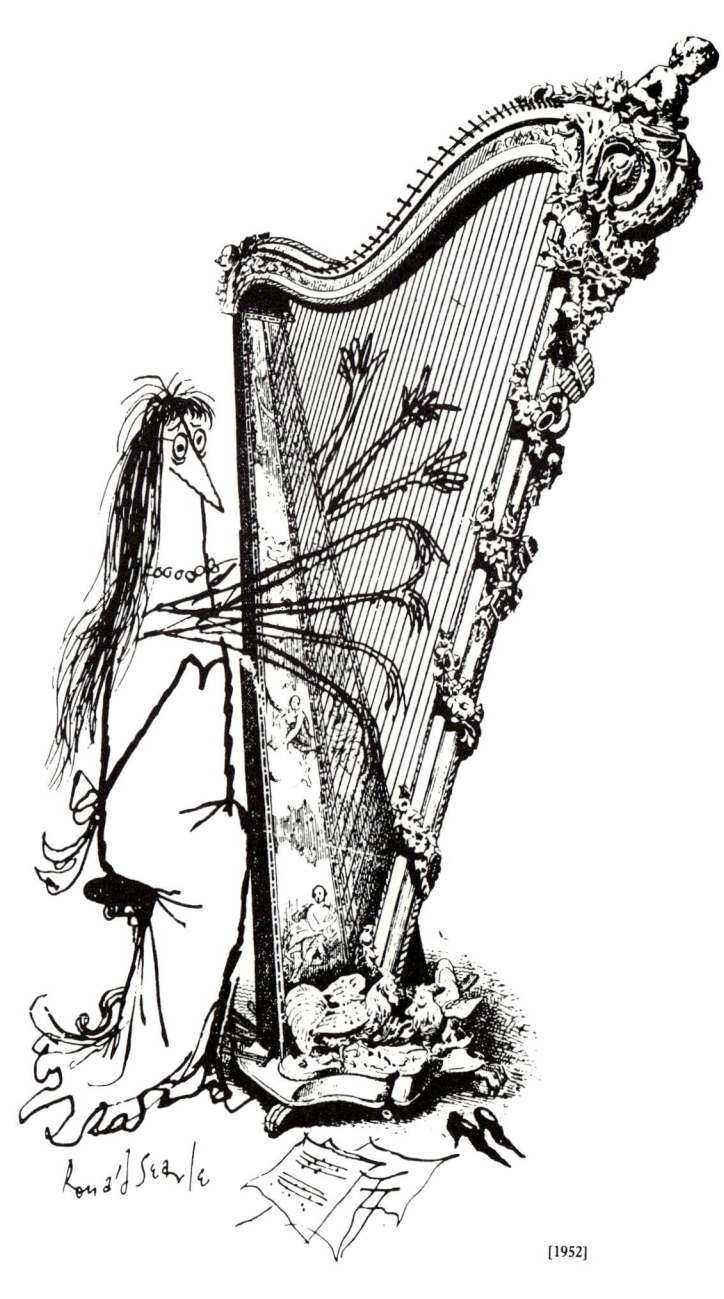

[1952]

[1952]

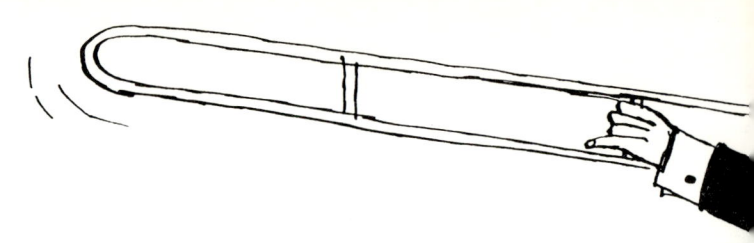

Ronald Searle

[1956]

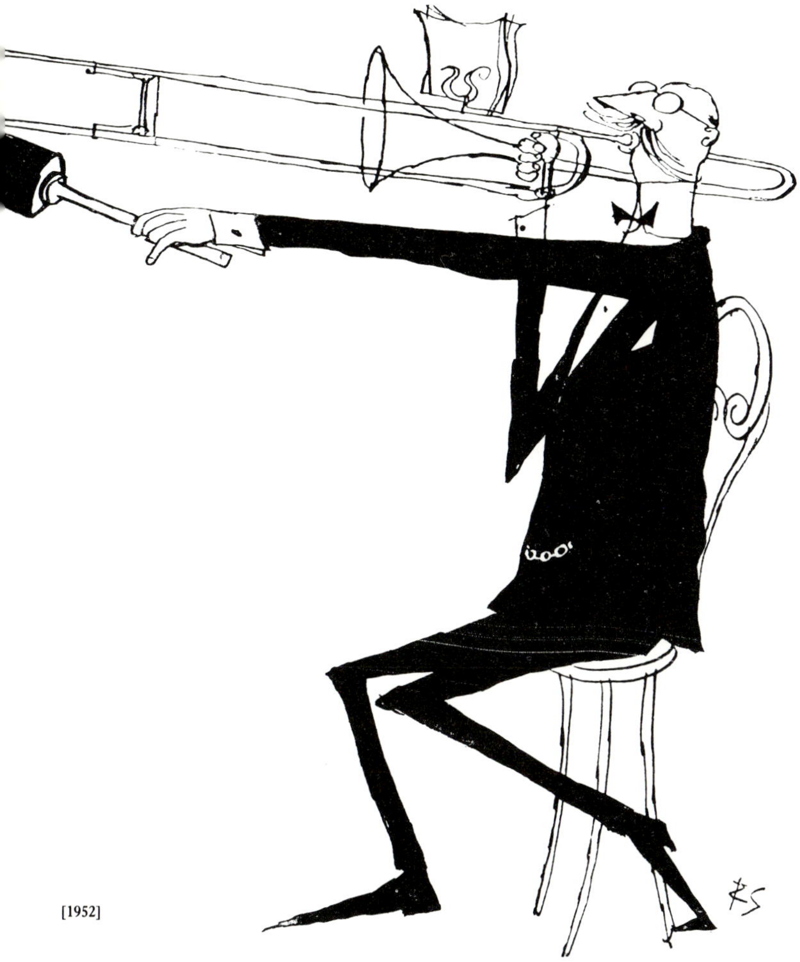

[1952]

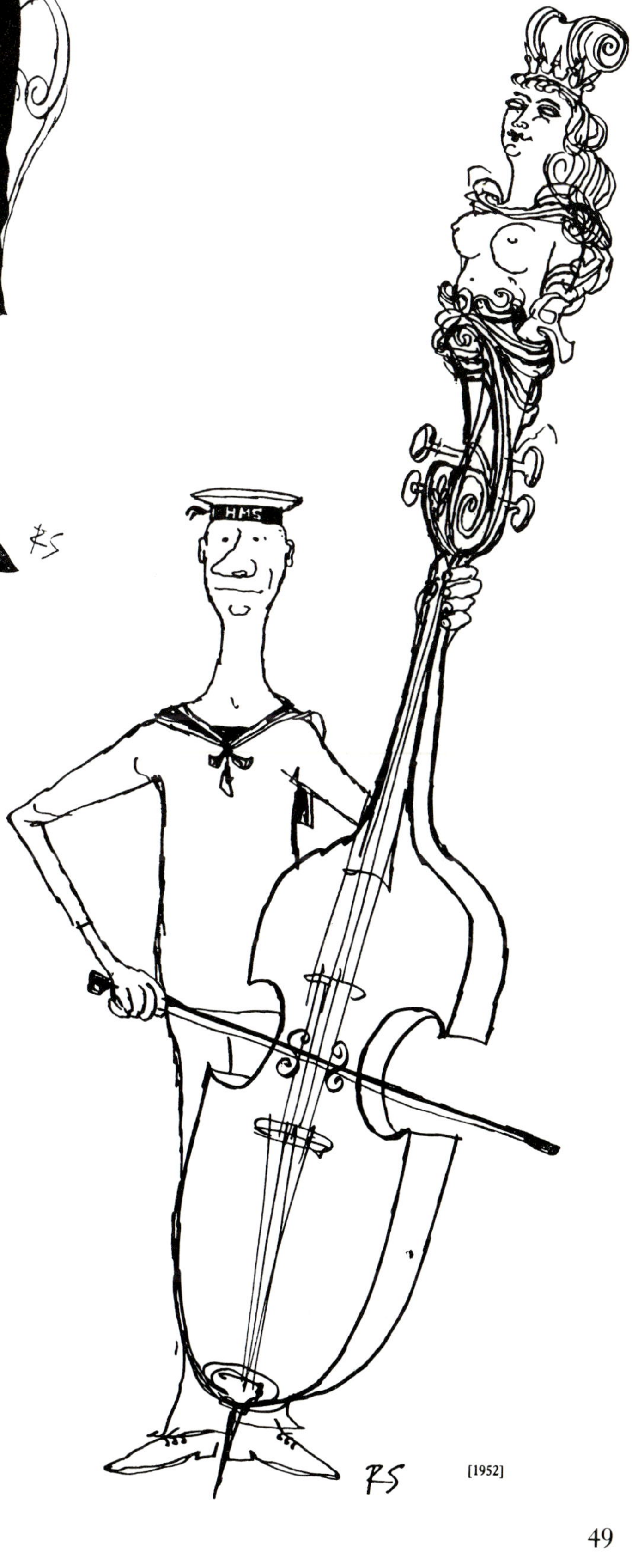
HMS

[1952]

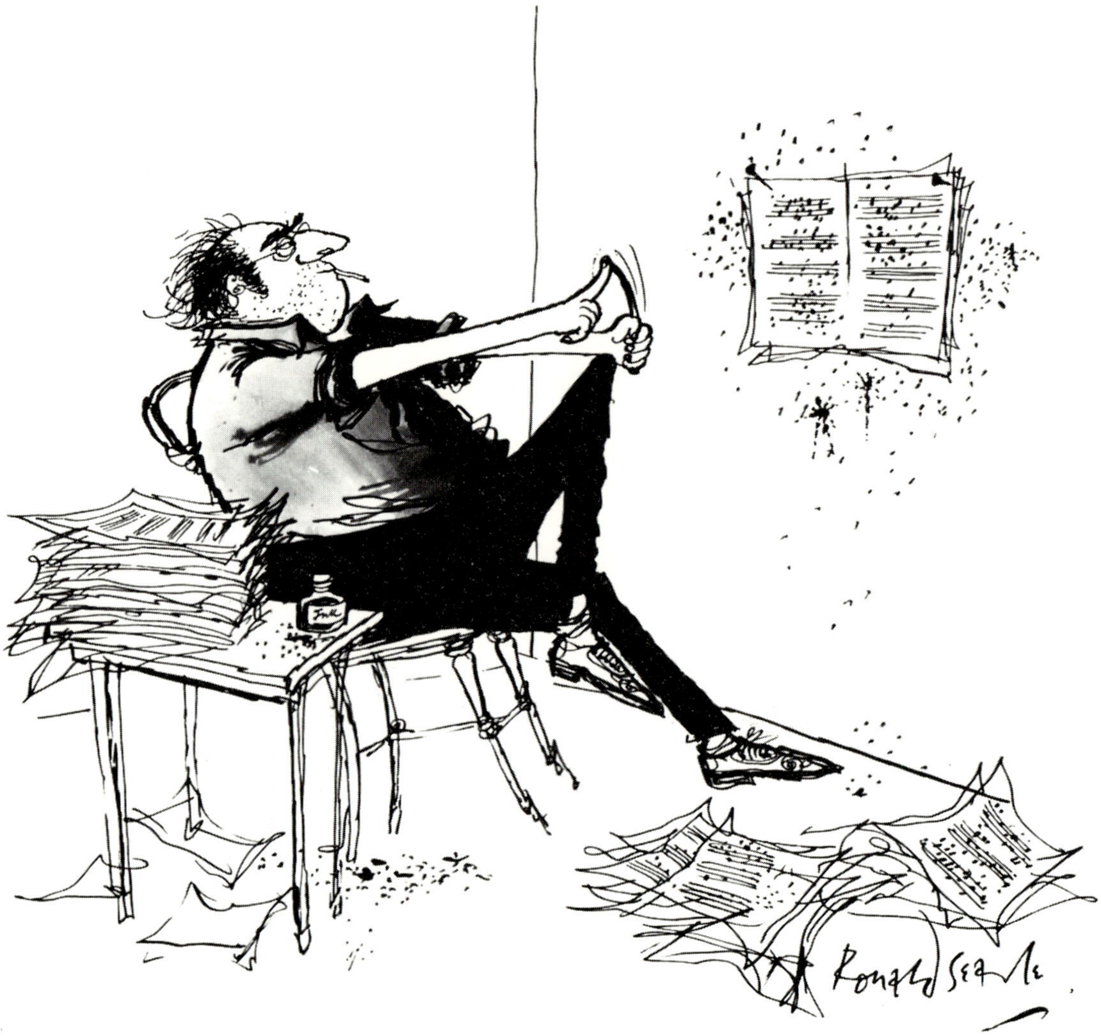
Ronald Searle

[1956]

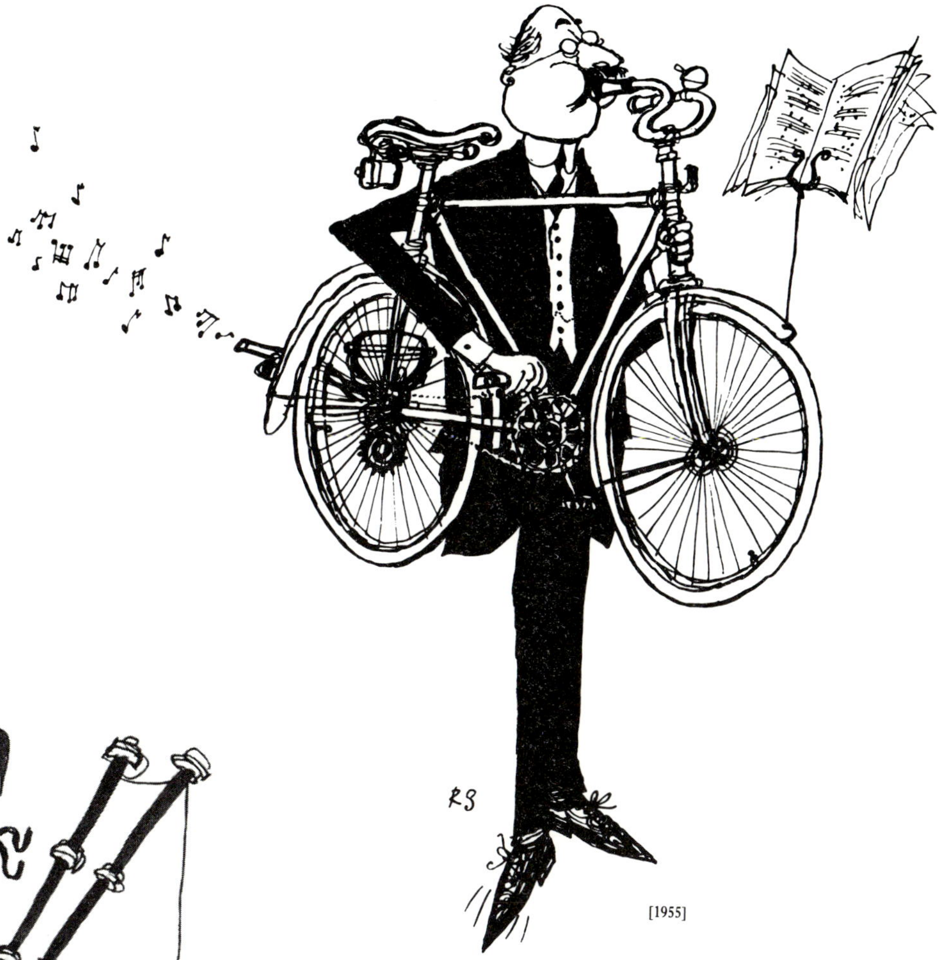

[1955]

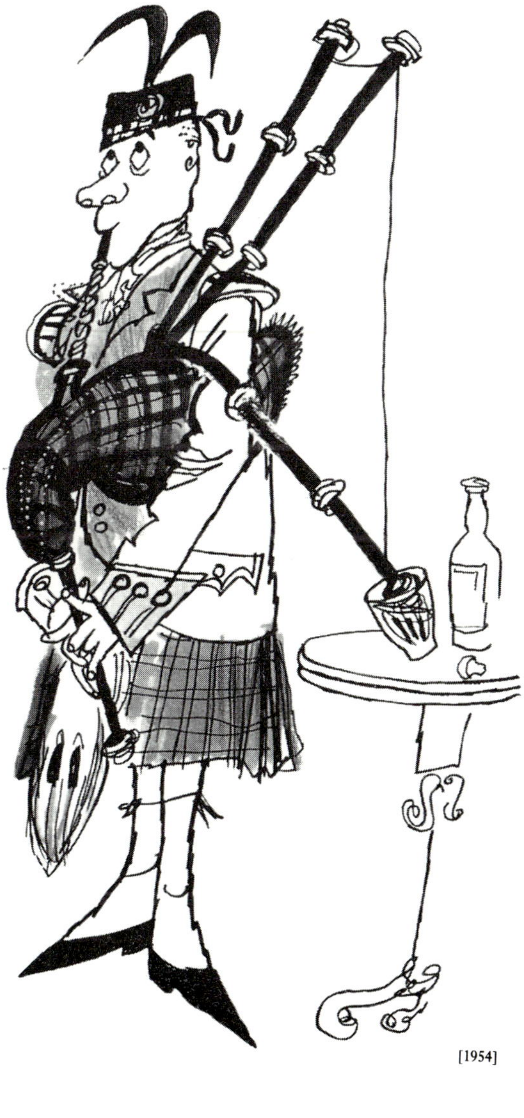

[1954]

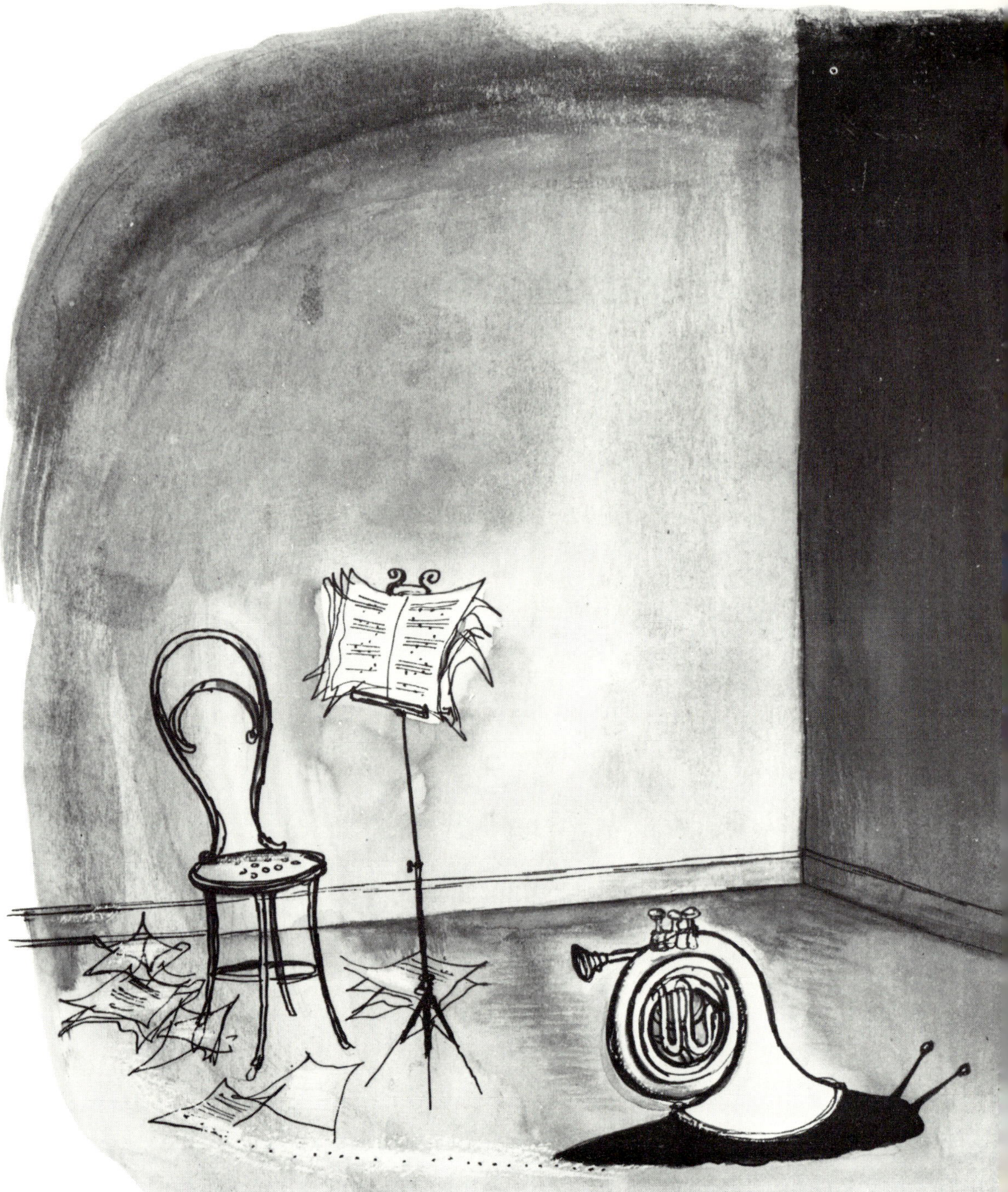
Ronald Searle

[1956]

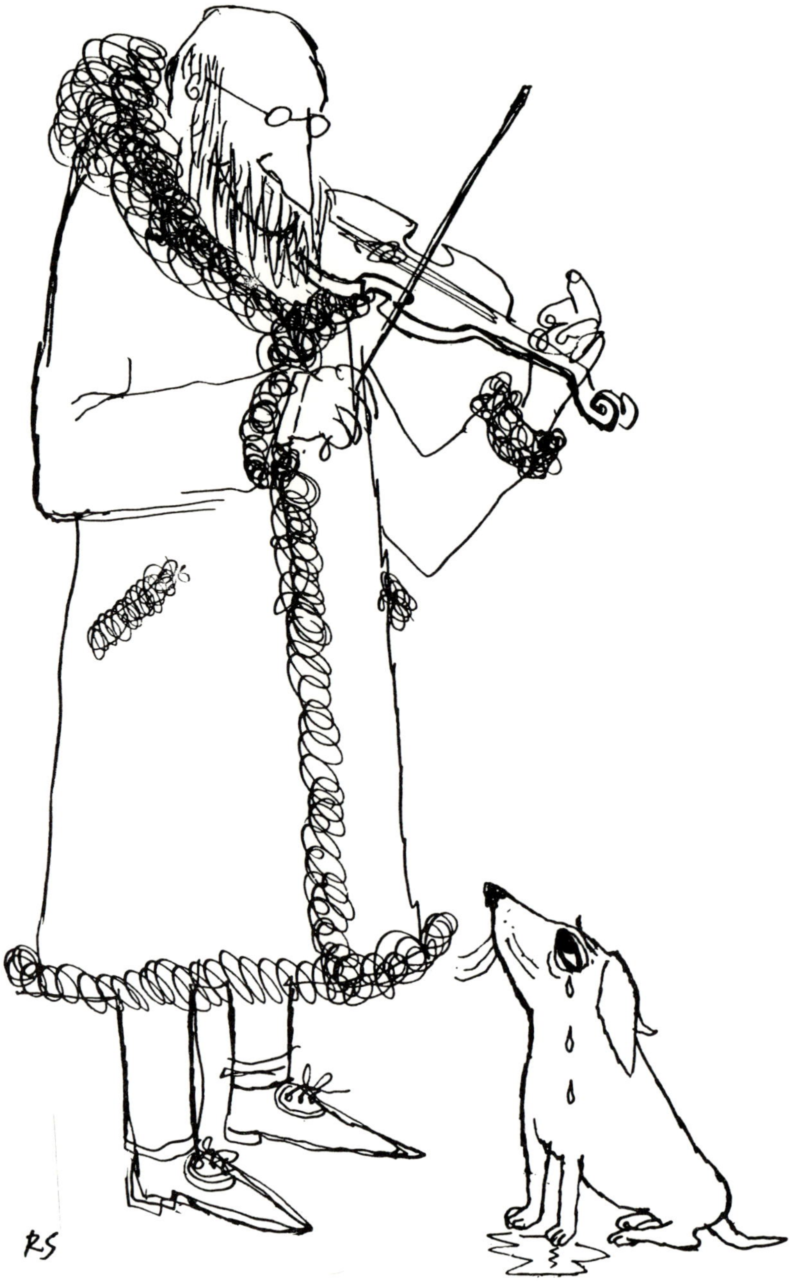
RS

[1952]

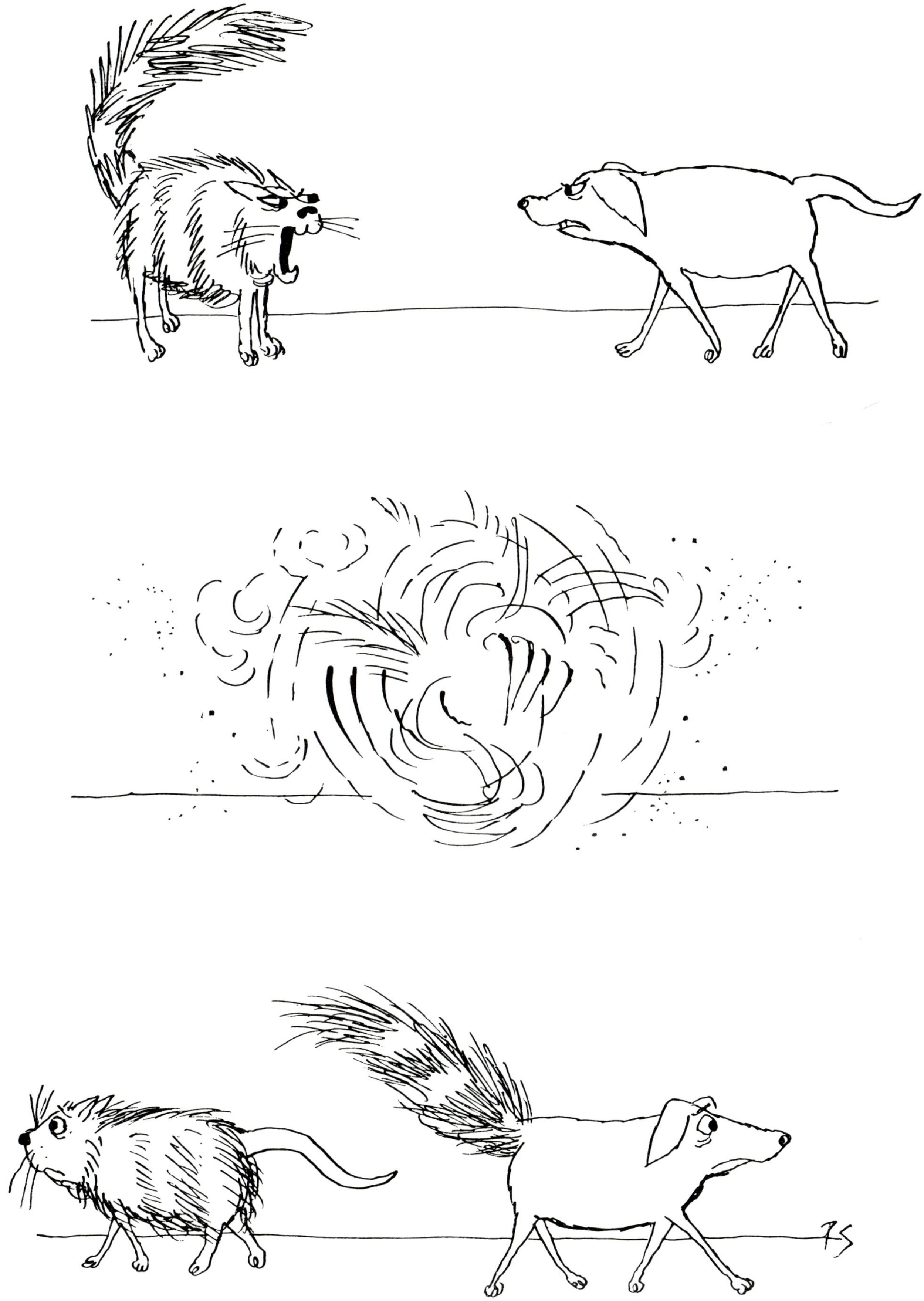

[1952]

[1954]

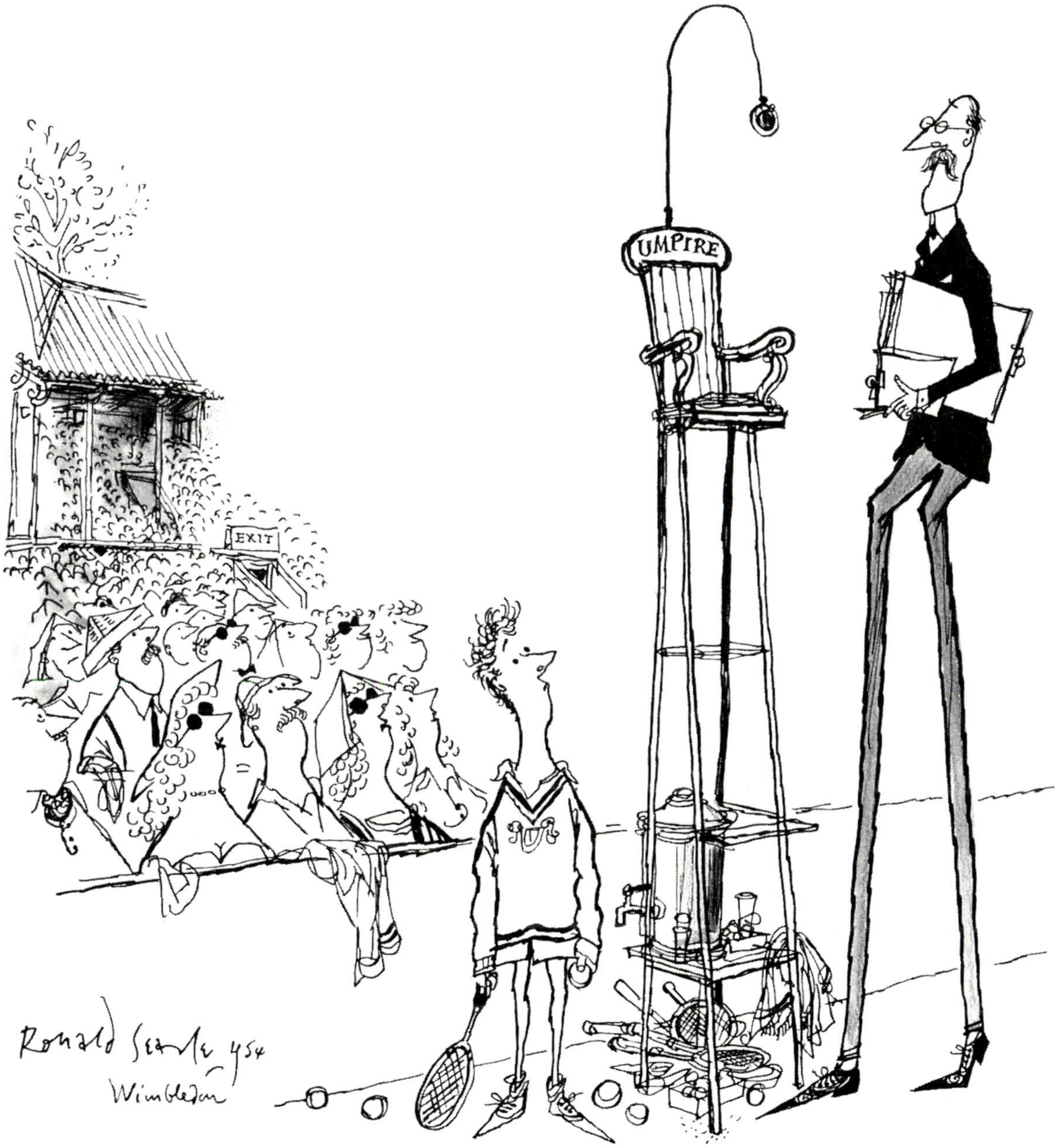
UMPIRE
EXIT
Ronald Searle '54
Wimbledon

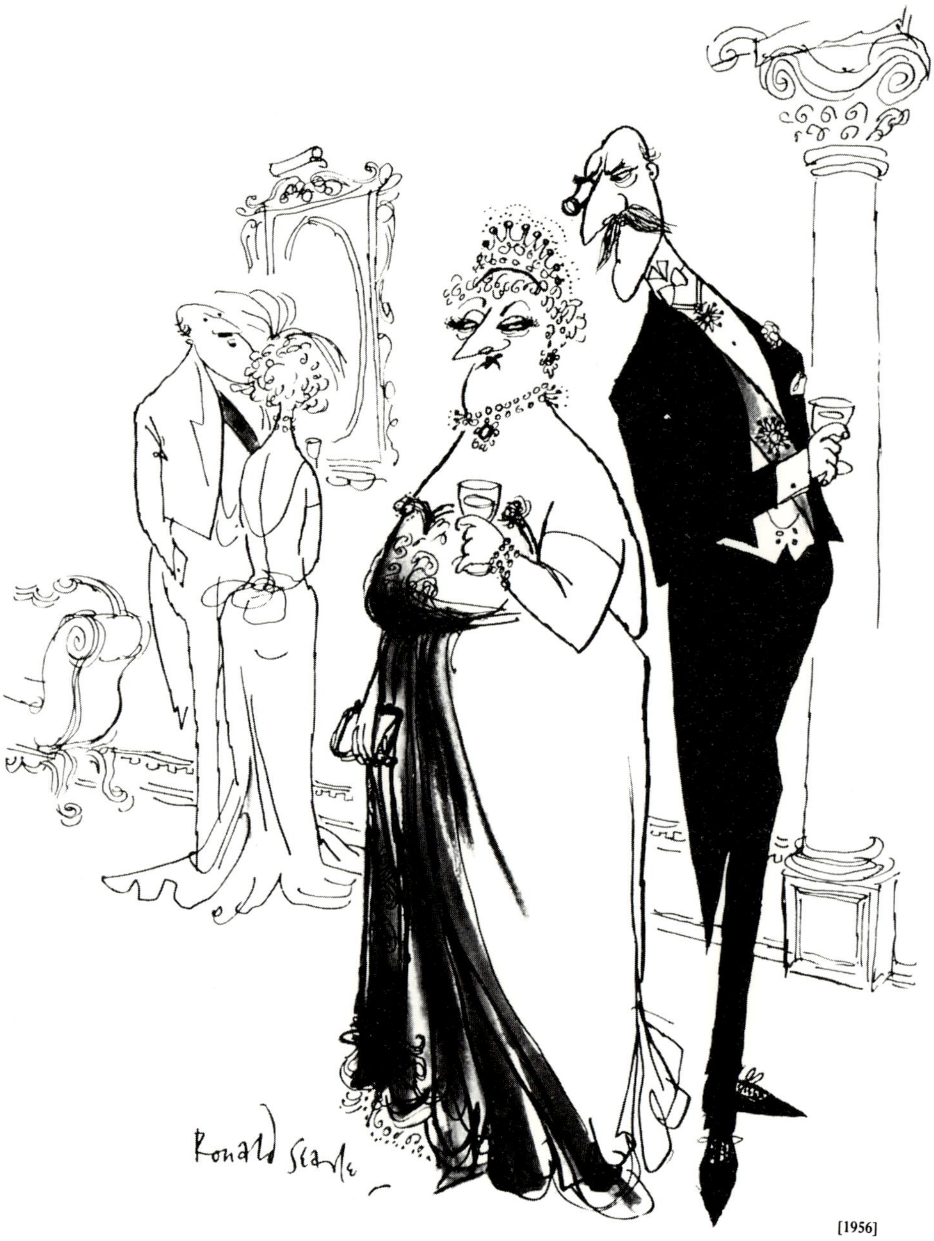
Ronald Searle

[1956]

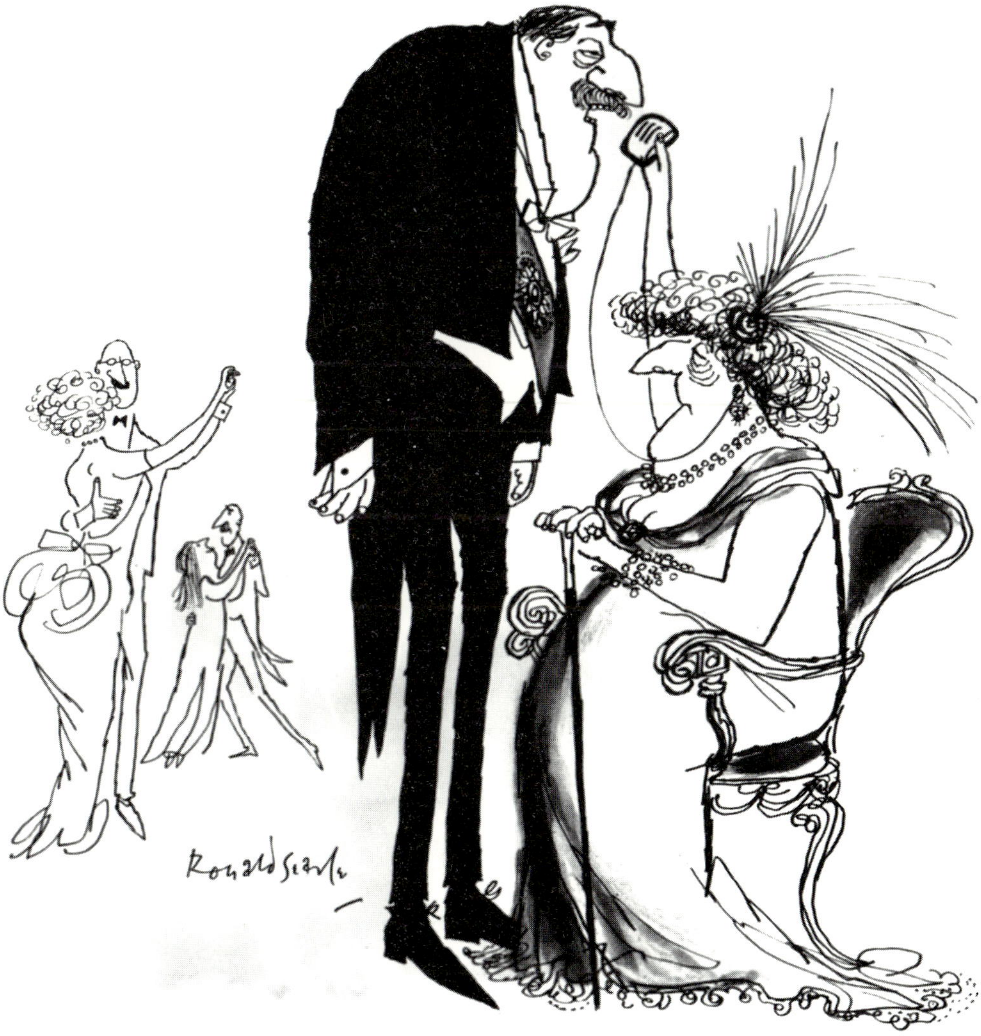
Ronald Searle

[1955]

'May I have the pleasure?'

[1955]

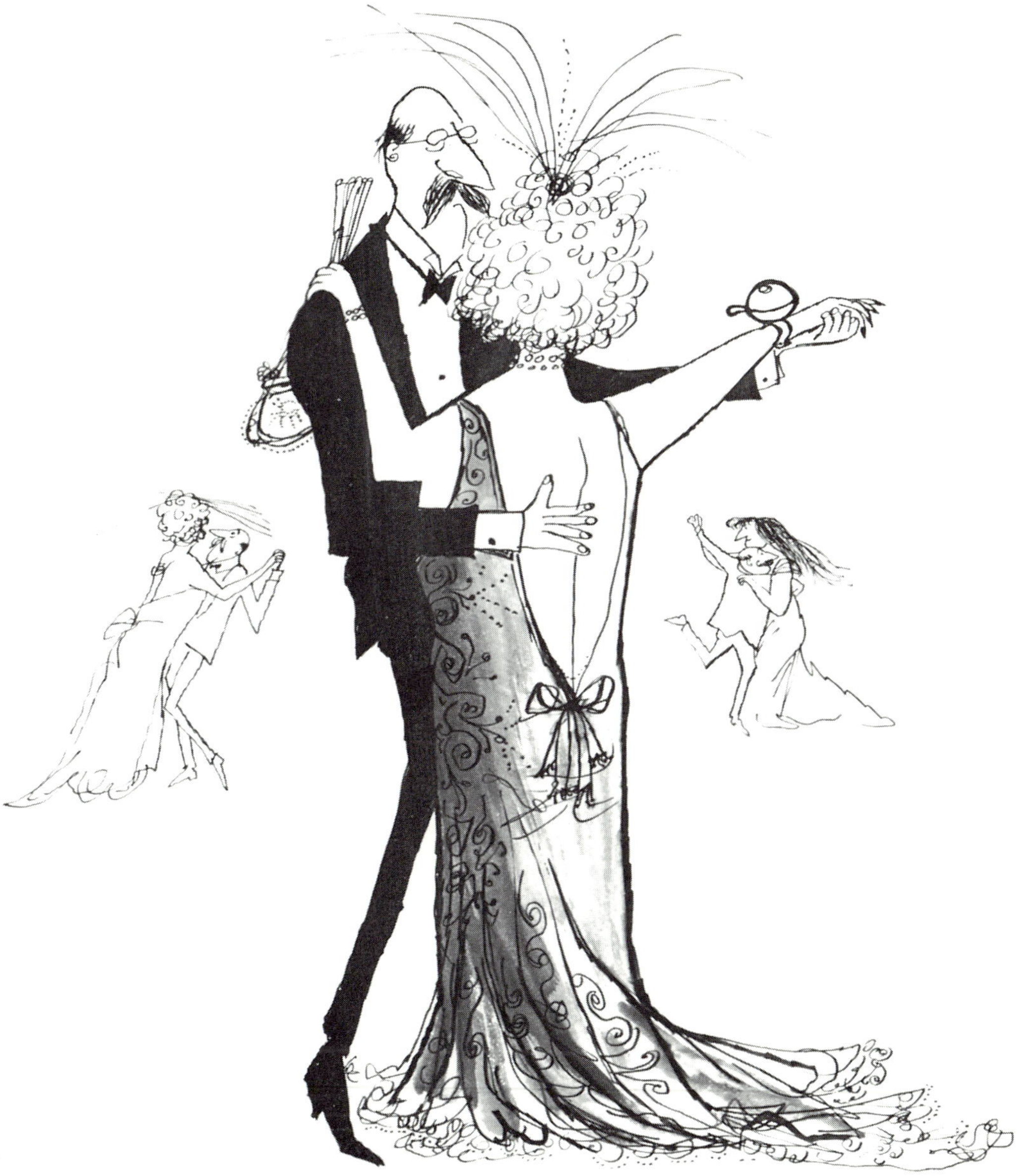

[1955]

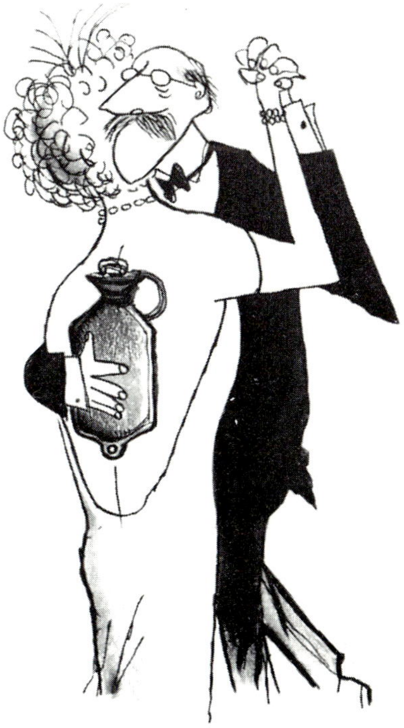

[1954]

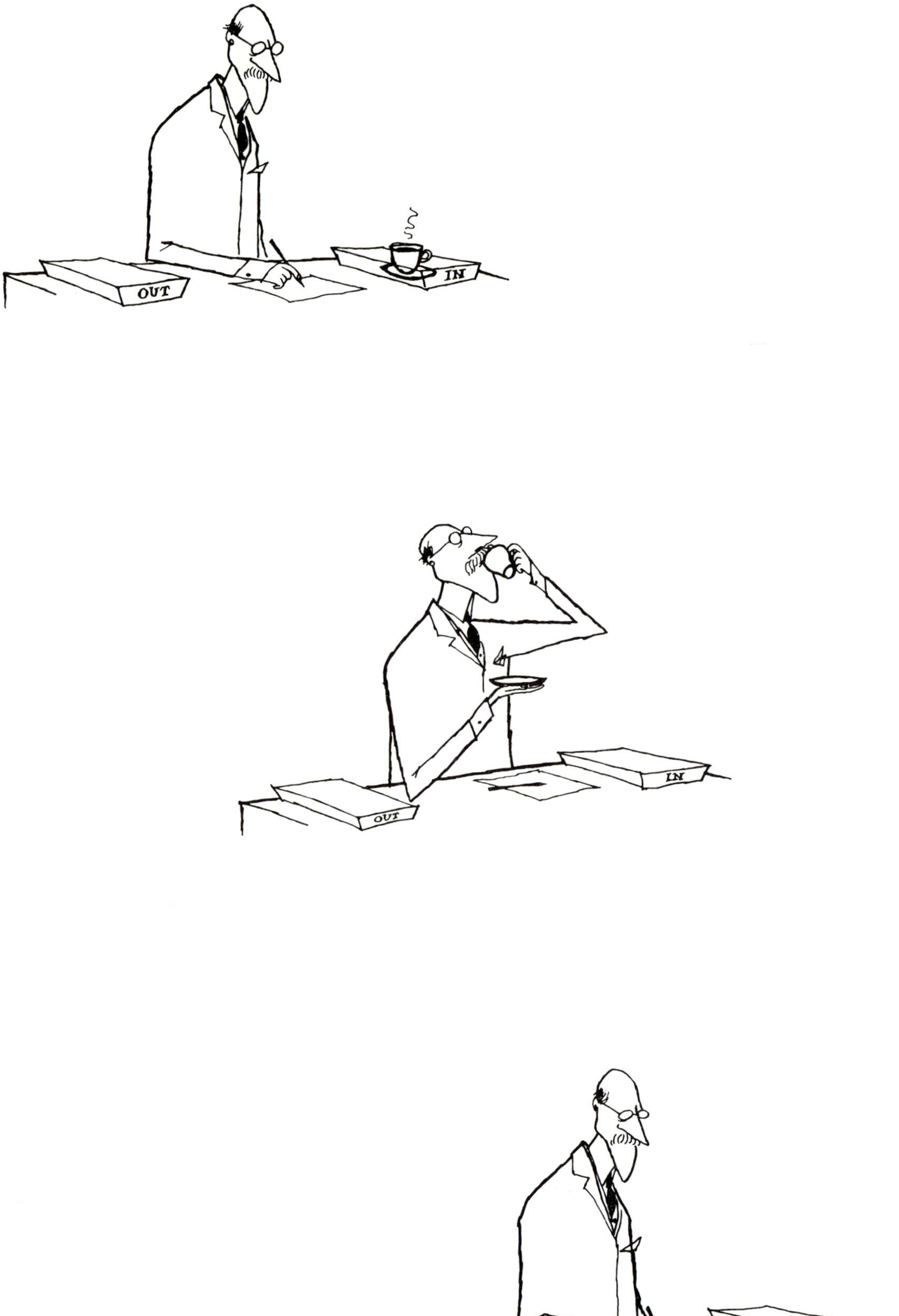
OUT
IN
OUT
IN
OUT
IN

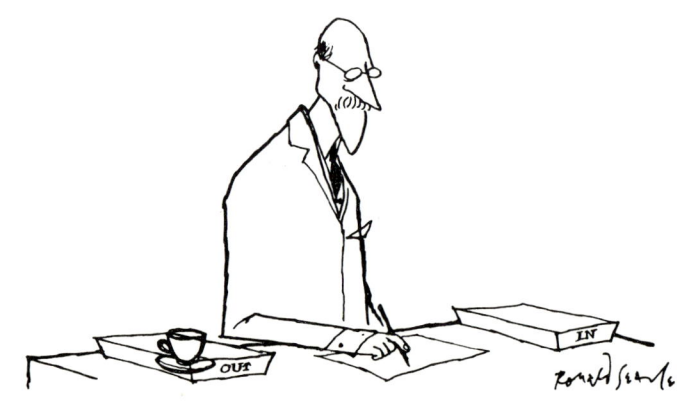

[1954]

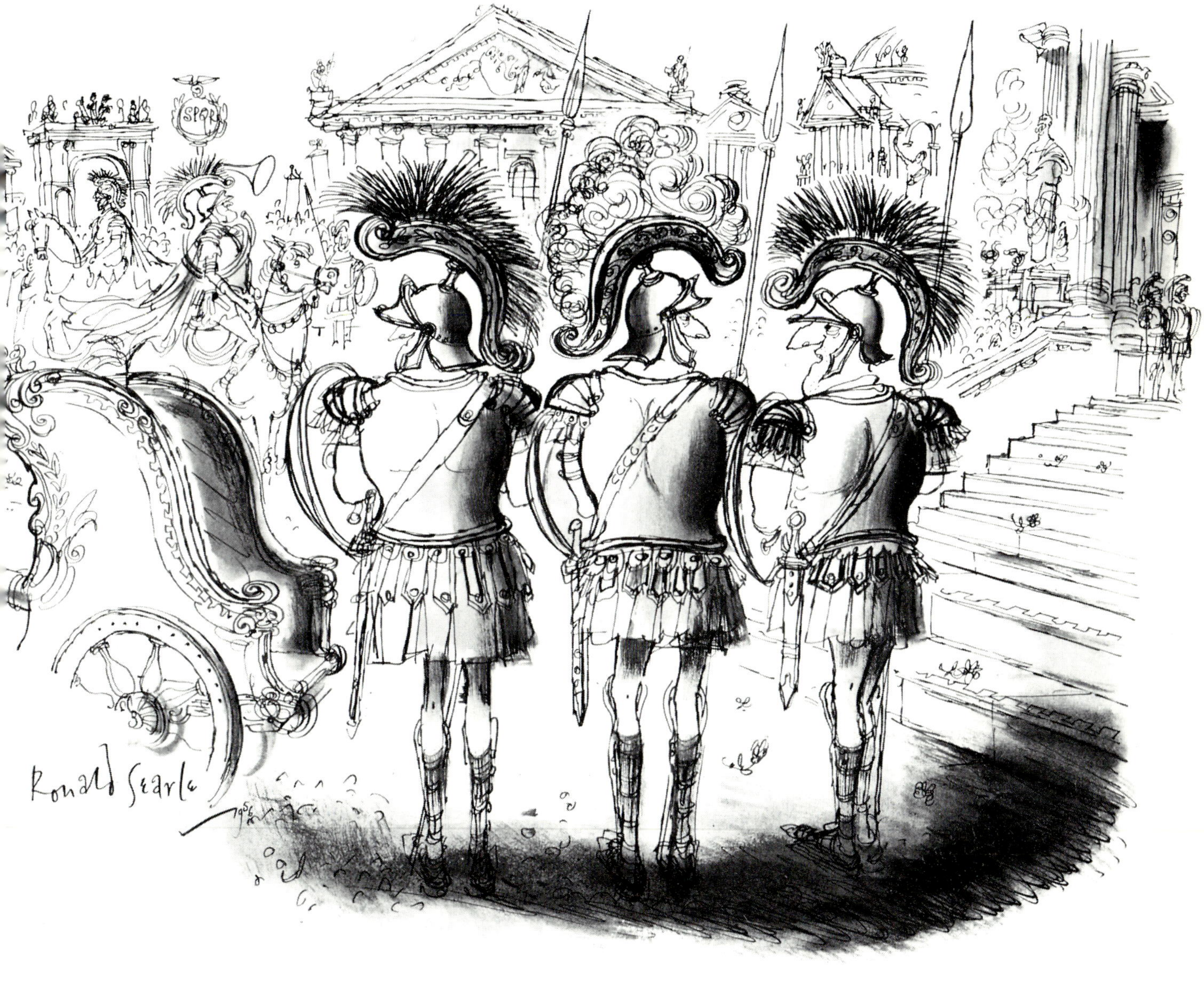
SPQR
Ronald Searle

'Of course, you're lucky, yours curls naturally.'

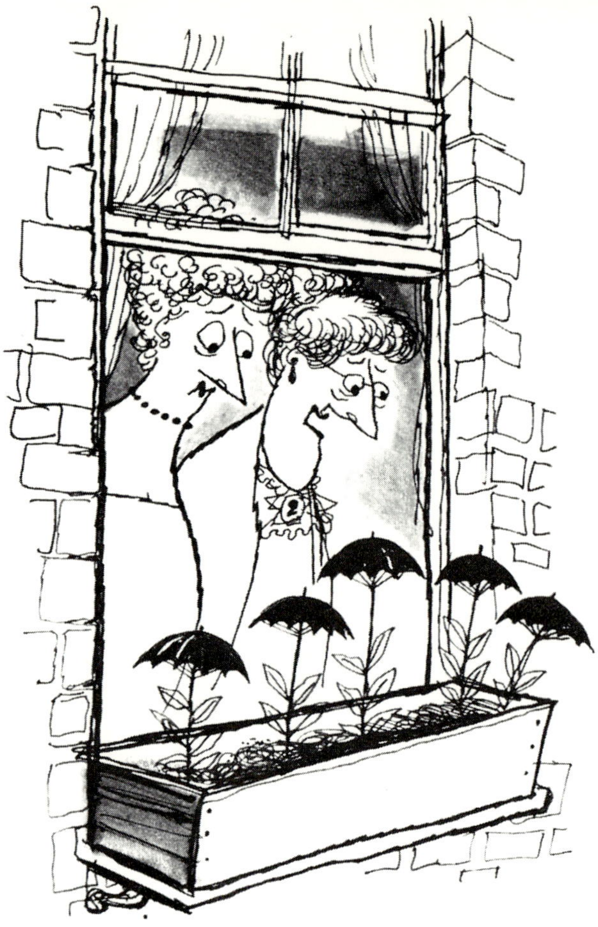

'I'm afraid it's the weather.'

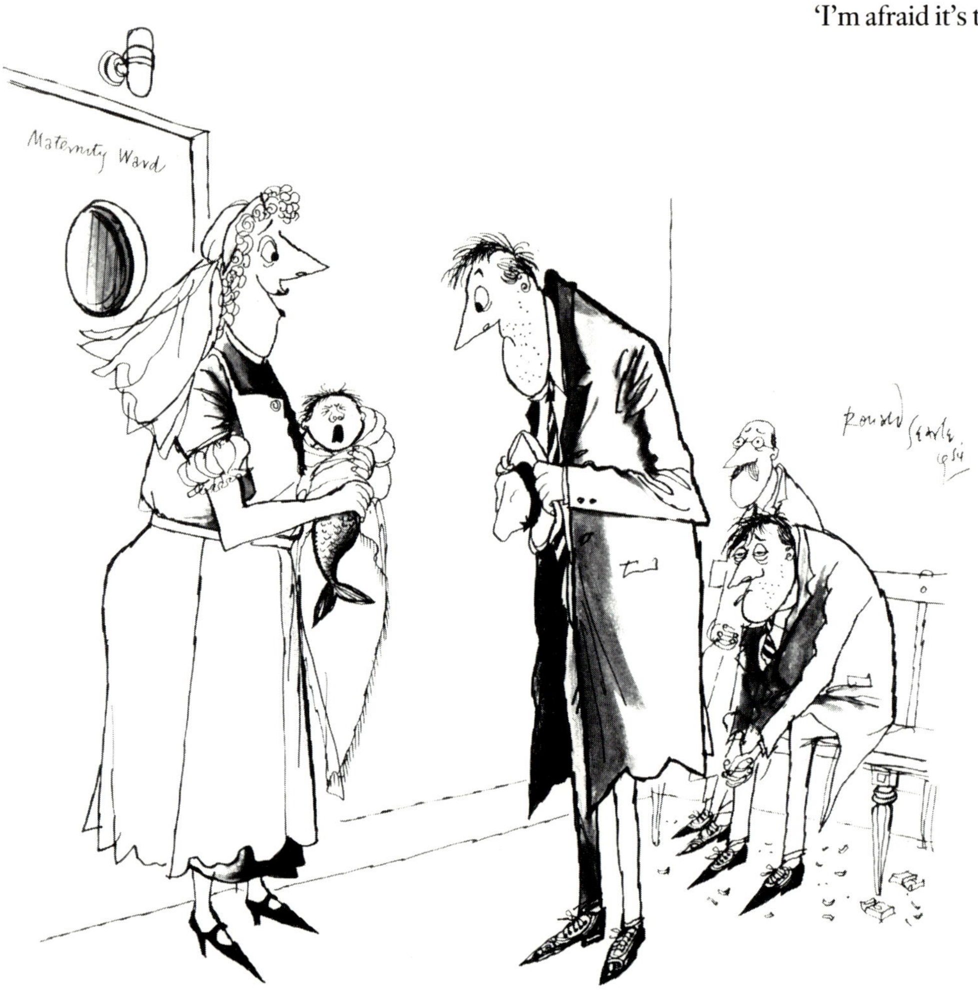
Maternity Ward

'I'm afraid it's the weather.'

beware

[1954]

[1952]

'One of my earlier works…'

BATH

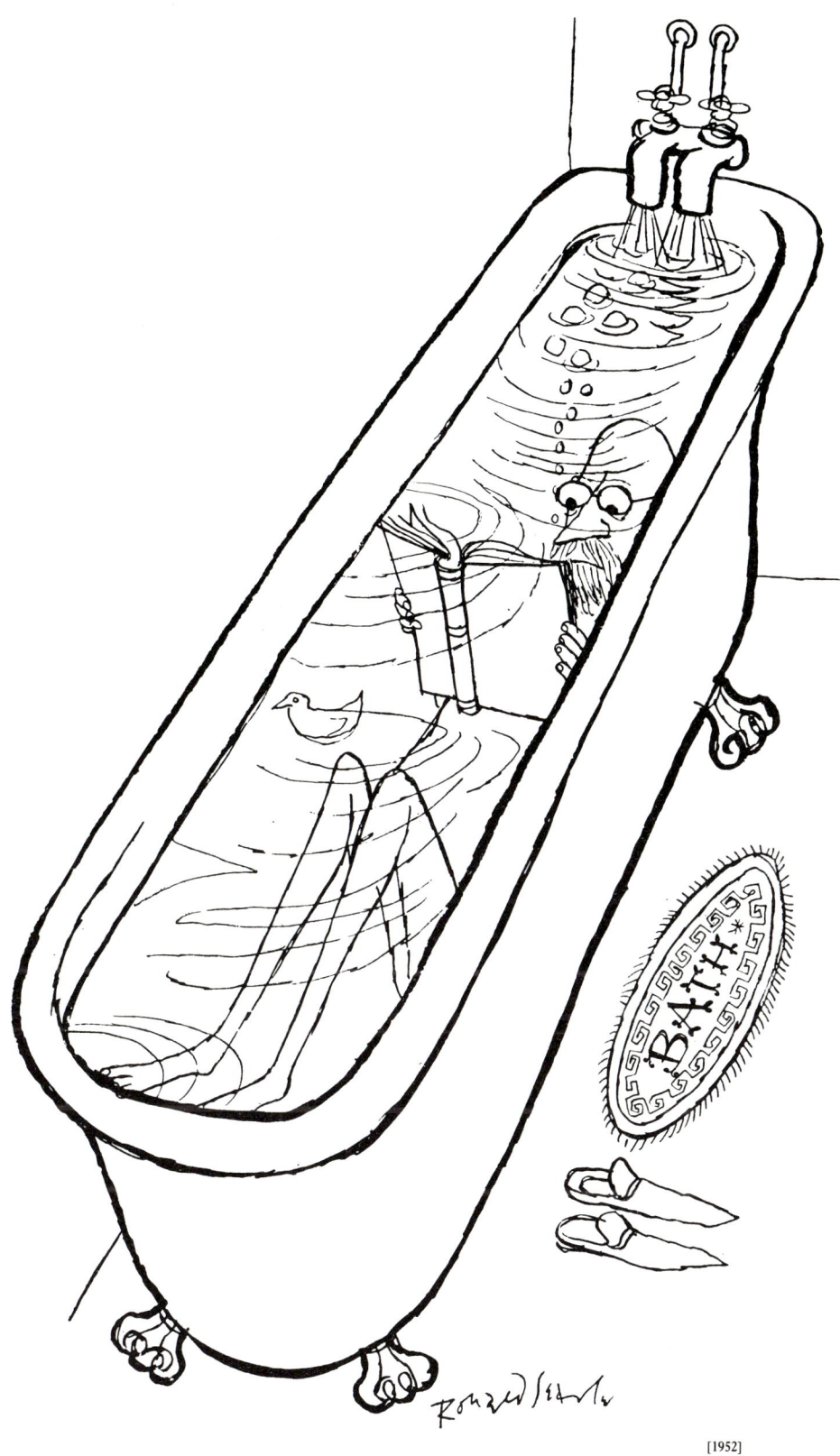

[1952]

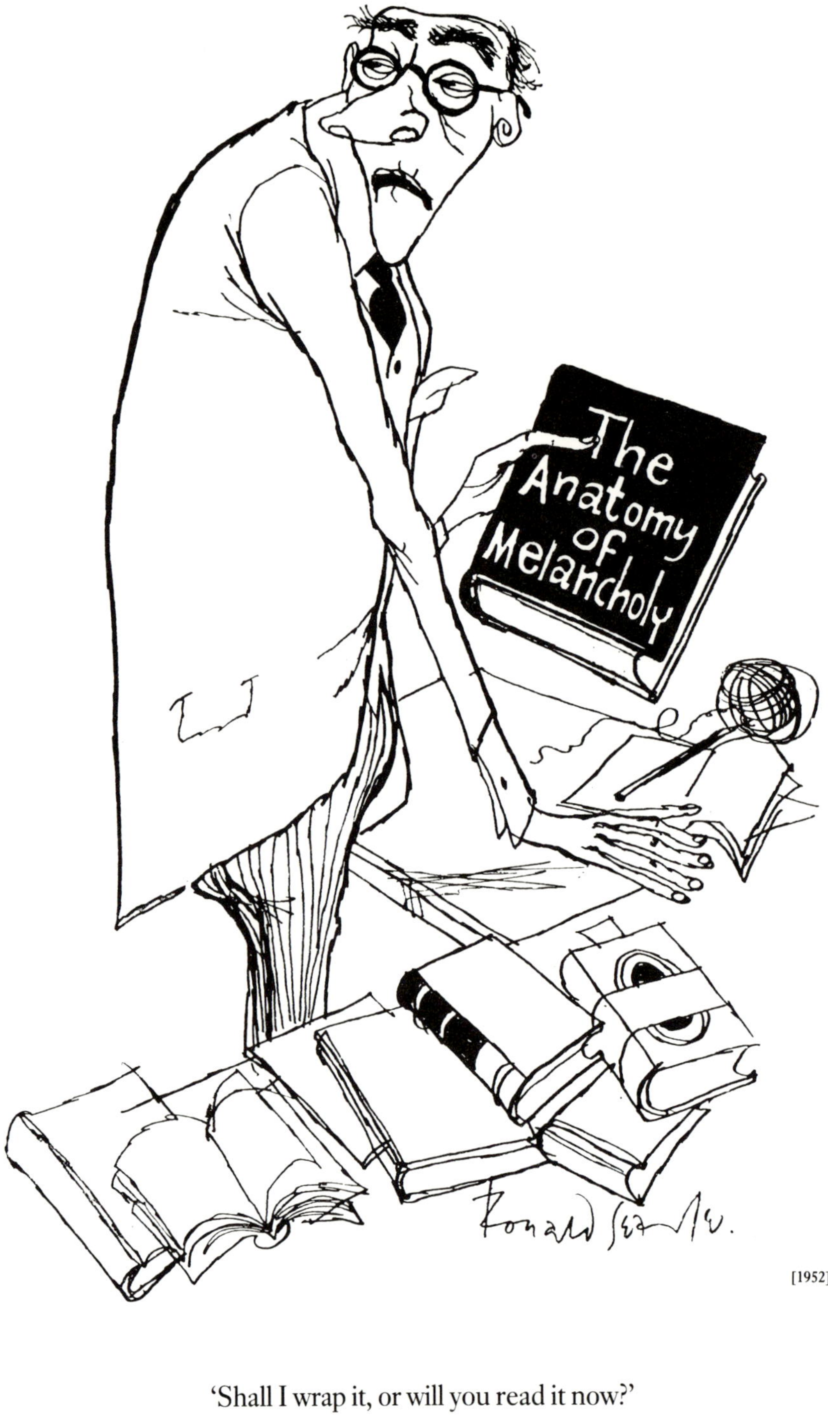
The Anatomy of Melancholy
Ronald Searle.

[1952]

'Shall I wrap it, or will you read it now?'

[1952]

'We read it together –
an unforgettable experience.'

[1951]

'Excuse me, your Proust is showing.'

[1952]

'Mine's a Tristram Shandy.'

[1952]

'My God! Roget's Thesaurus.'

'A to C, stupid, not A to Z!'

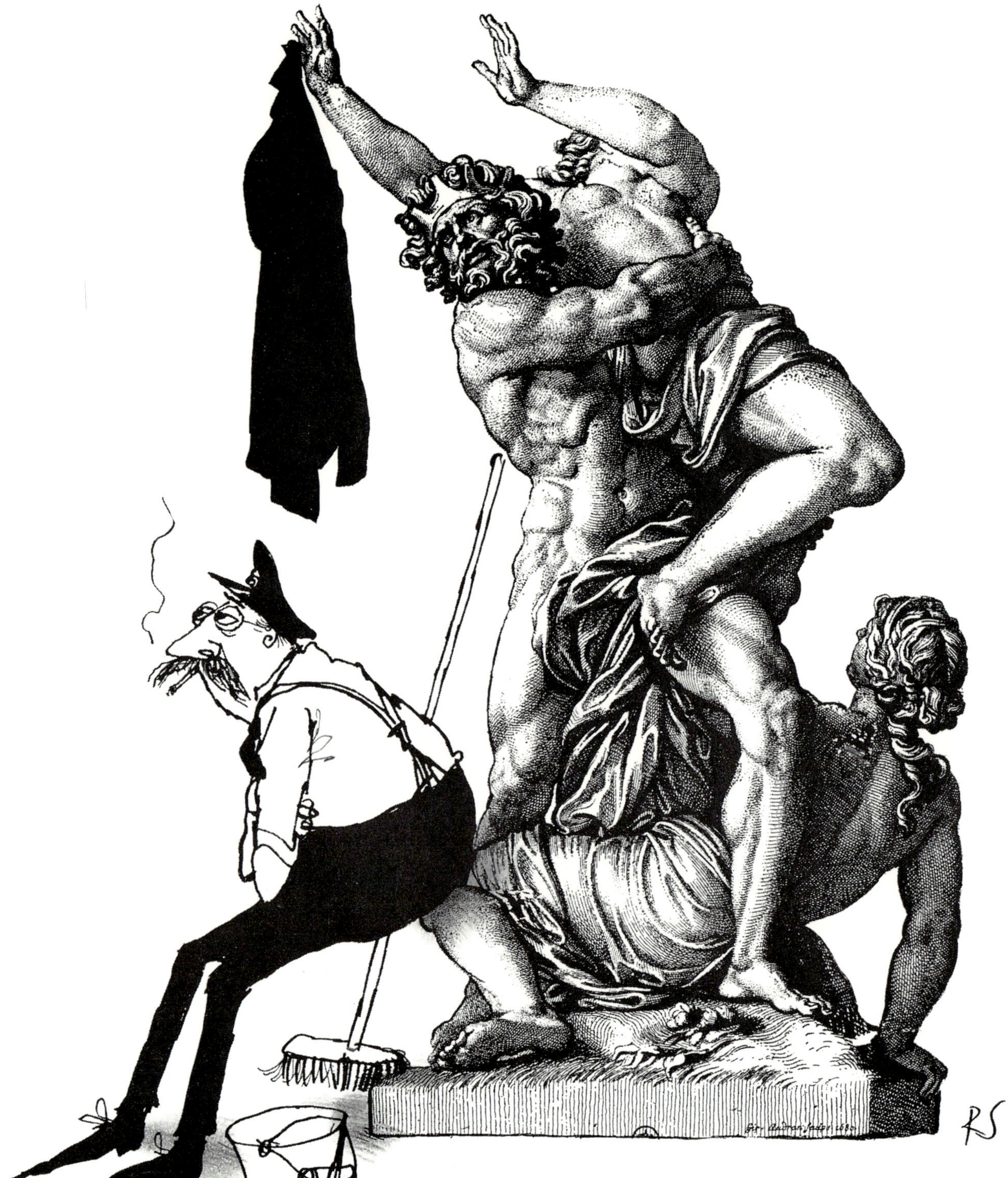

[1952]

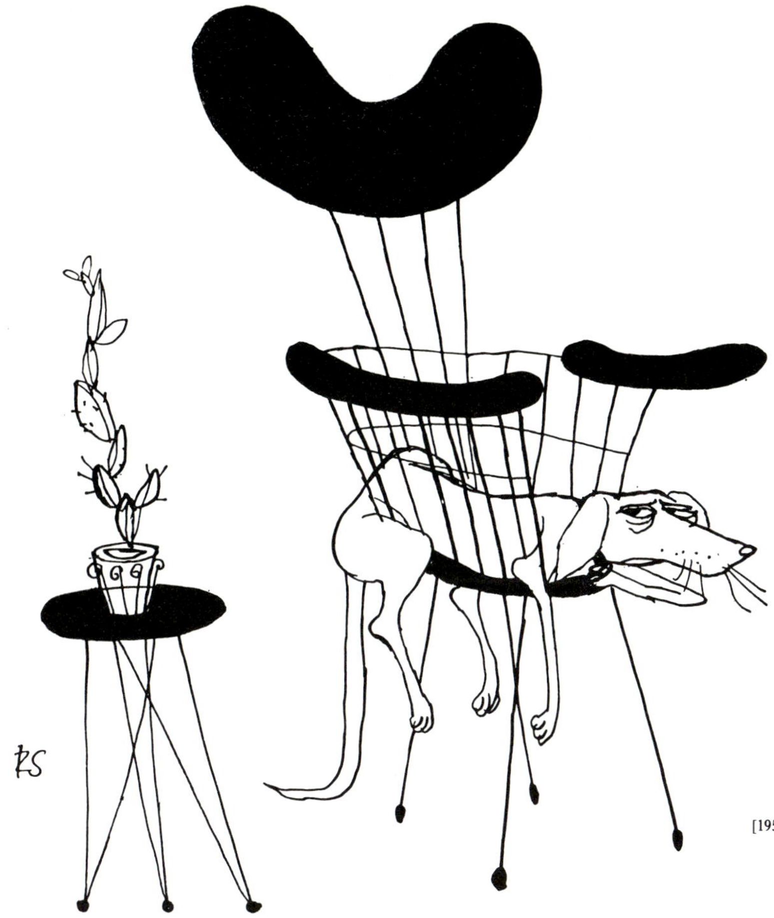

[1952]

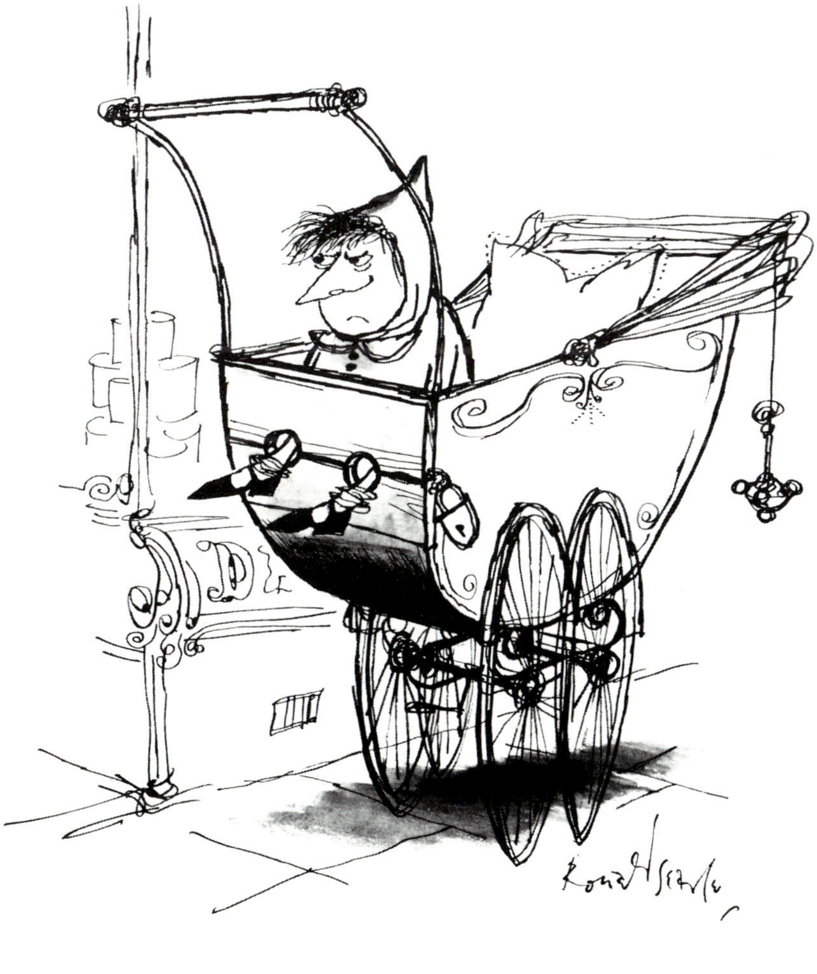

[1956]

Signing Off . . .

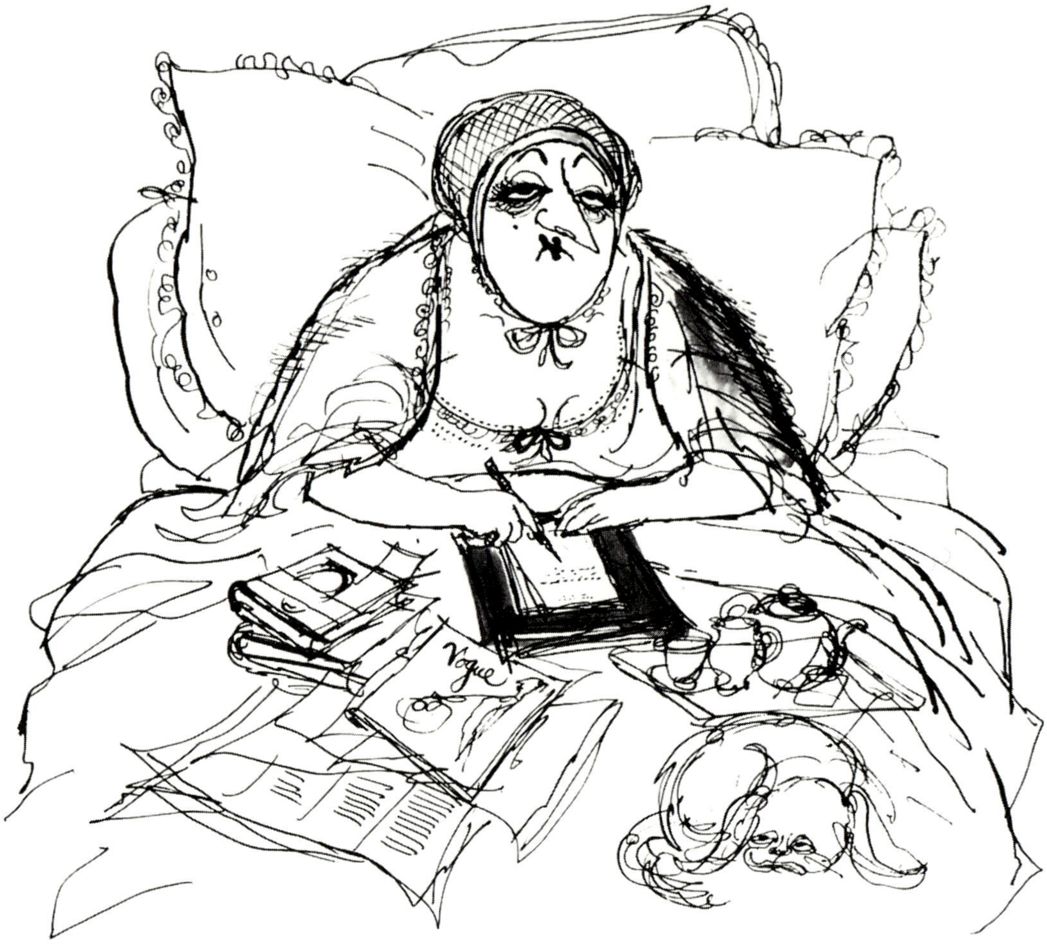
Vogue

[1956]

Yours in haste

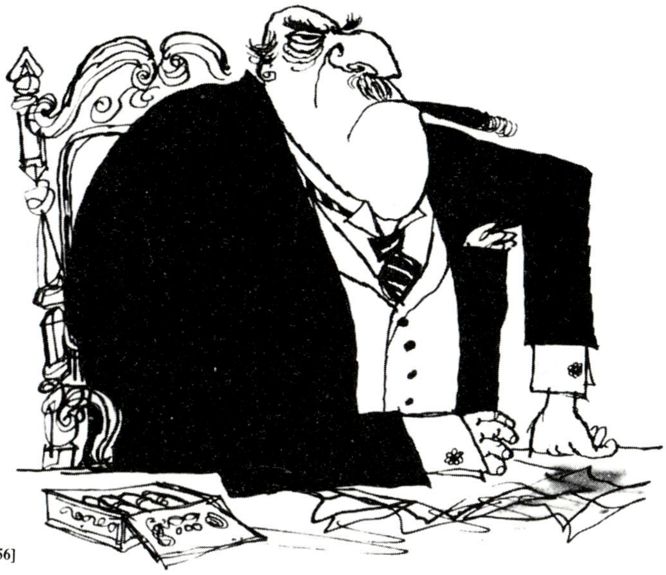

[1956]

Your most obedient servant

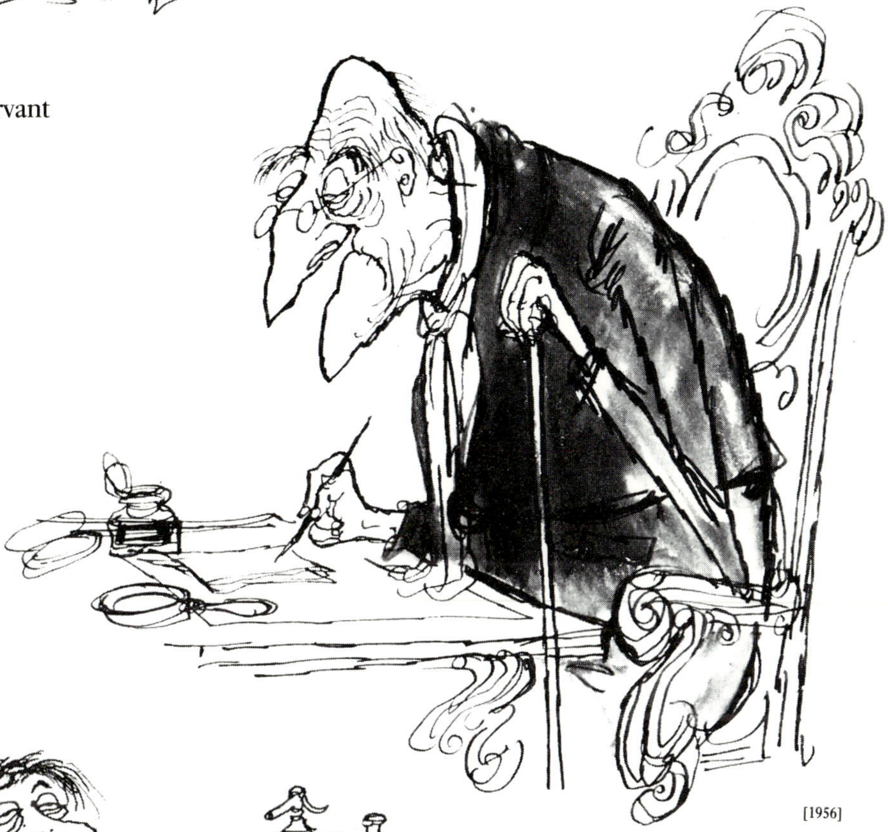

[1956]

Your loving son

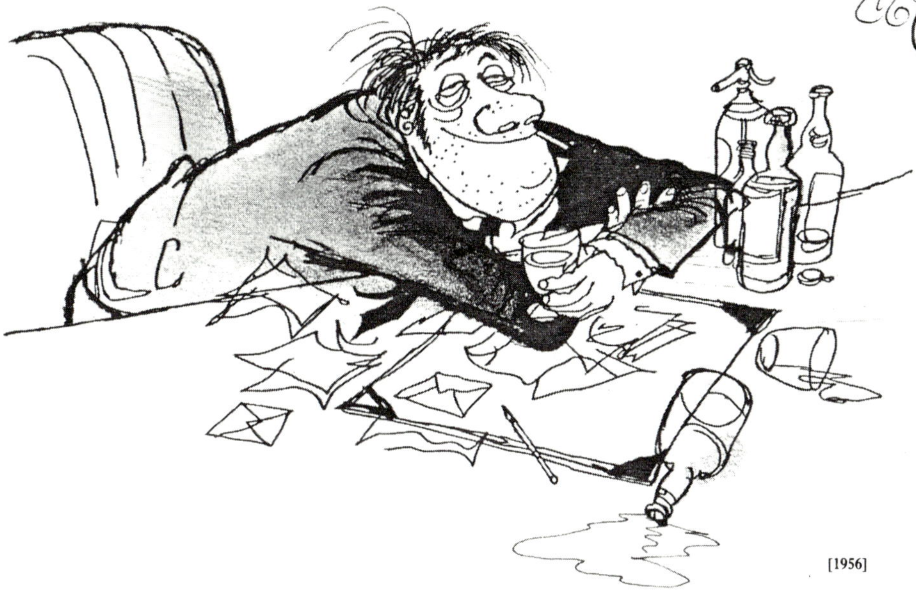

[1956]

Cordially yours

[1956]

Yours ever

[1956]

Yours sincerely

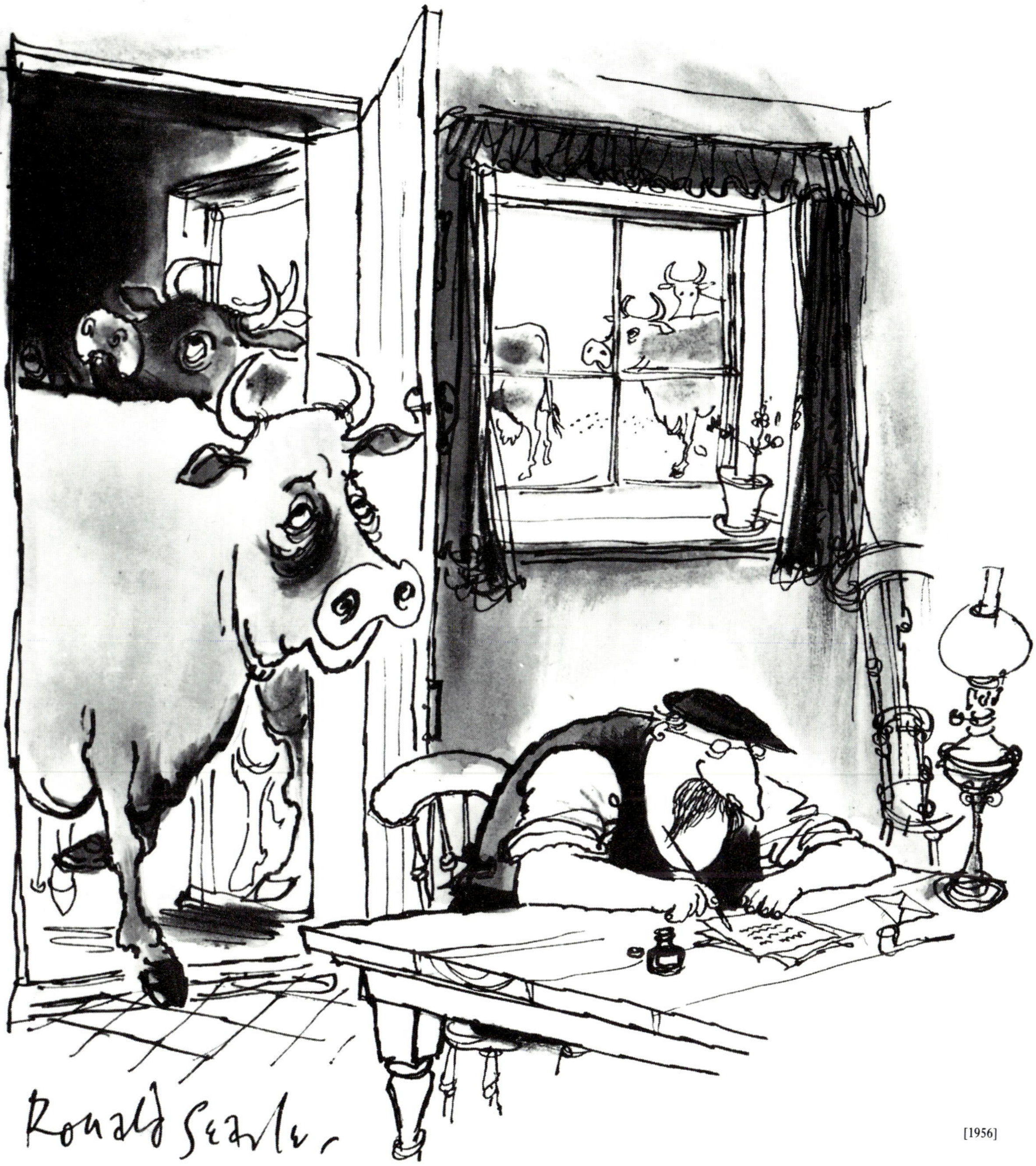
Ronald Searle

[1956]

Yours till the cows come home

[1956]

Yours faithfully

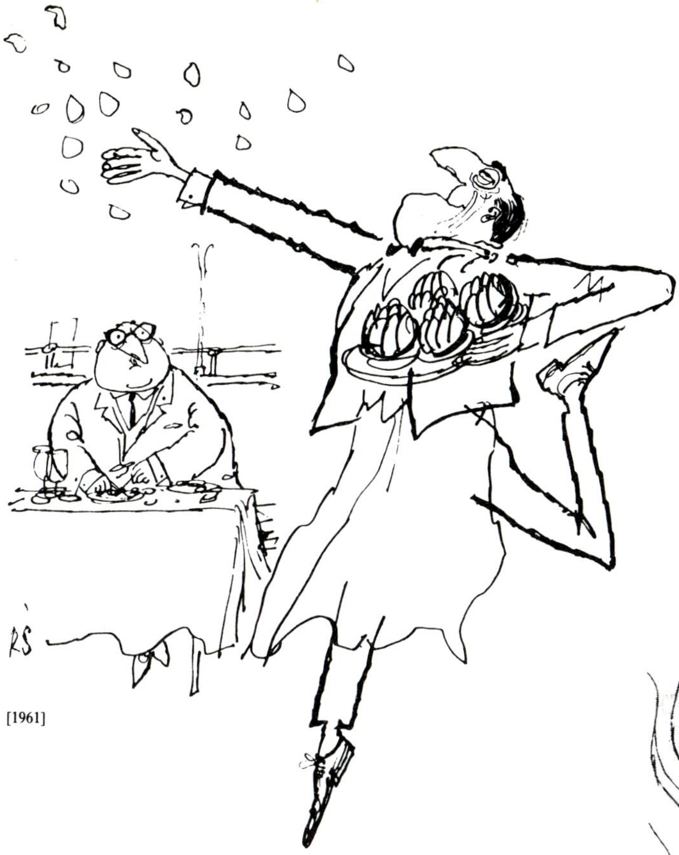

[1961]

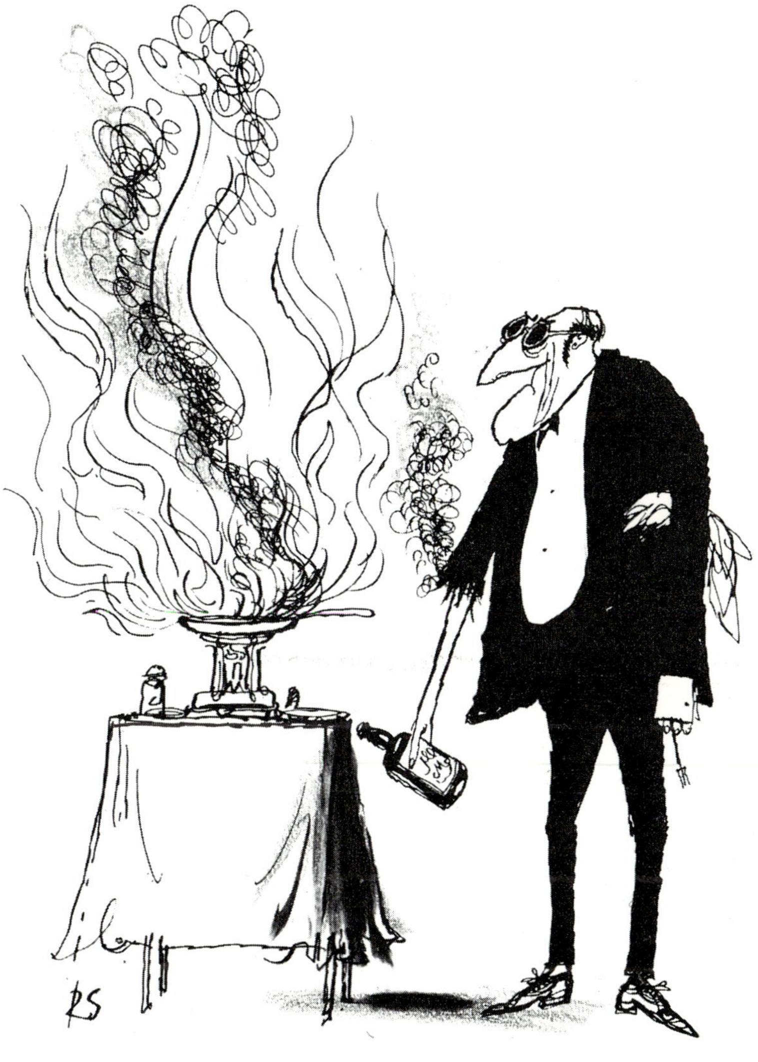

[1960]

Food is just fuel after all…

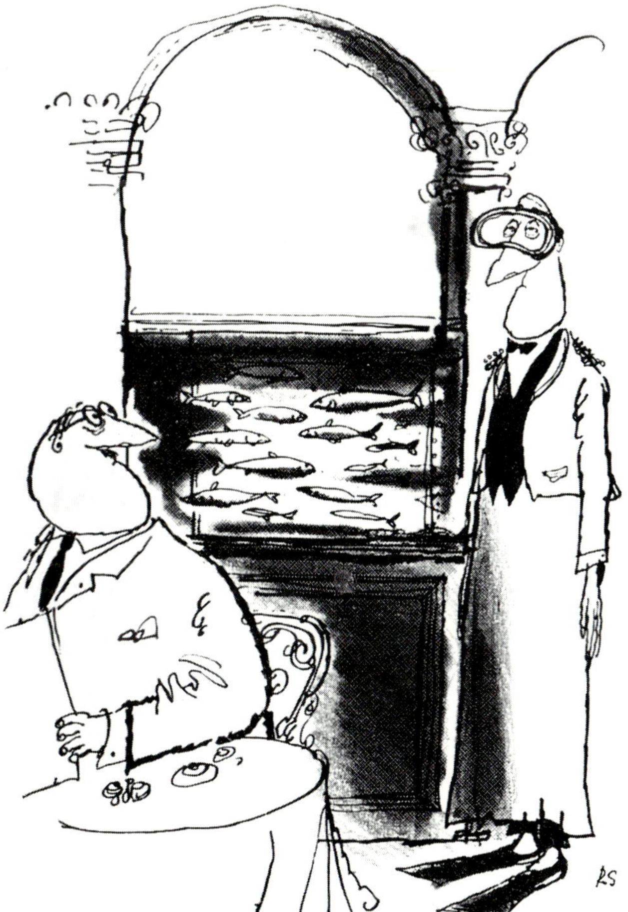

[1961]

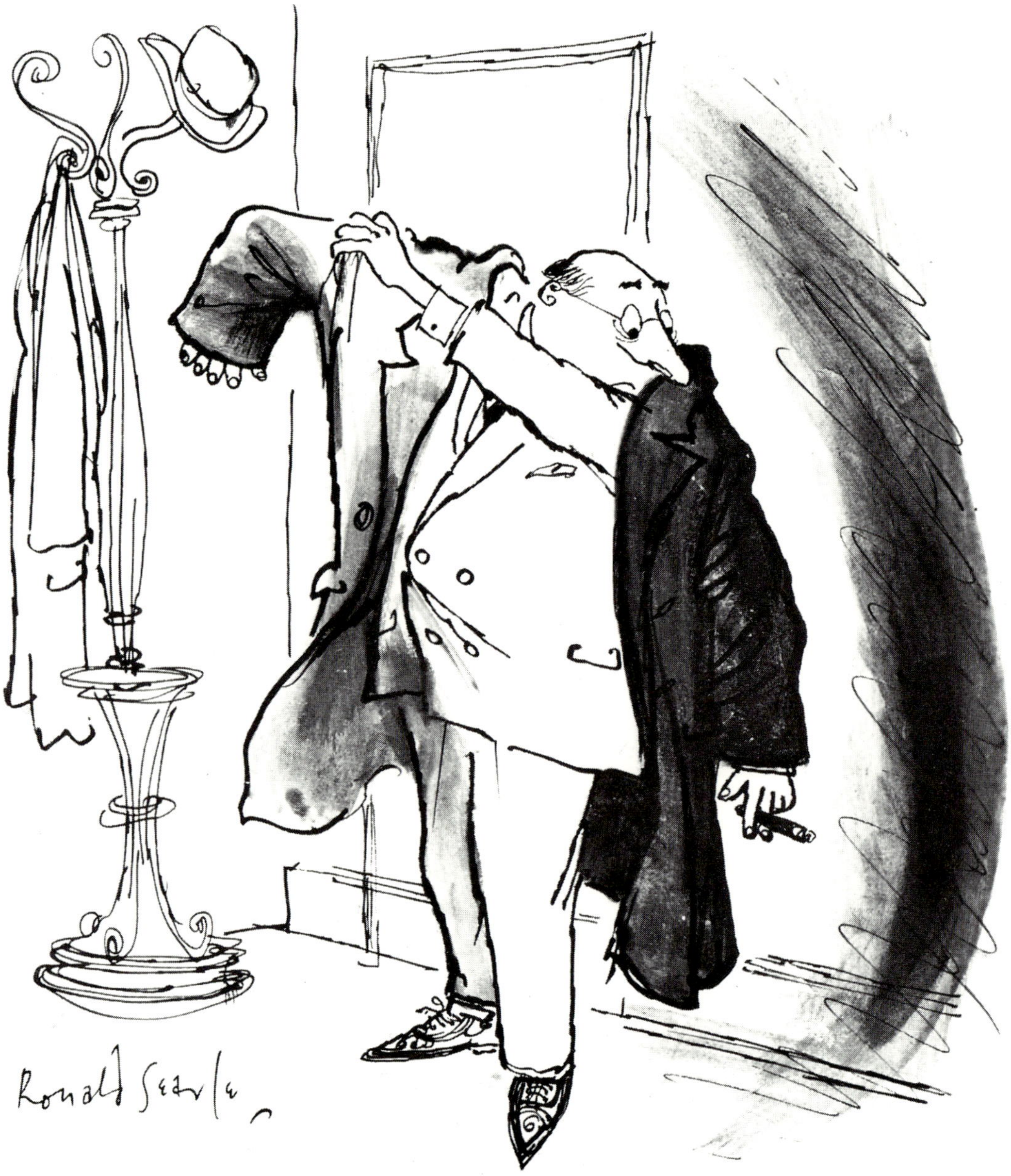
Ronald Searle

[1957]

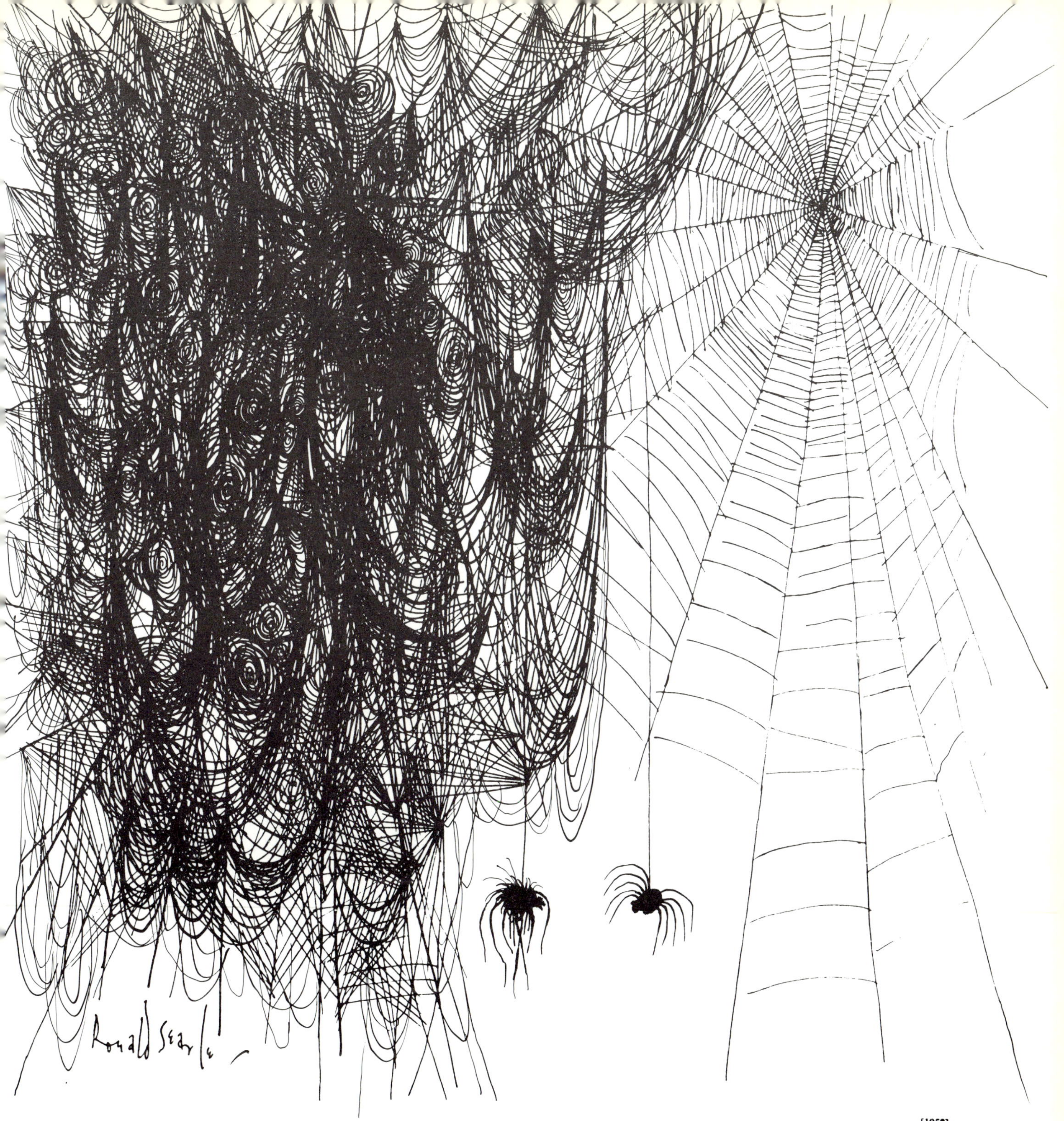
Ronald Searle

[1958]

'Could you tell me the name of your psychiatrist?'

[1952]

St. Trinian's

1941 – 1953

Though St. Trinian's lie in ruins, the St. Trinian's spirit
will rise from her ashes, like a vulture from the feast.

C. Day Lewis [1953]

St.Trinia
School for g

[1952]

84

A Short Dirge for St. Trinian's

Where are the girls of yesteryear? How strange
To think they're scattered East, South, West and North –
Those pale Medusas of the Upper Fourth,
Those Marihuanas of the Moated Grange.

No more the shrieks of victims, and no more
The fiendish chuckle borne along the breeze!
Gone are the basilisk eyes, the bony knees.
Mice, and not blood, run down each corridor.

Now poison ivy twines the dorm where casks
Were broached and music mistresses were flayed,
While on the sports ground where the pupils played
The relatively harmless adder basks.

Toll for St. Trinian's, nurse of frightful girls!
St. Trinian's, mother of the far too free!
No age to come (thank God) will ever see
Such an academy as Dr. Searle's.

C. Day Lewis [1953]

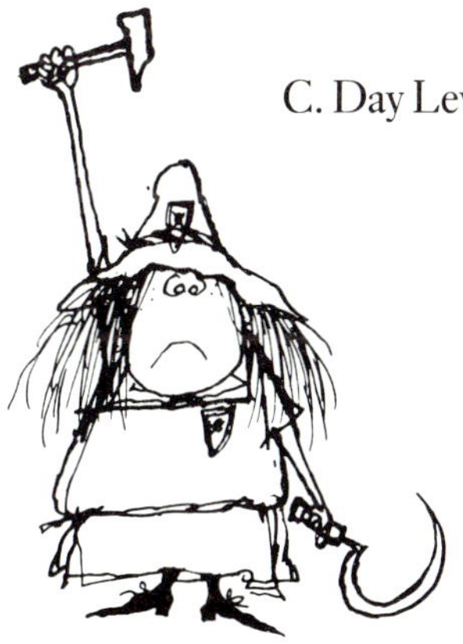

Our Philosophy
(For those who came in late)

Maidens of St. Trinian's
Gird your armour on.
Grab the nearest weapon
Never mind which one!
The battle's to the strongest
Might is always right.
Trample on the weakest
Glory in their plight!
St. Trinian's! St. Trinian's!
Our battle cry.
St. Trinian's! St. Trinian's!
Will never die!
Stride towards your fortune,
Boldly on your way.
Never once forgetting
There's one born every day.
Let our motto be broadcast
'Get your blow in first',
She who draws the sword last
Always comes off worst.

Sidney Gilliat [1954]

Now read on 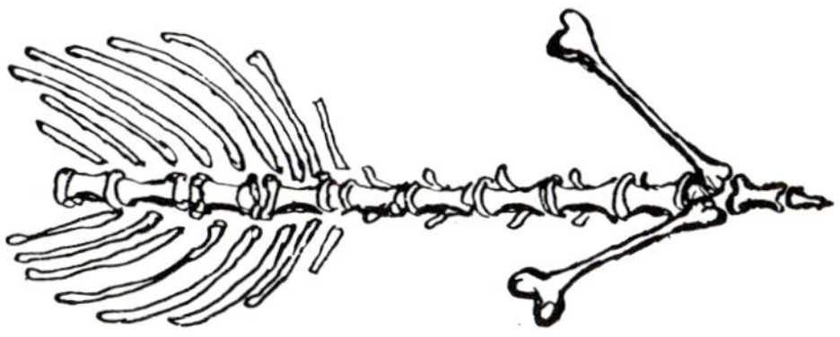

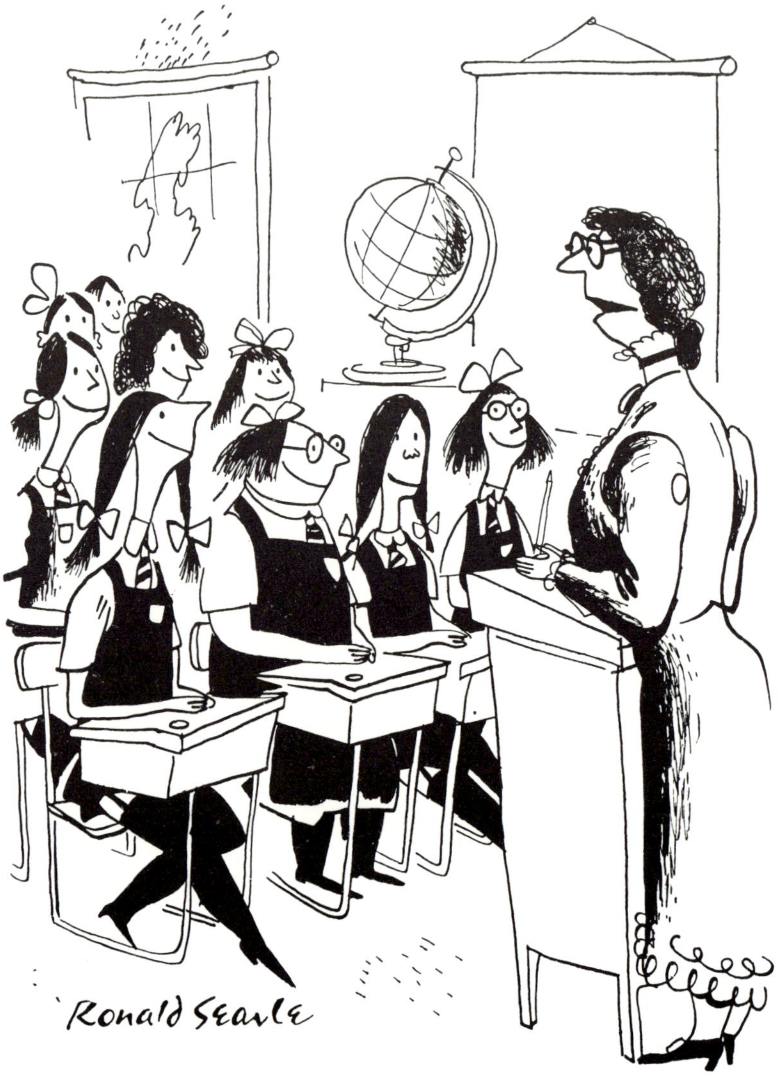
Ronald Searle

'Hand up the girl who burnt down the East Wing last night.'

The second St. Trinian's cartoon, drawn in Changi gaol, Singapore, around 1944 and published in April 1946, five years after the first.

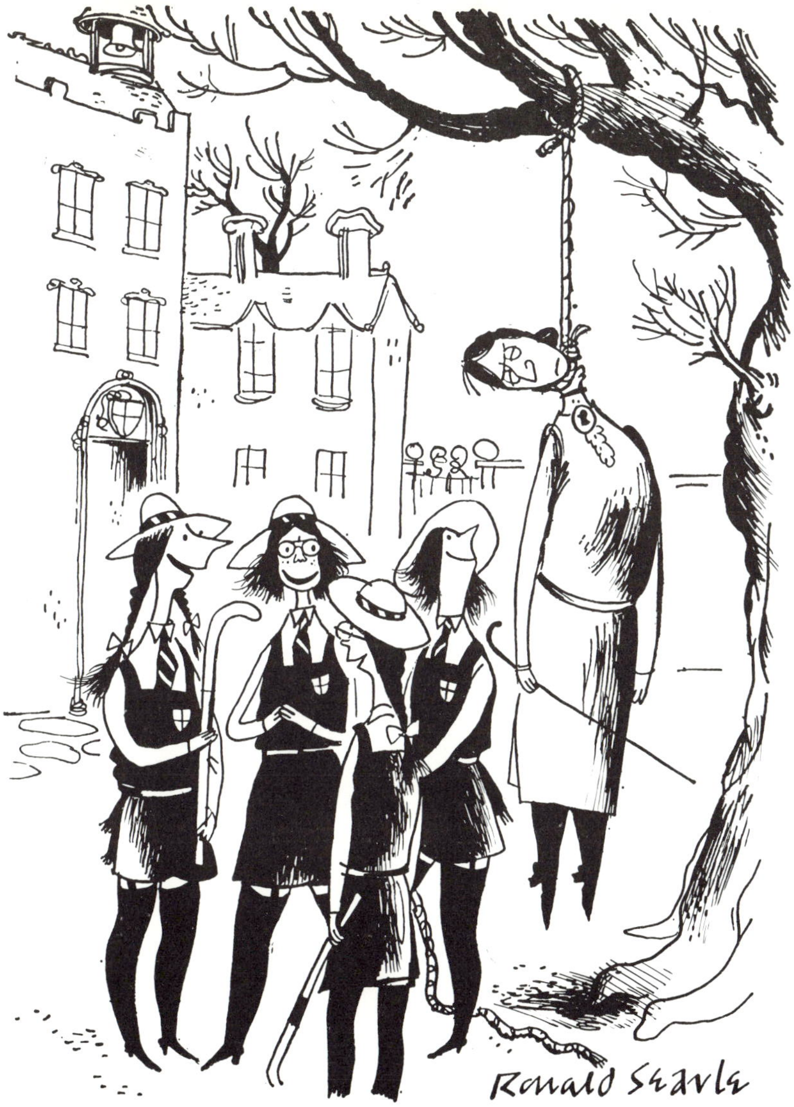
Ronald Searle

[1946]

'Well, that's O.K. – now for old "Stinks".'

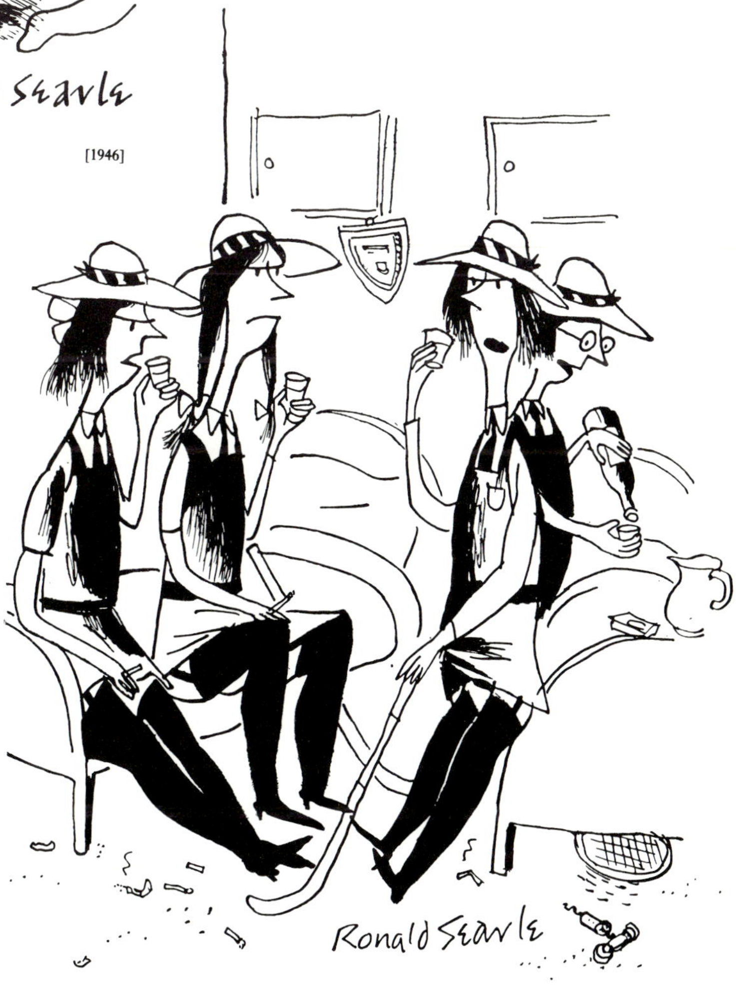
Ronald Searle

[1947]

'Oh my God, she's put water with it again.'

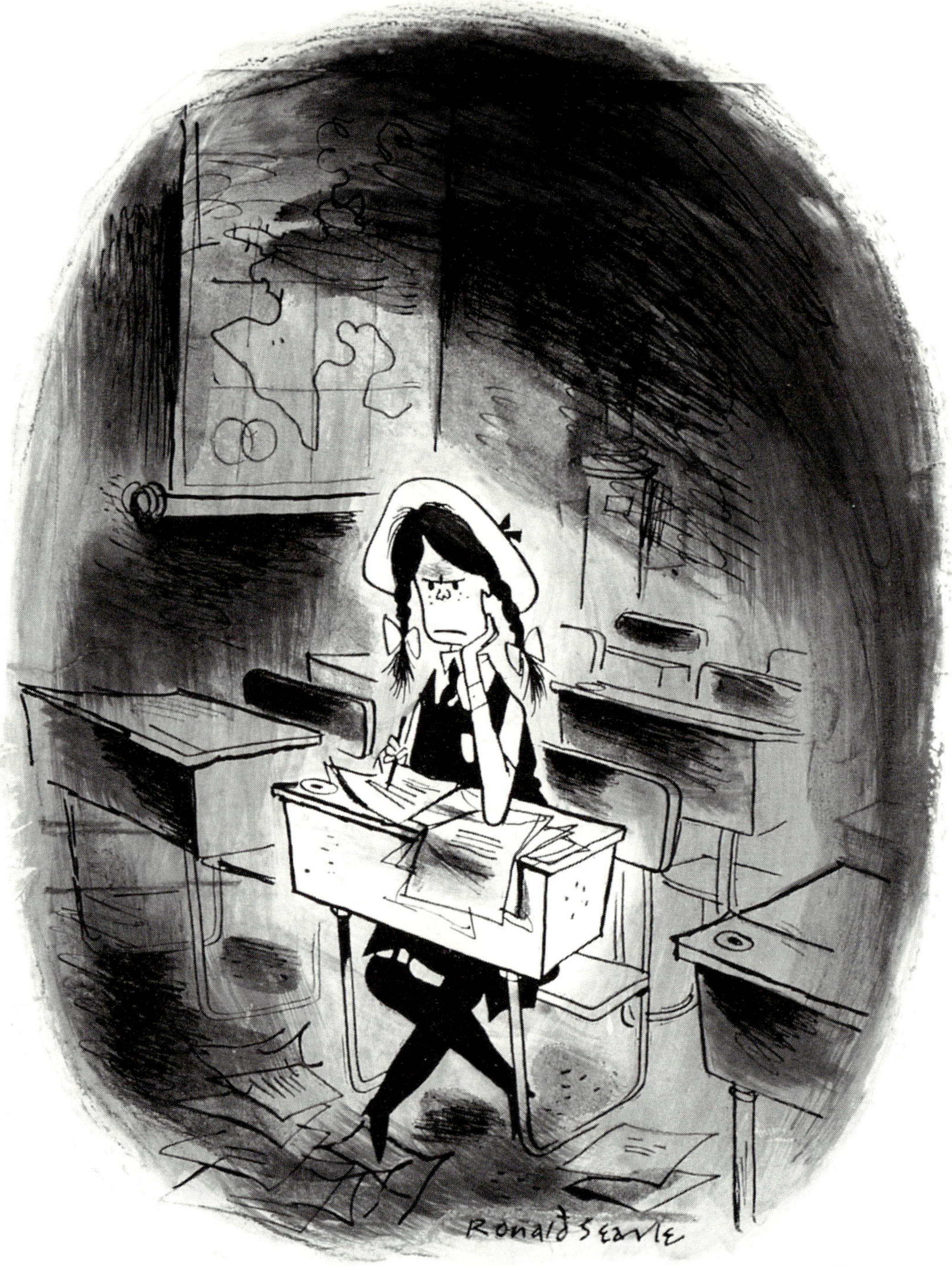
Ronald Searle

[1947]

'I must not smoke Pot during prayers.
I must not smoke Pot during...'

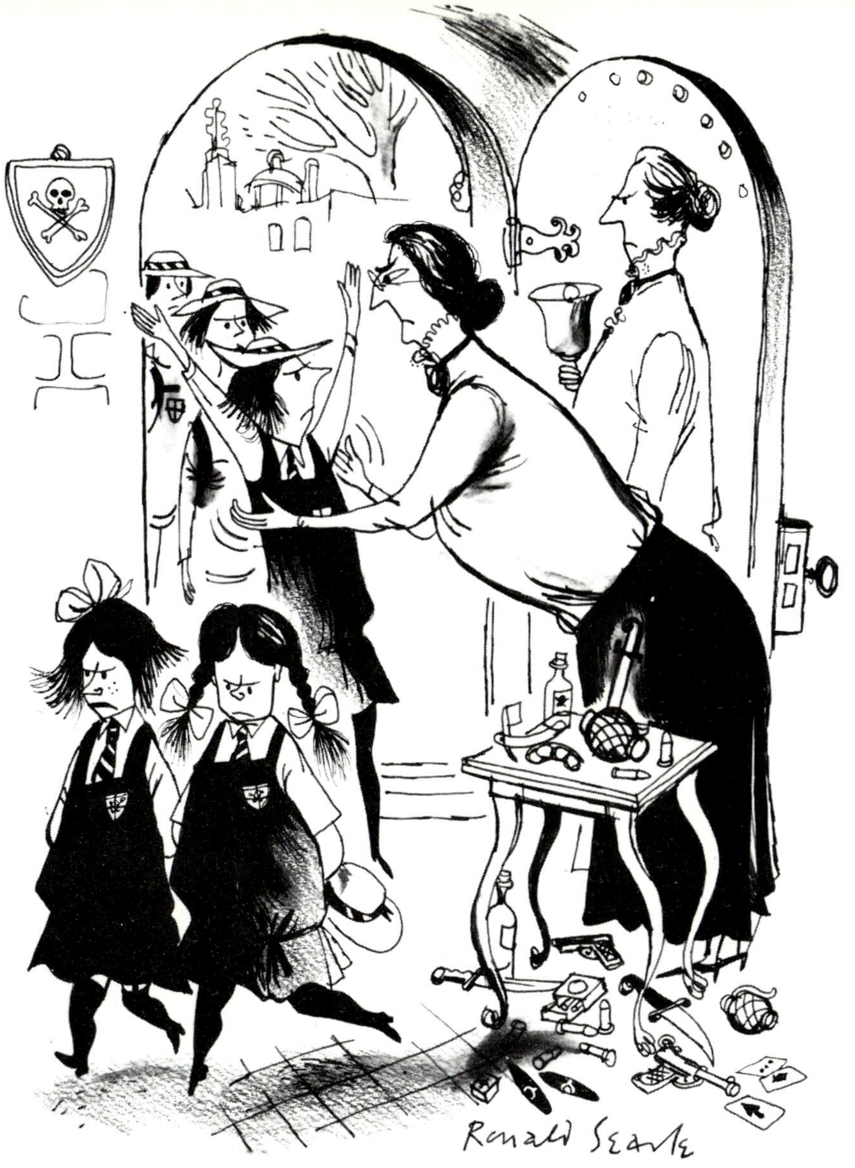
Ronald Searle

[1948]

'Bang goes another pair of knuckledusters.'

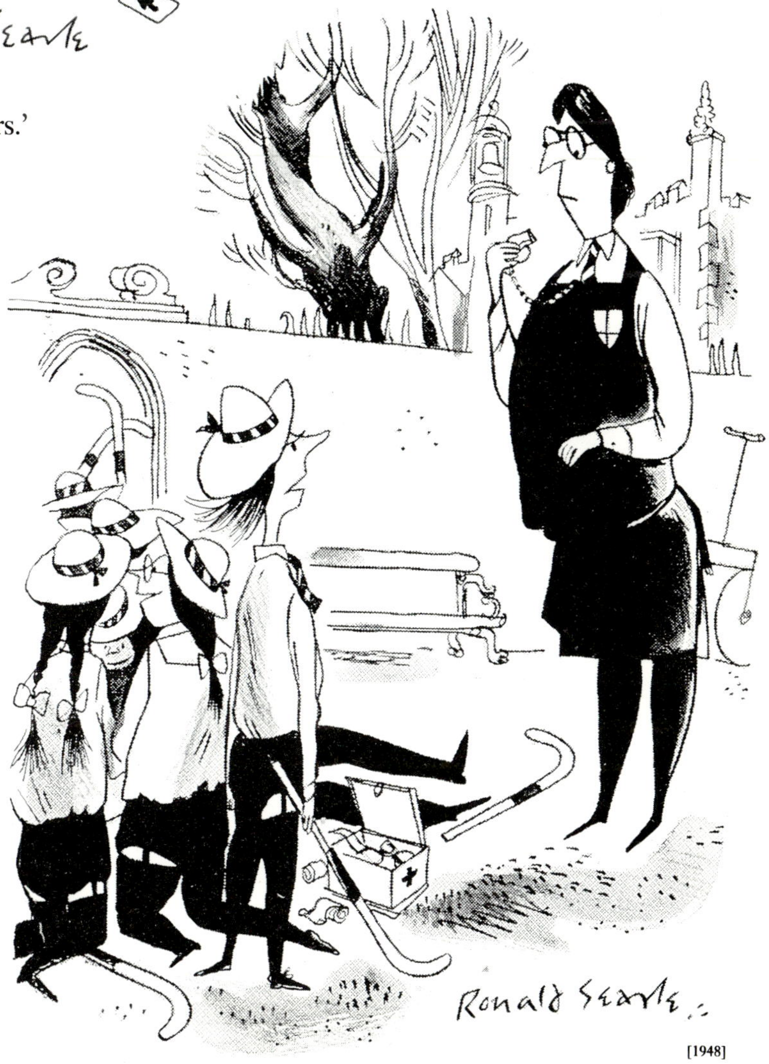
Ronald Searle

'But I only broke her leg, Miss.'

[1948]

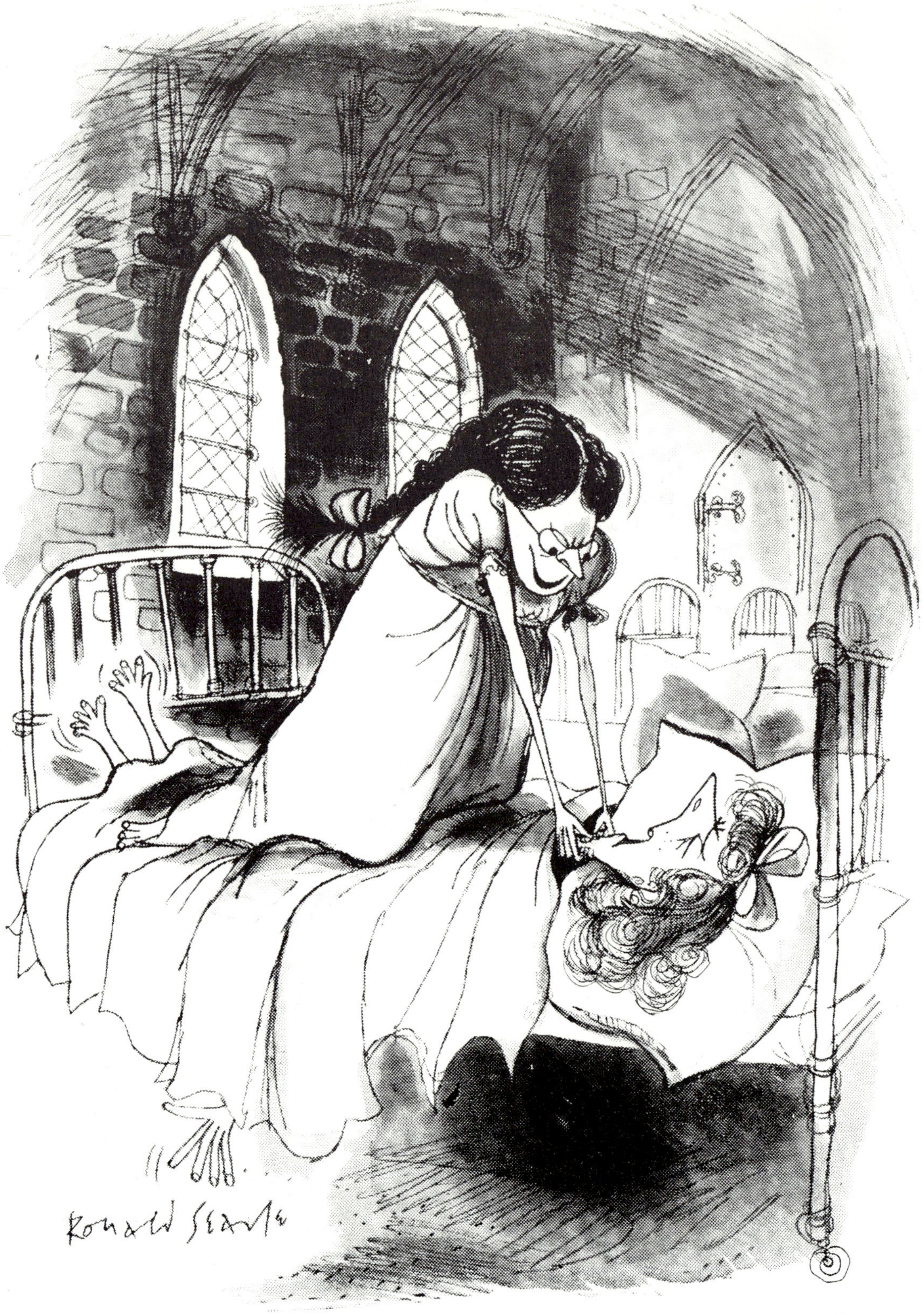
Ronald Searle

[1951]

'Go on, say it – "I promise to leave my body to Science".'

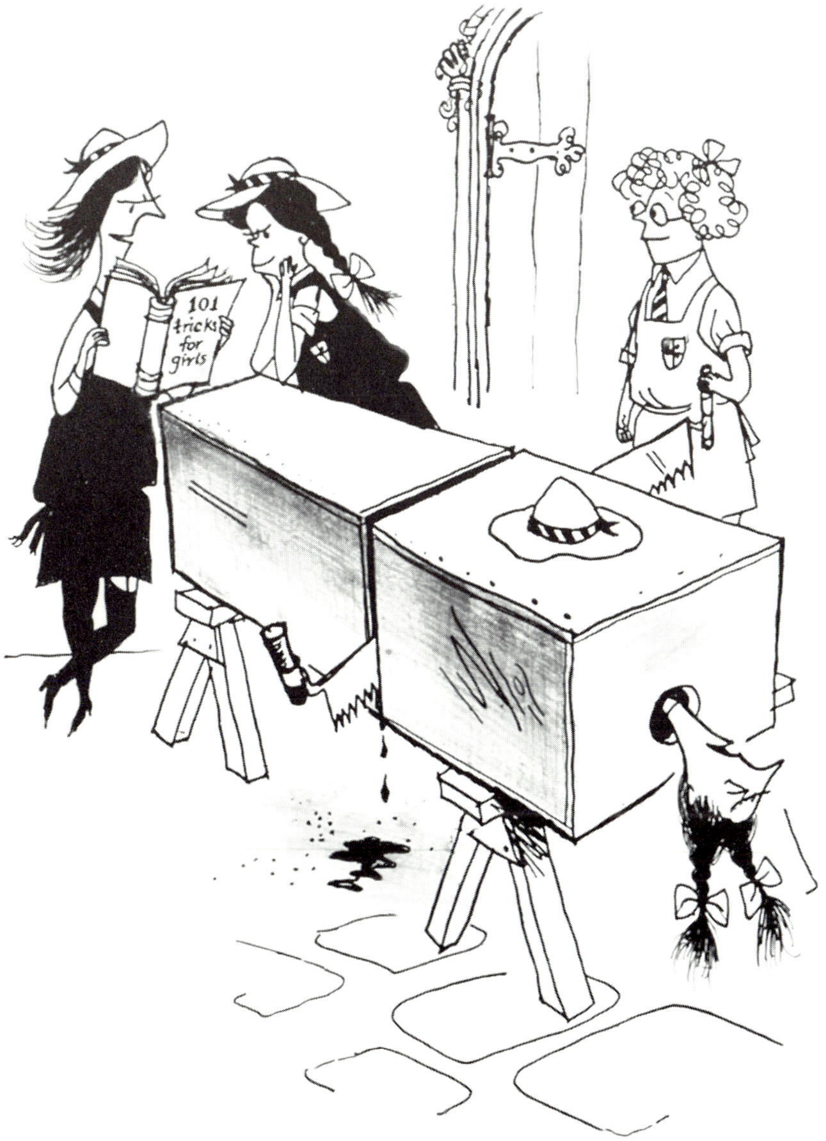
101
tricks
for
girls

[1948]

[1950]

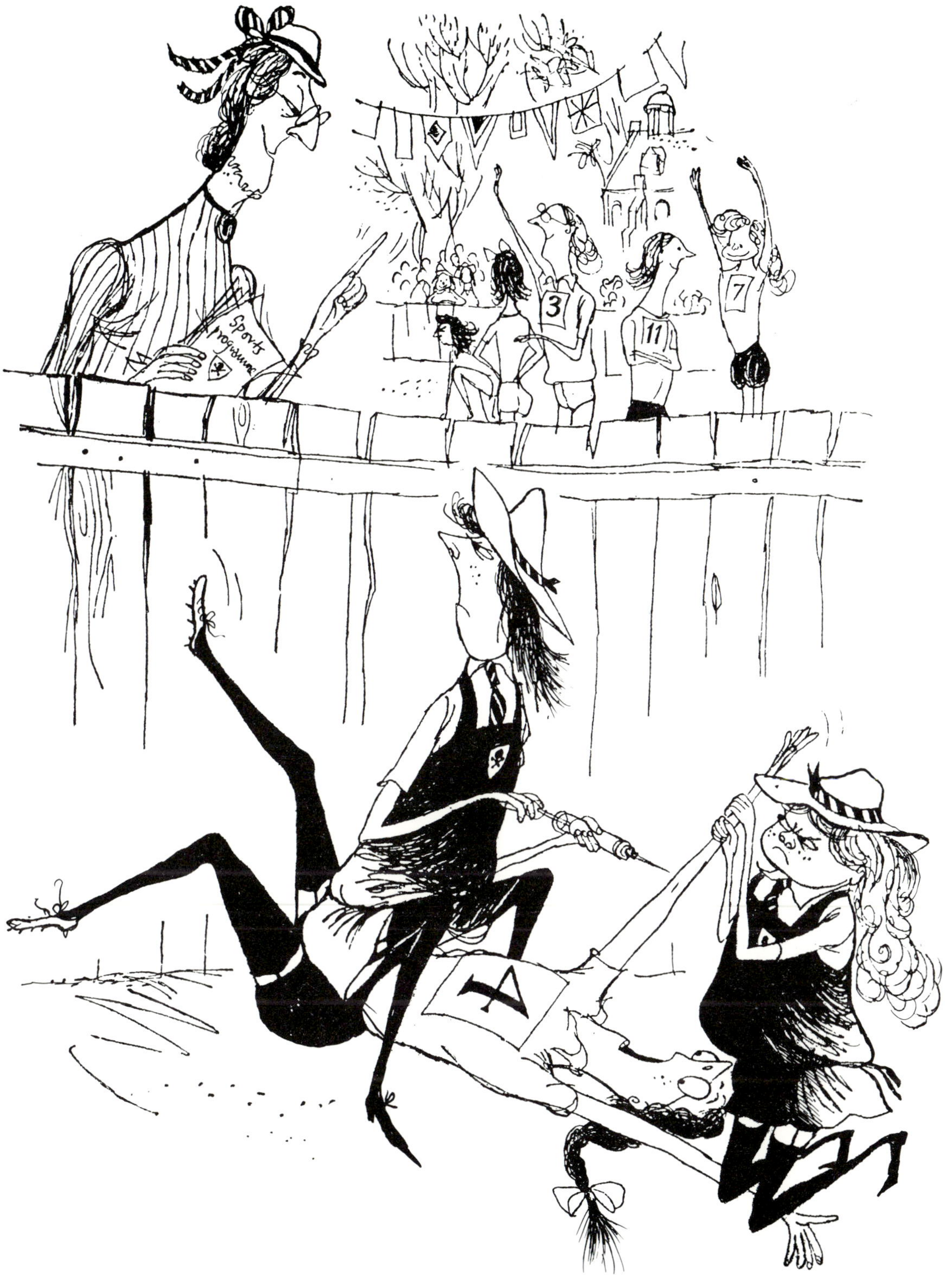
Sports programme
3
11
7

[1950]

'Fair play, St. Trinian's, use a clean needle.'

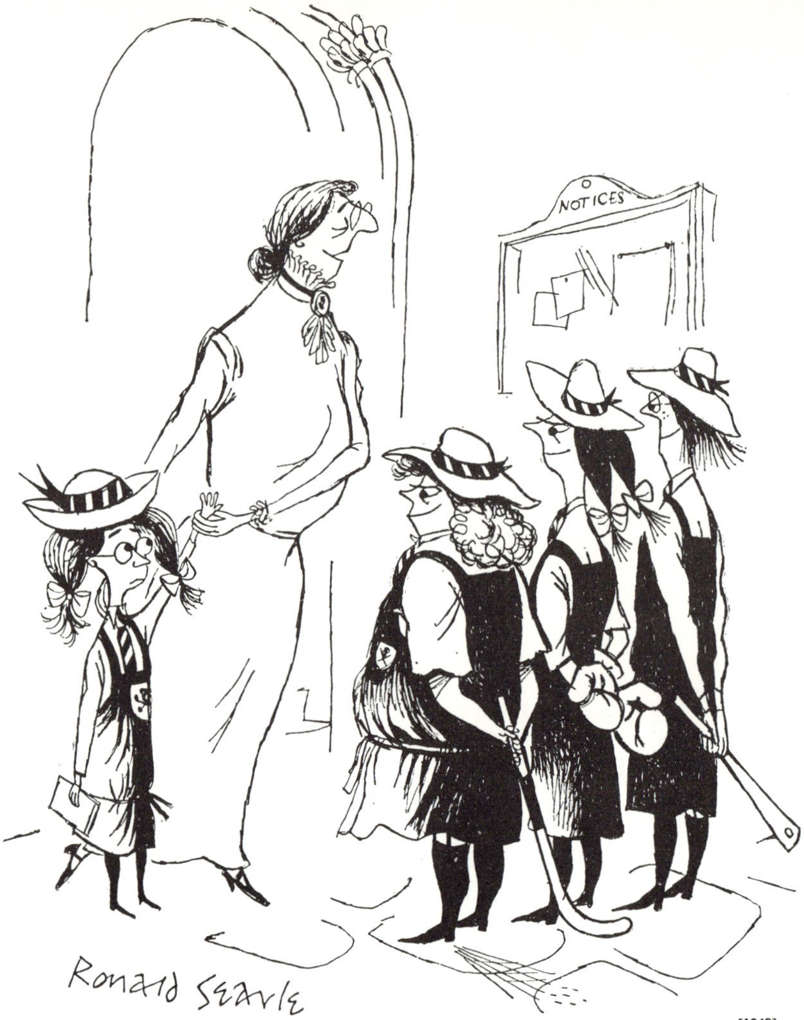
NOTICES
Ronald Searle

[1949]

'Prudence is new to St. Trinian's, I want you to take care of her, girls.'

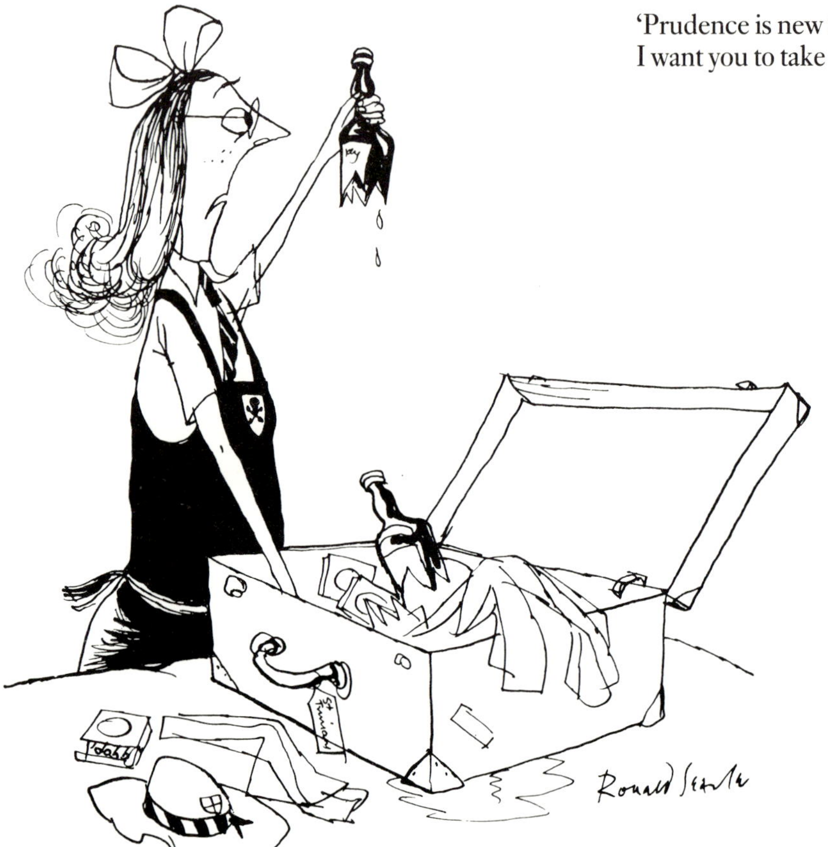
Ronald Searle

[1949]

'Hell! My best scotch.'

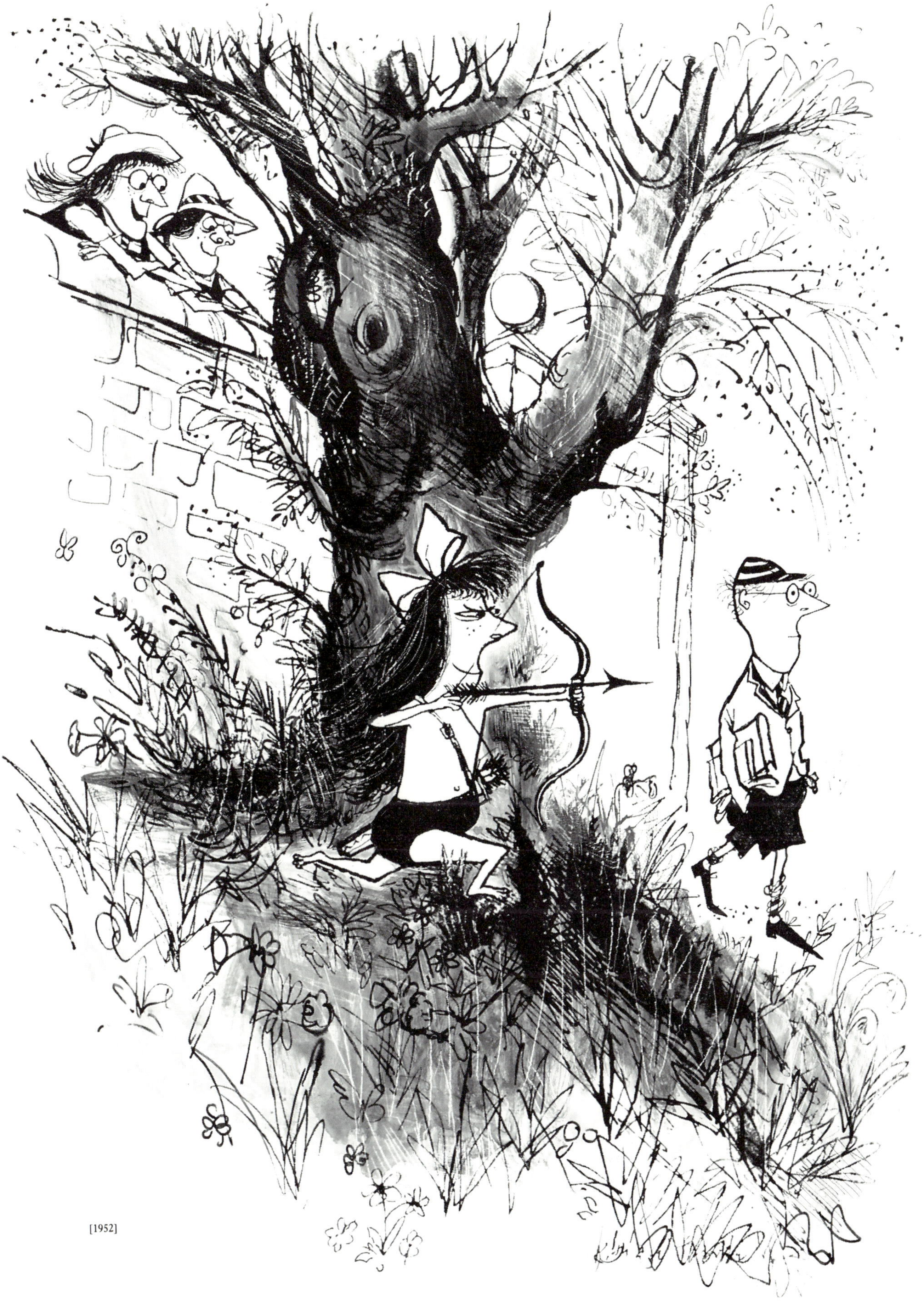

[1952]

'Oh my God, she's in love.'

[1949]

'Life will be just a hollow mockery without you, Drusilla.'

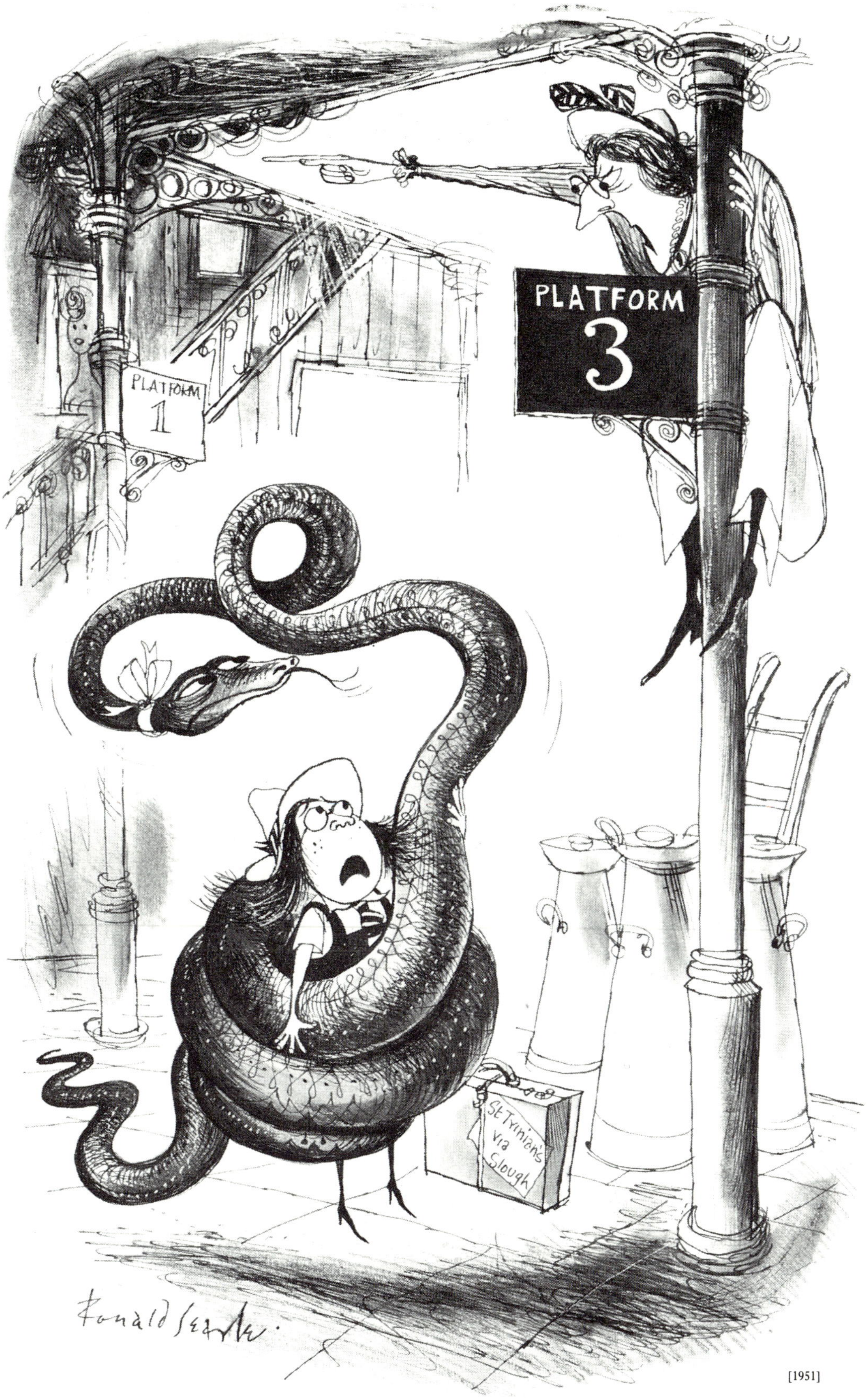
PLATFORM
3
PLATFORM
1
St Trinian's
via
Slough
Ronald Searle.
[1951]

'But, Miss Merryweather, you *said* we could bring our pets back with us.'

[1951]

'Little Maisy's our problem child.'

'Come along, prefects. Playtime over.'

[1950]

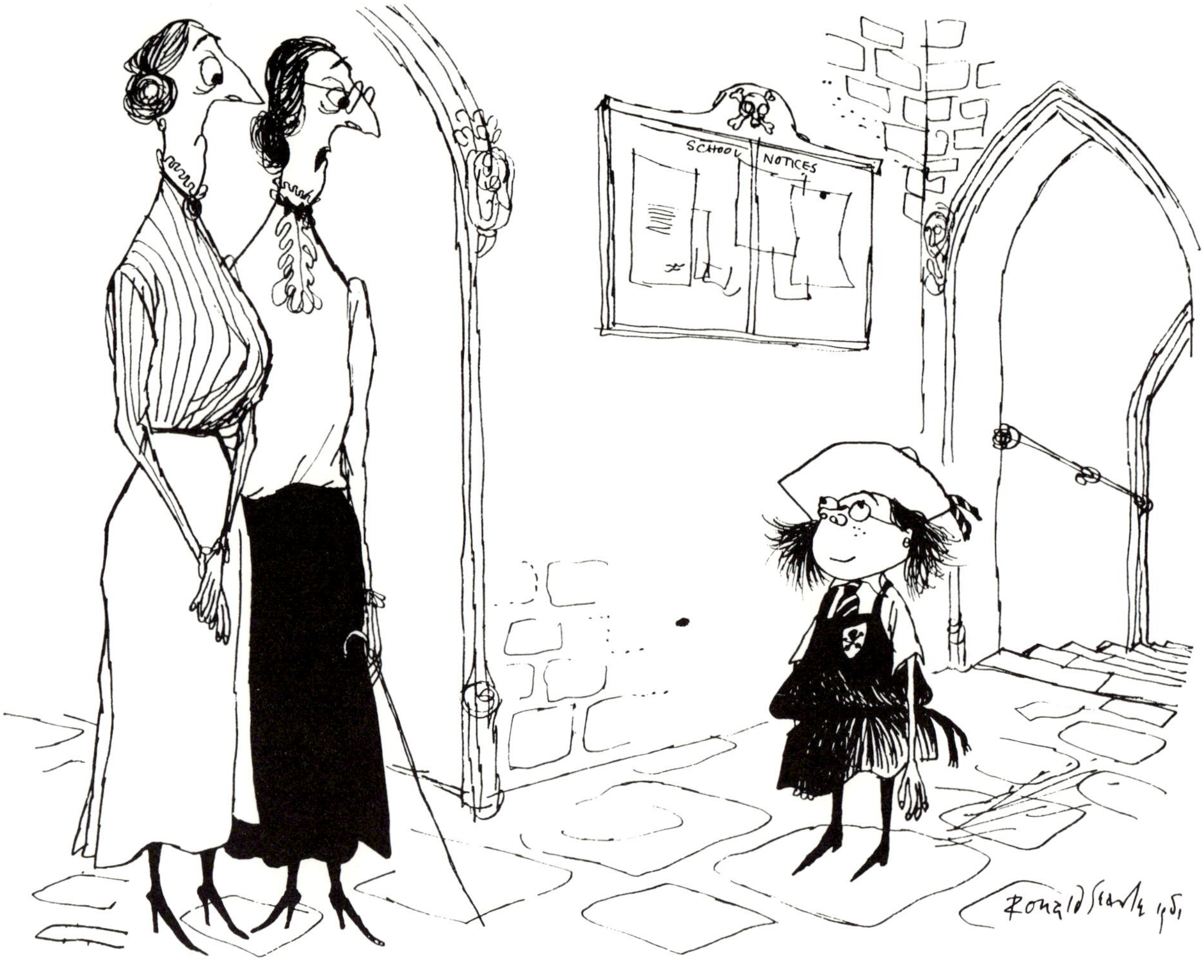
SCHOOL NOTICES

'We'd better have her examined, she's resolved to be good.'

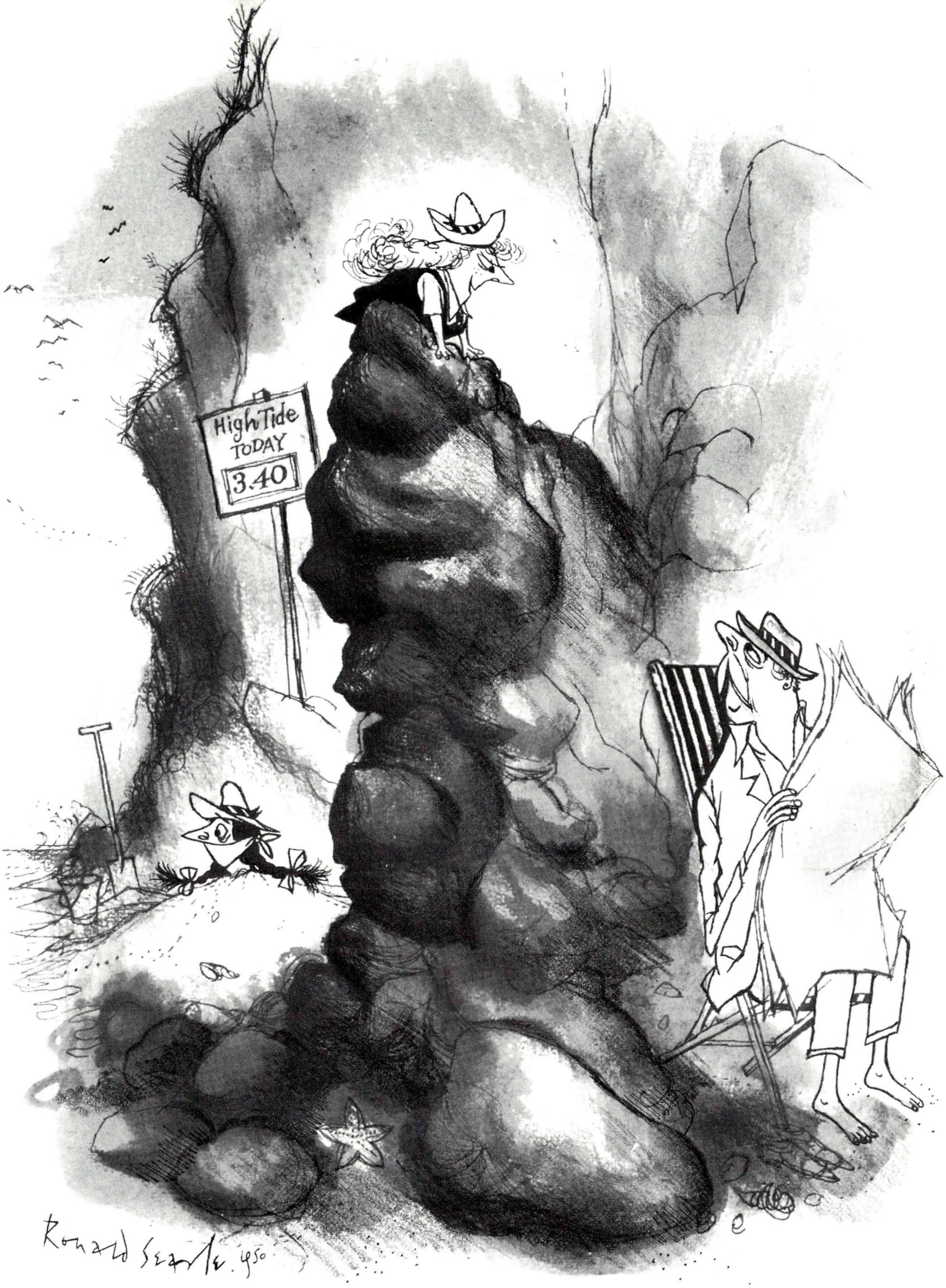
High Tide
TODAY
3.40
Ronald Searle 1950

'Could you tell me the time, please?'

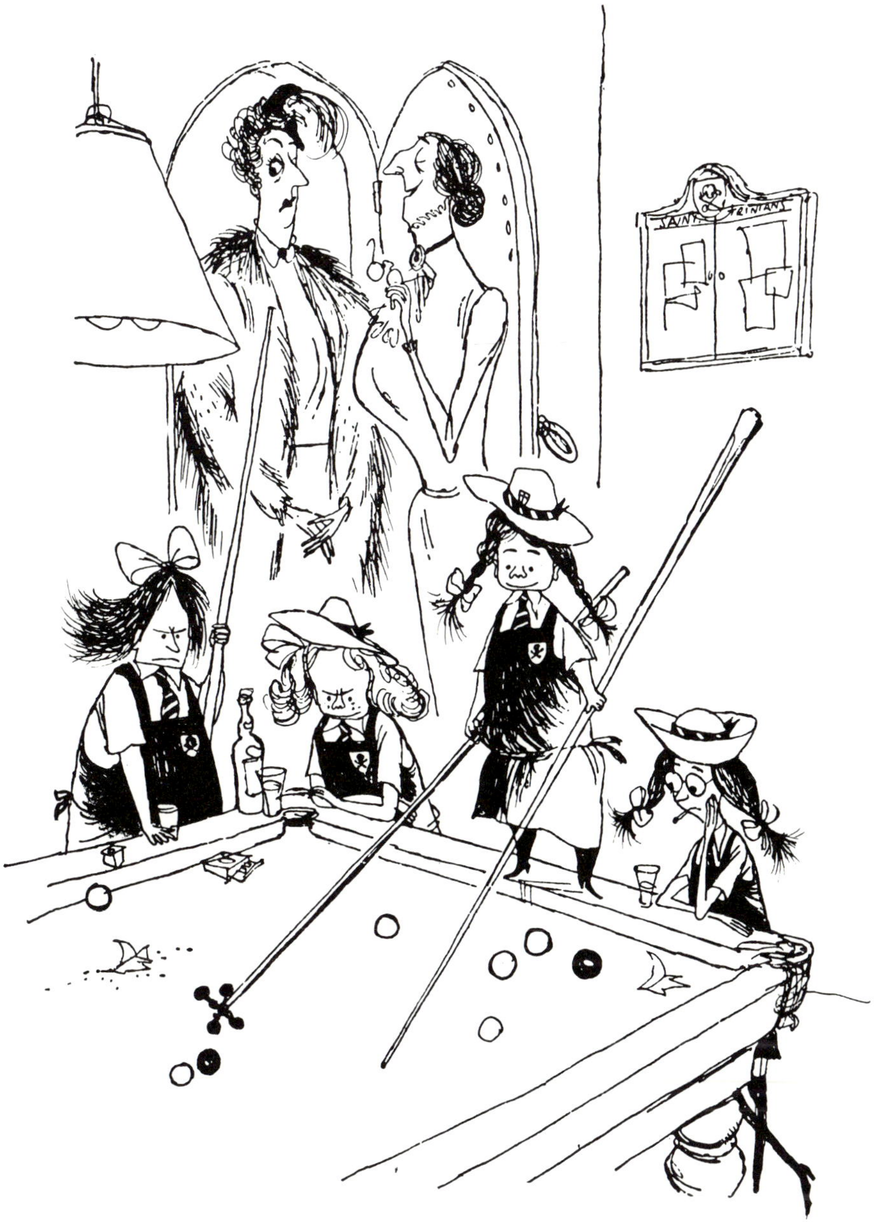

[1949]

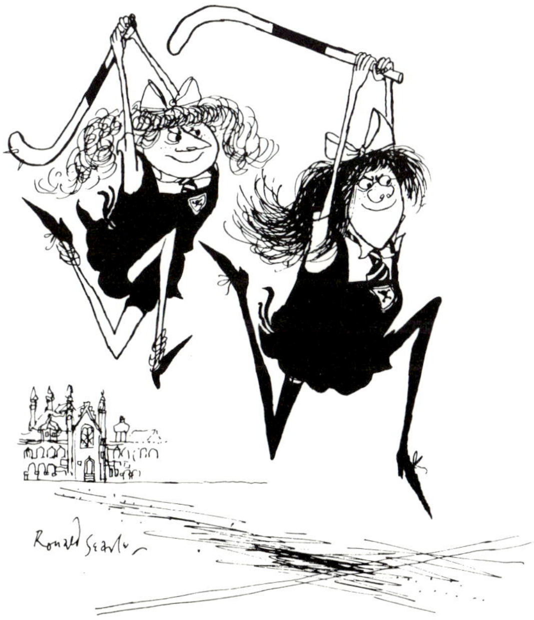
Ronald Searle

'...of course indoor games are an extra.'

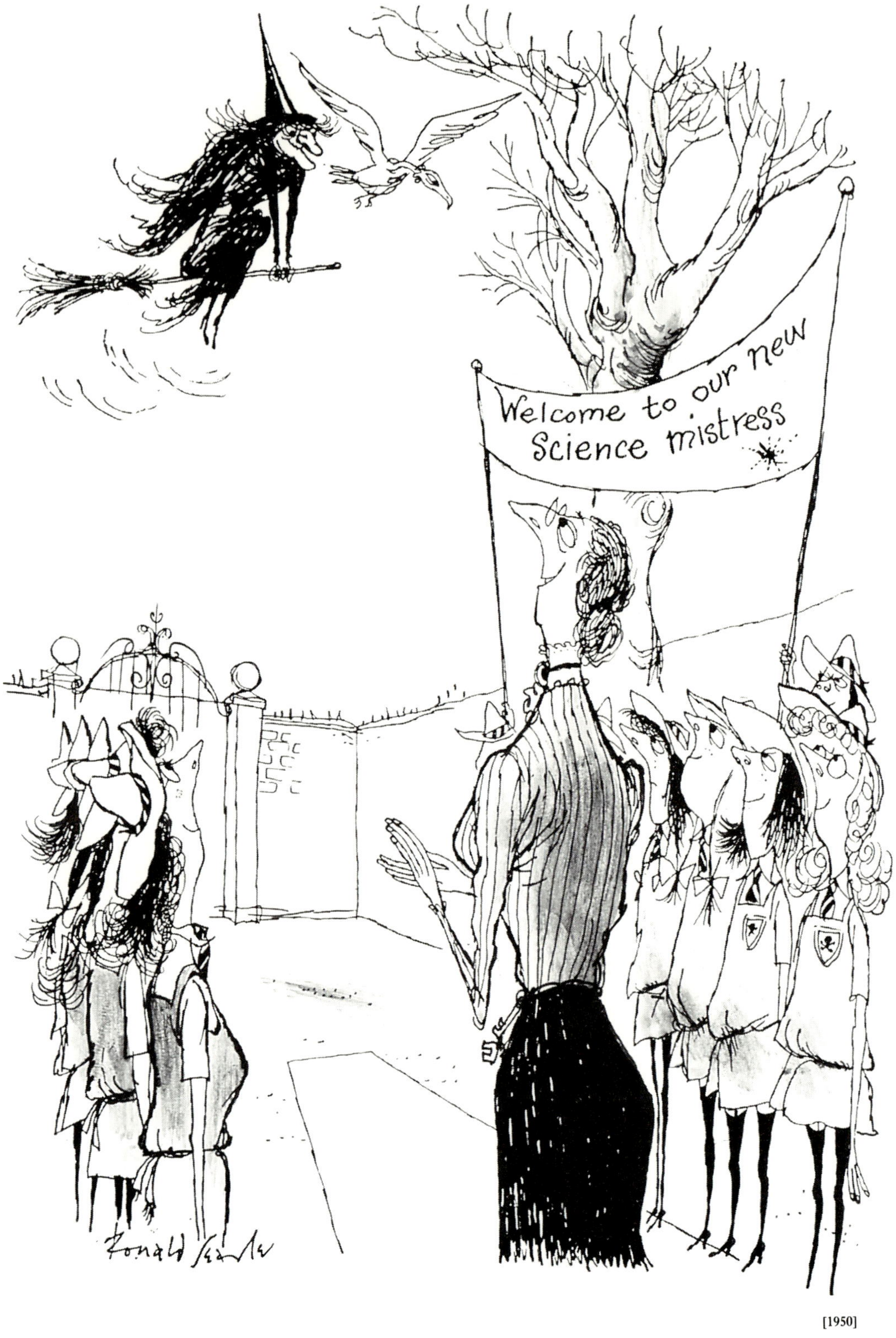
Welcome to our new
Science mistress
Ronald Searle

[1950]

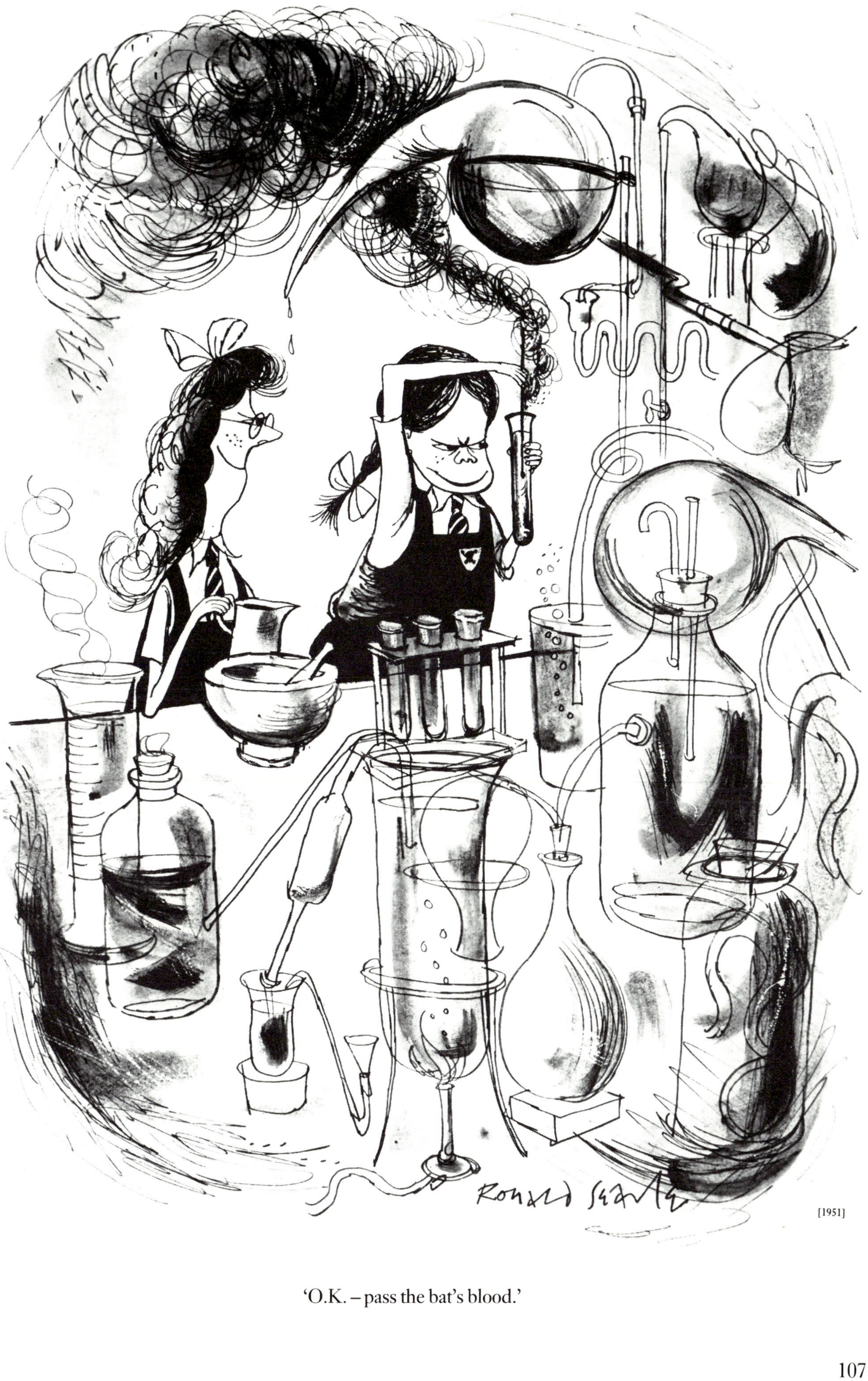
RONALD SEARLE

[1951]

'O.K. – pass the bat's blood.'

'Who's there?'

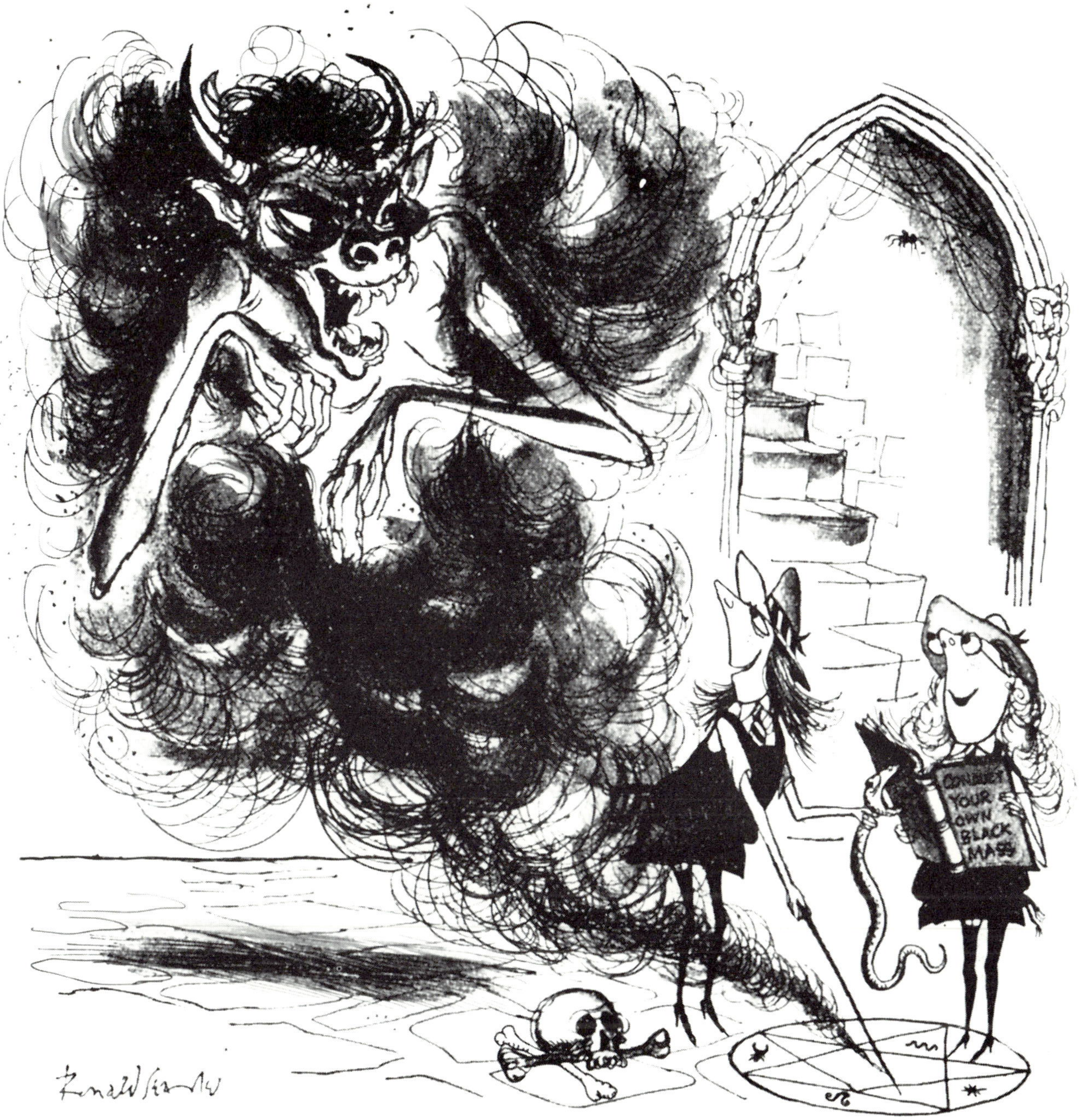
CONDUCT YOUR OWN BLACK MASS

[1950]

'Now ask him to abolish homework.'

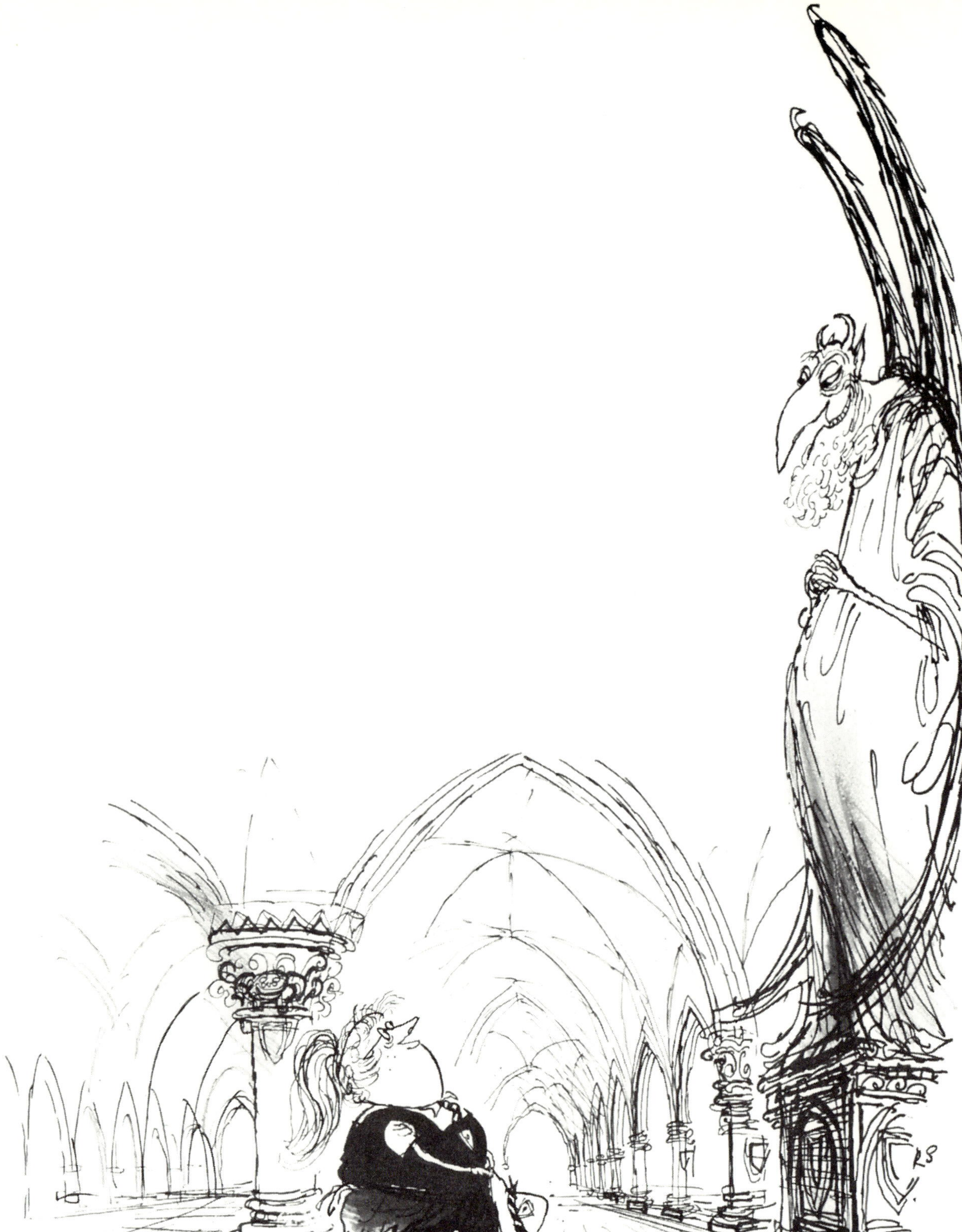

[1959]

'And please rain fire and brimstone on the lot.'

[1950]

'All right! All right! I'll join the union.'

[1953]

[1953]

'Honestly, darling, you don't look a day over nine.'

[1952]

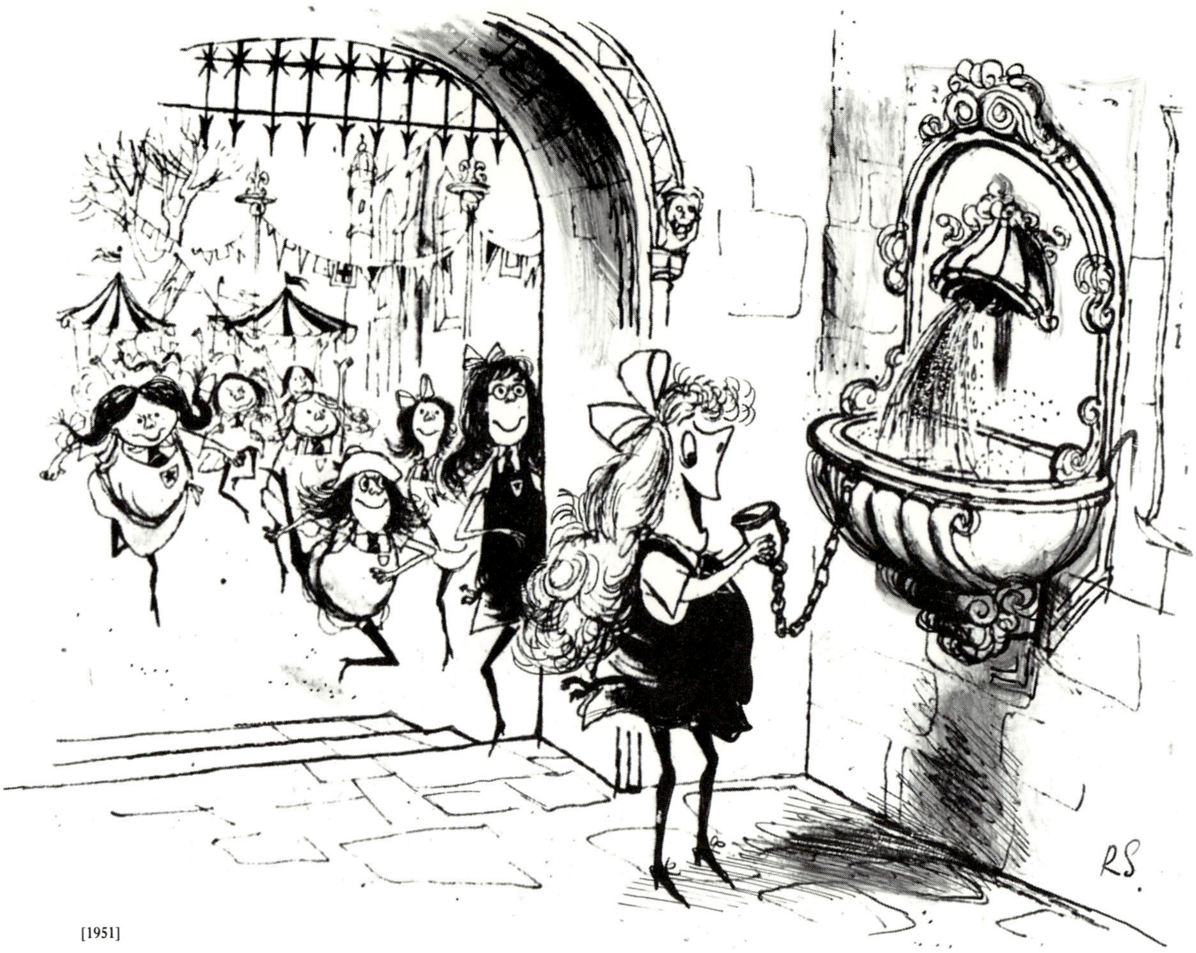
R.S.

[1951]

'It's WINE!'

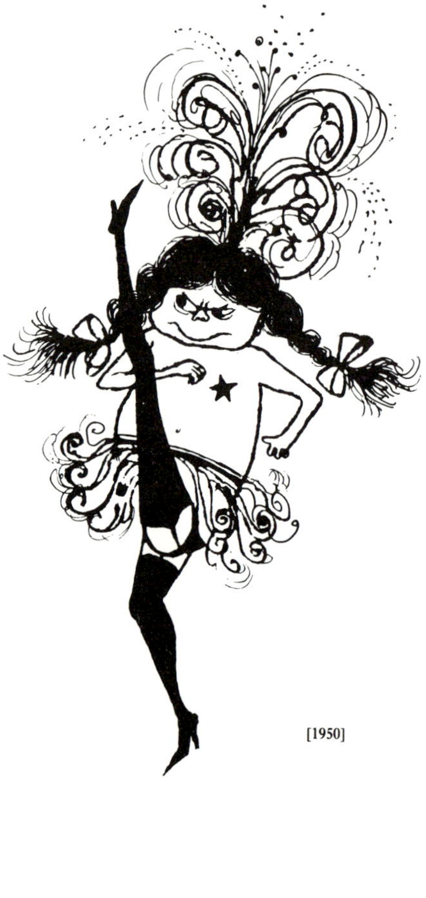

[1950]

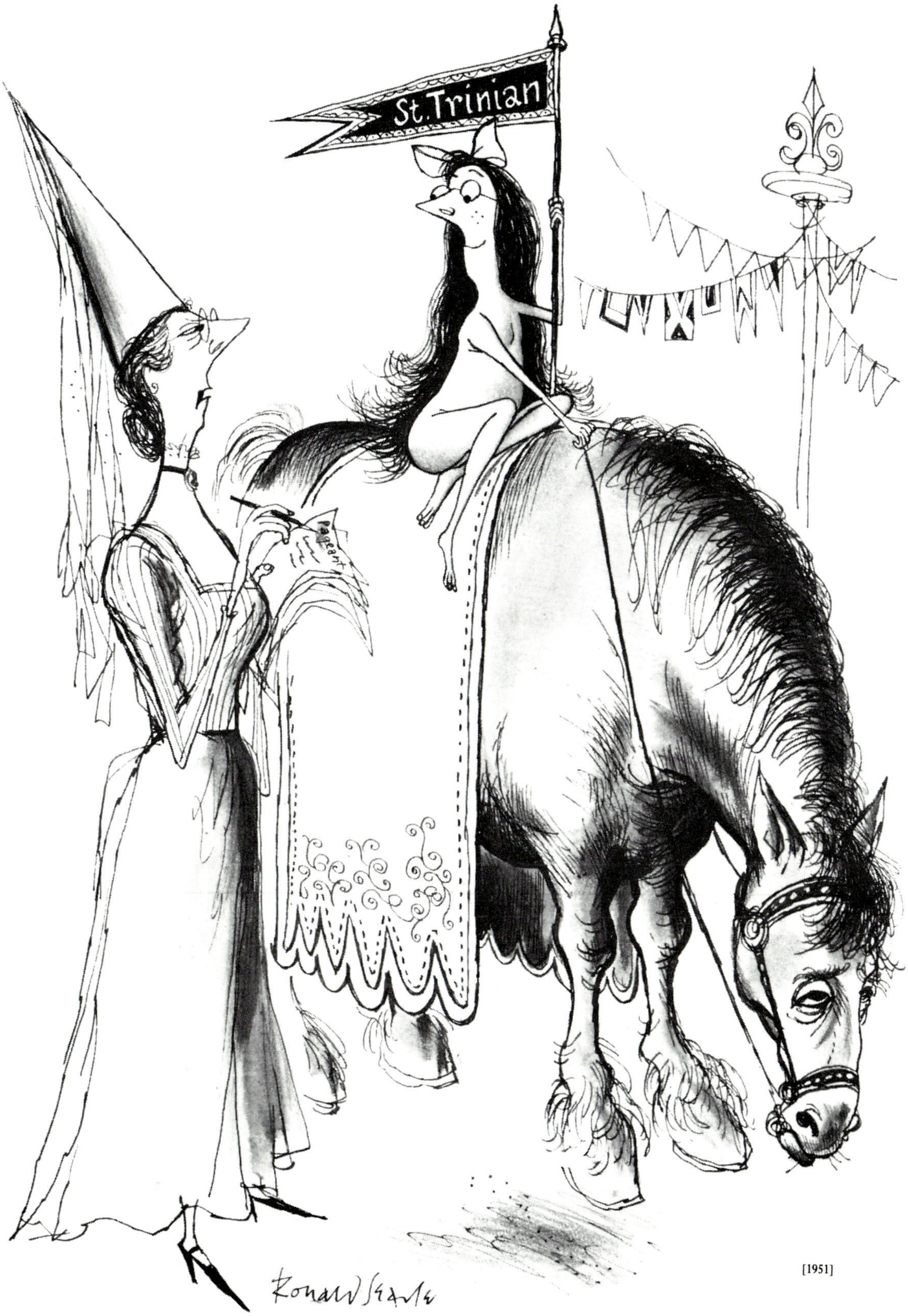
St. Trinian
Pageant
Ronald Searle
[1951]

'Eunice, dear, aren't we rather muddling our patron saints?'

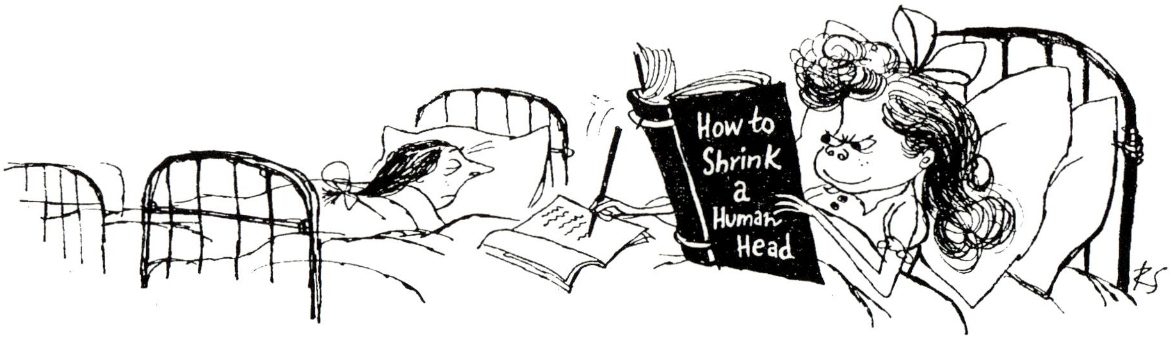
How to
Shrink
a
Human
Head

[1950]

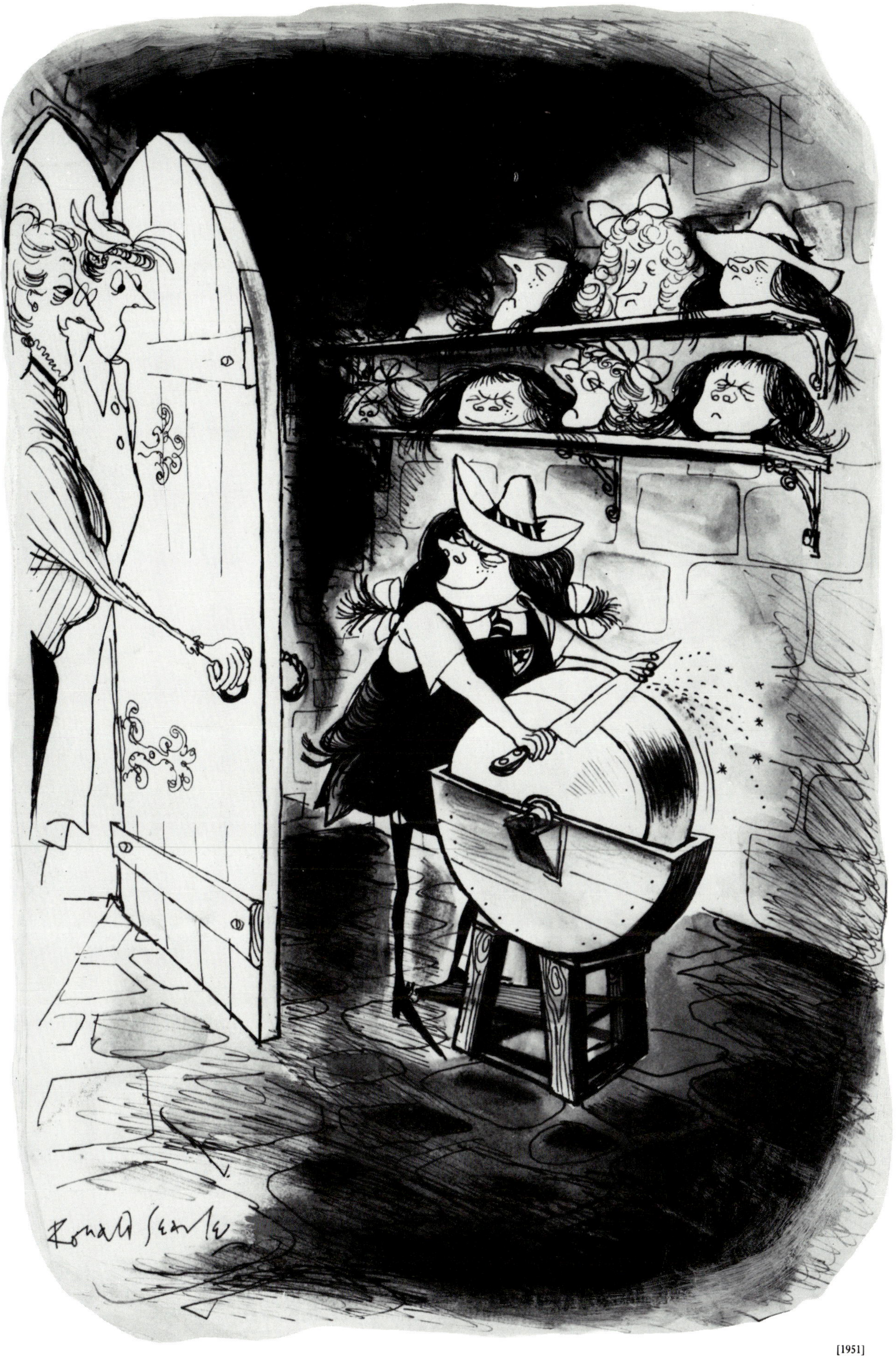
Ronald Searle

[1951]

'And this is Rachel, our head girl.'

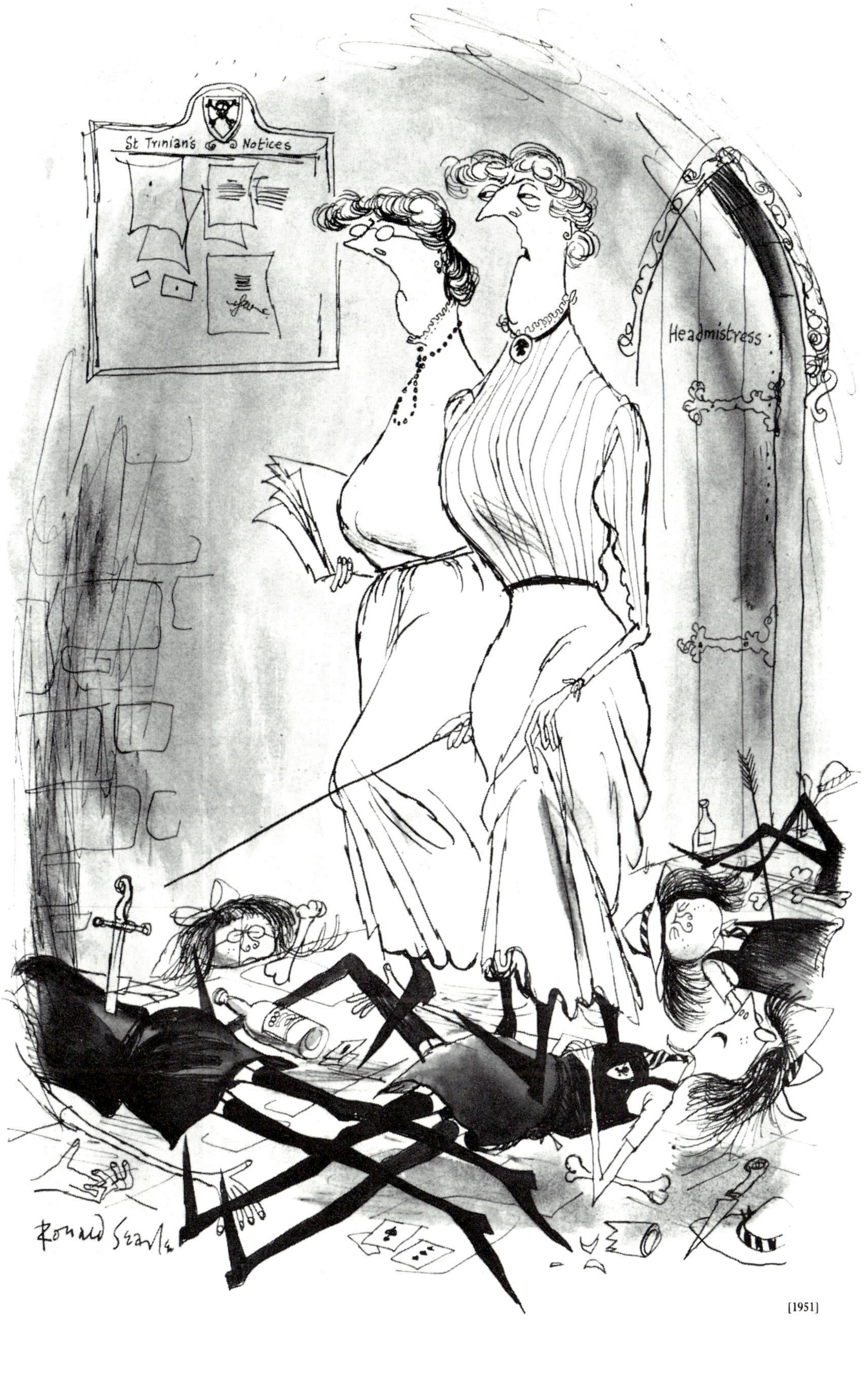
St Trinian's Notices
Headmistress
Ronald Searle

[1951]

'Cleaners getting slack, Horsefall.'

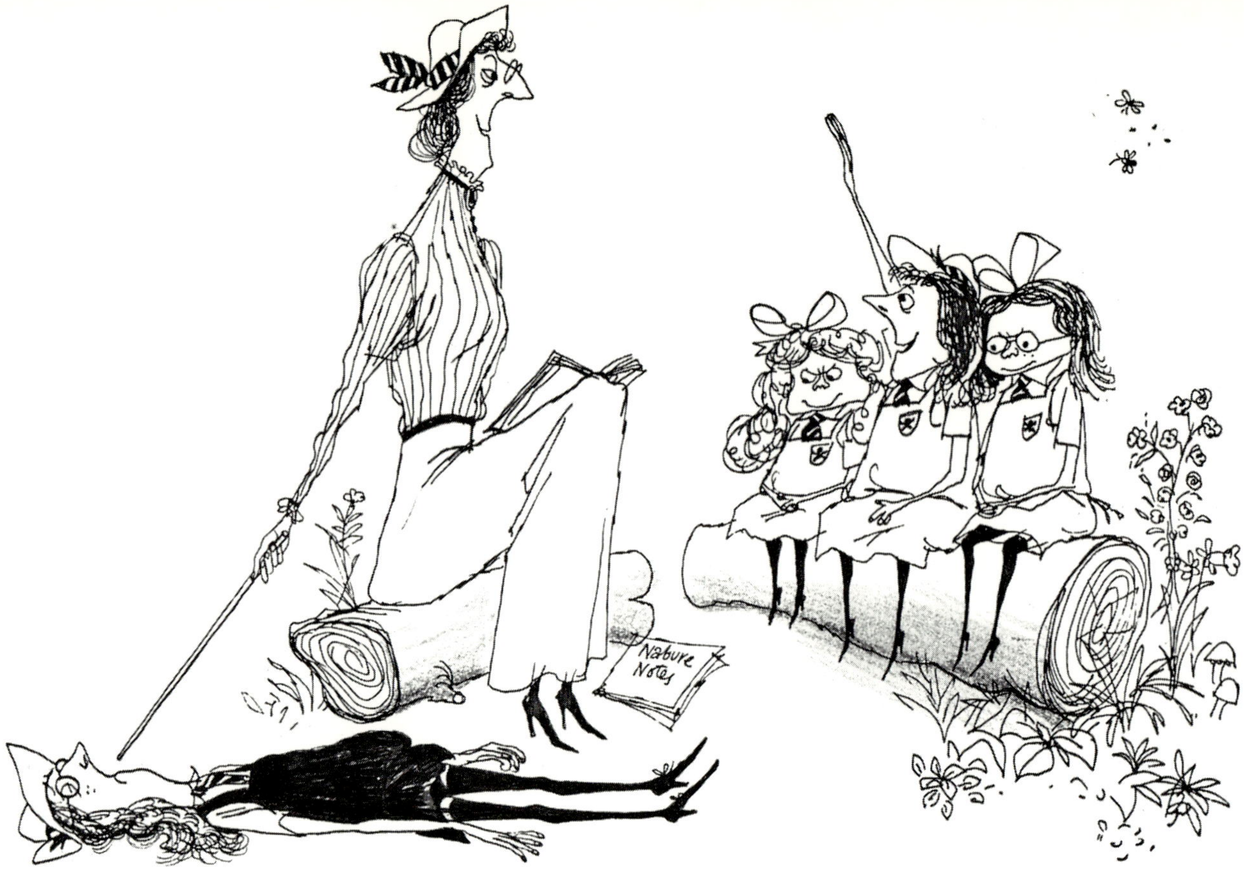
Nature Notes

[1951]

'Well done, Cynthia, it WAS Deadly Nightshade.'

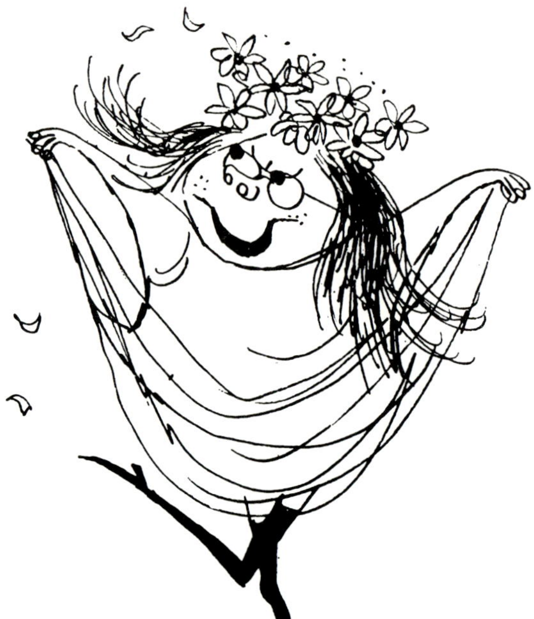

'Look, Miss, the spirit of Botony.'

[1951]

[1951]

'Dump those, they're harmless.'

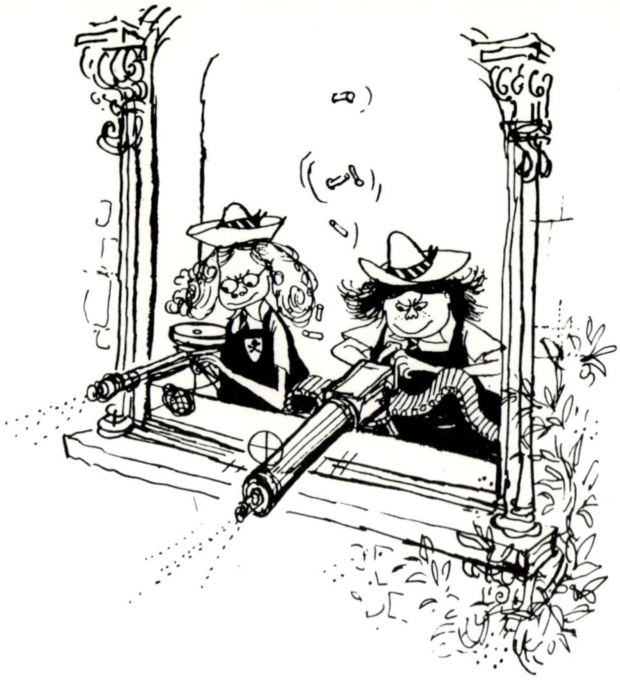

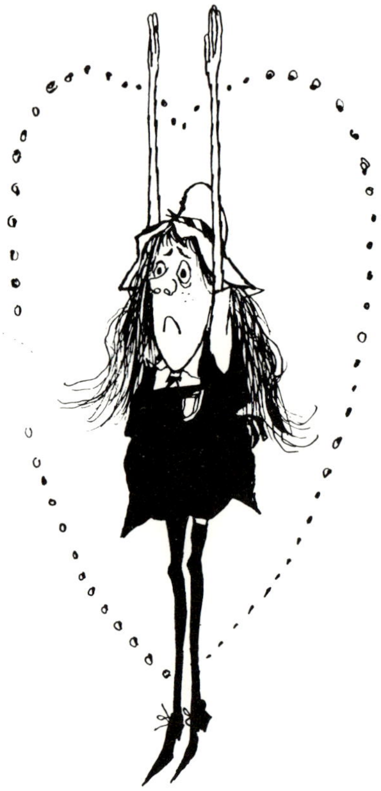

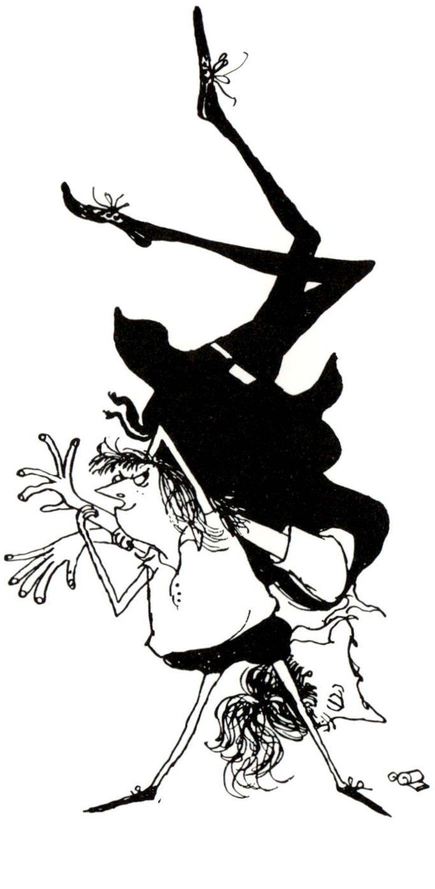

[1953]

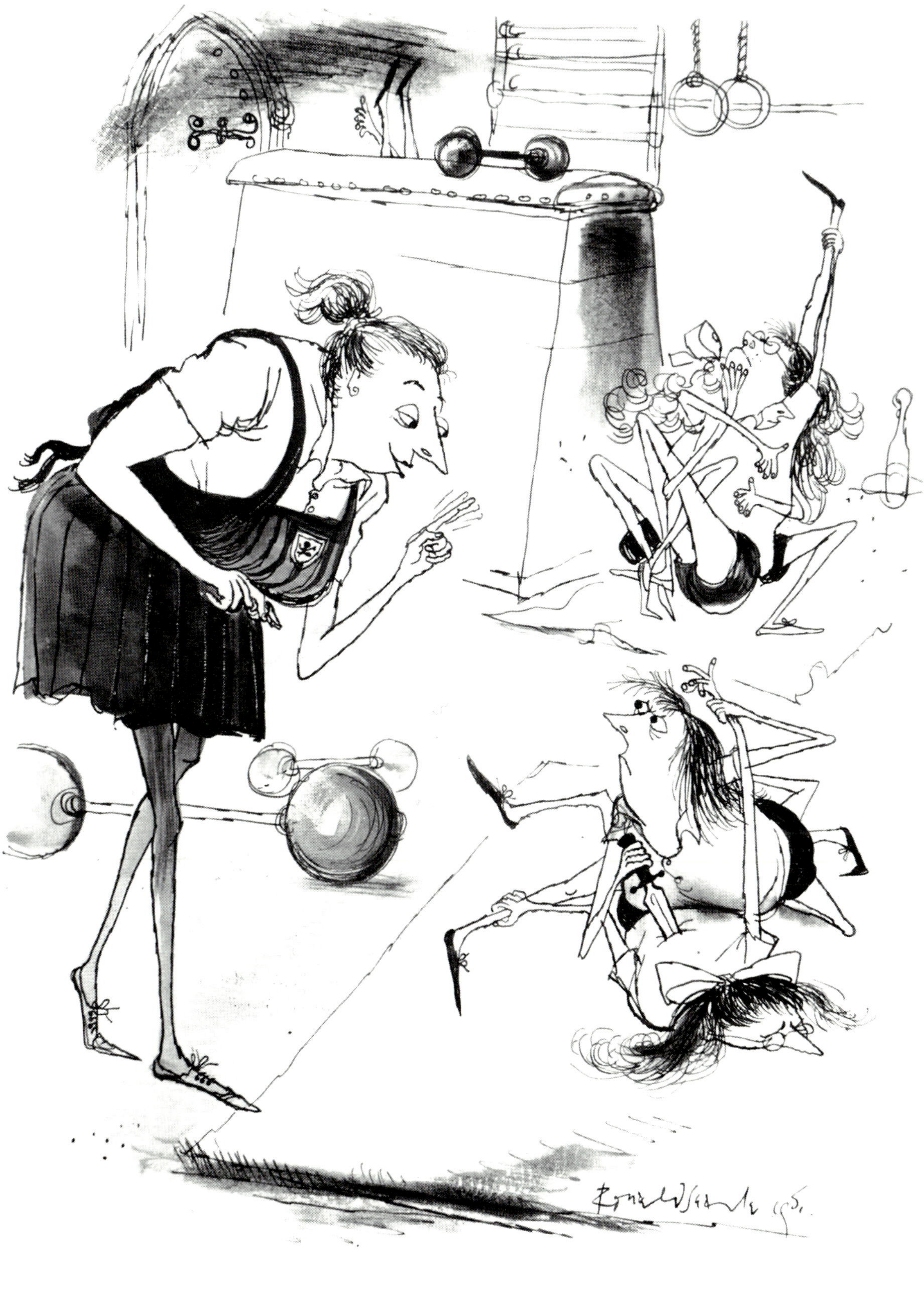

'Some little girl didn't hear me say "unarmed combat".'

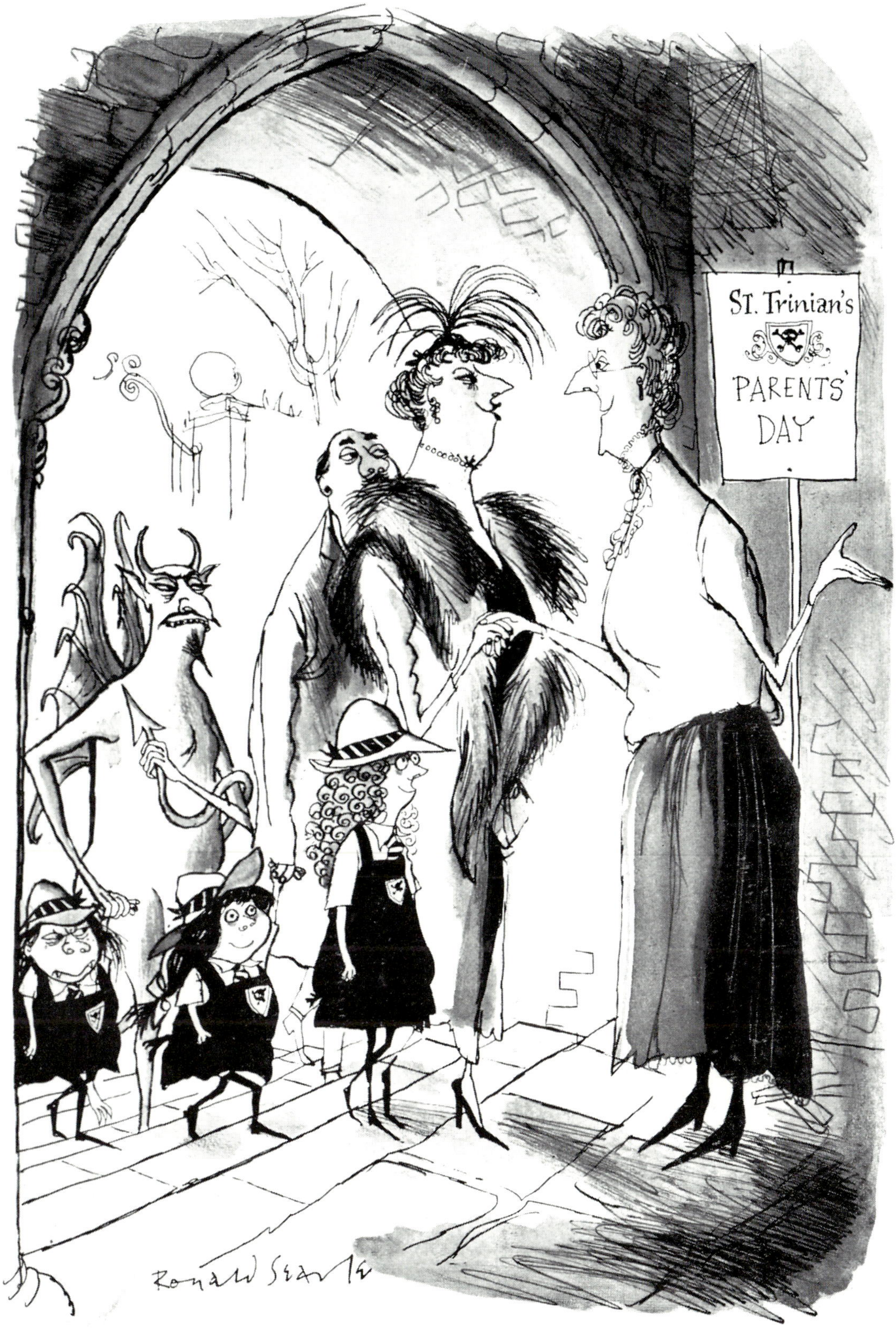
St. Trinian's
'PARENTS'
DAY
RONALD SEARLE

[1951]

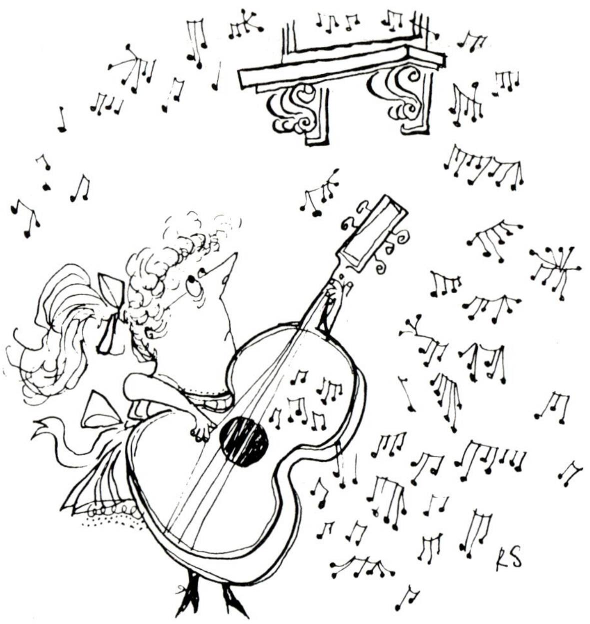

‘Why can’t he let down his hair, or something?’

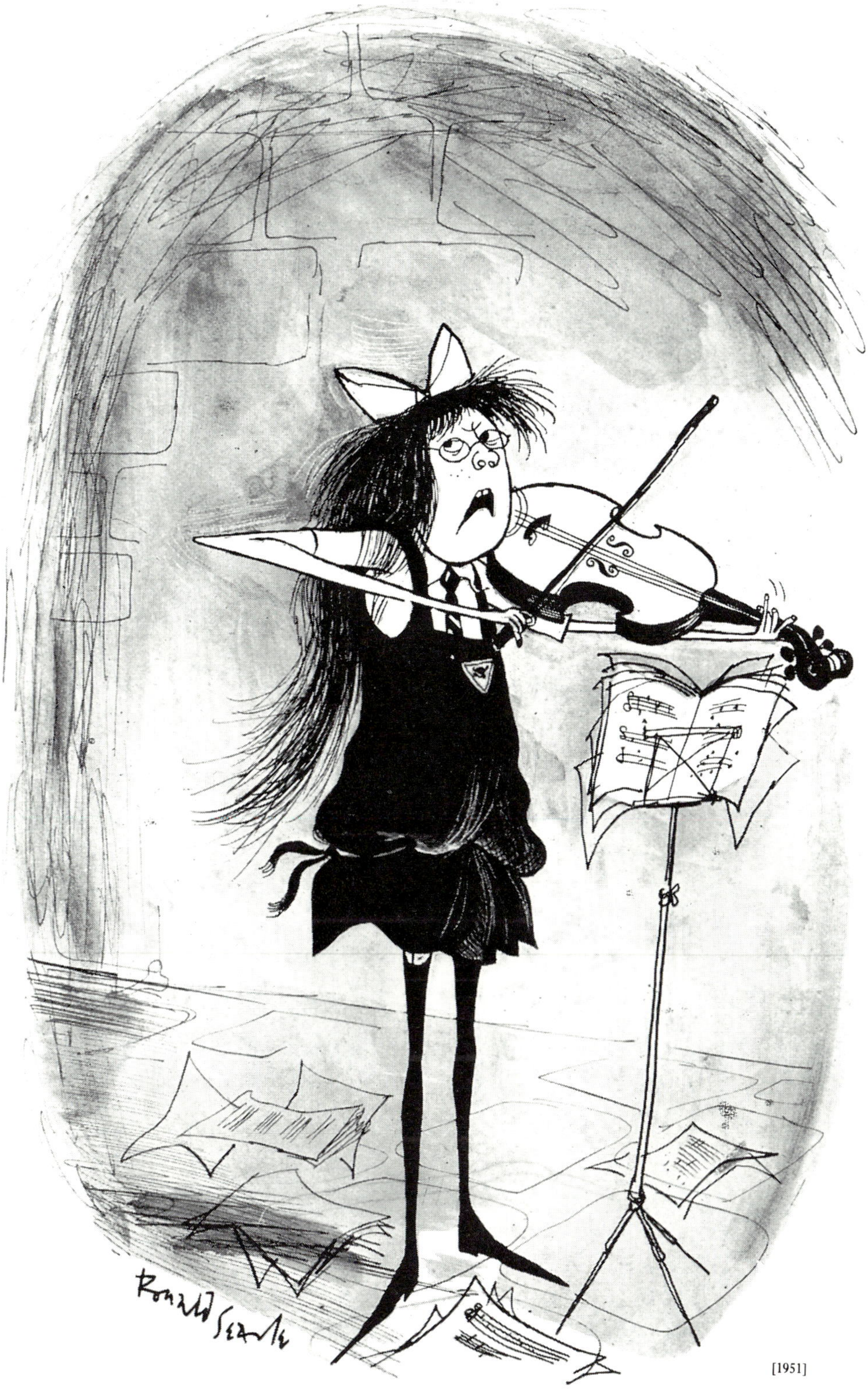
Ronald Searle

[1951]

'Well actually, Miss Tonks, my soul *is* in torment.'

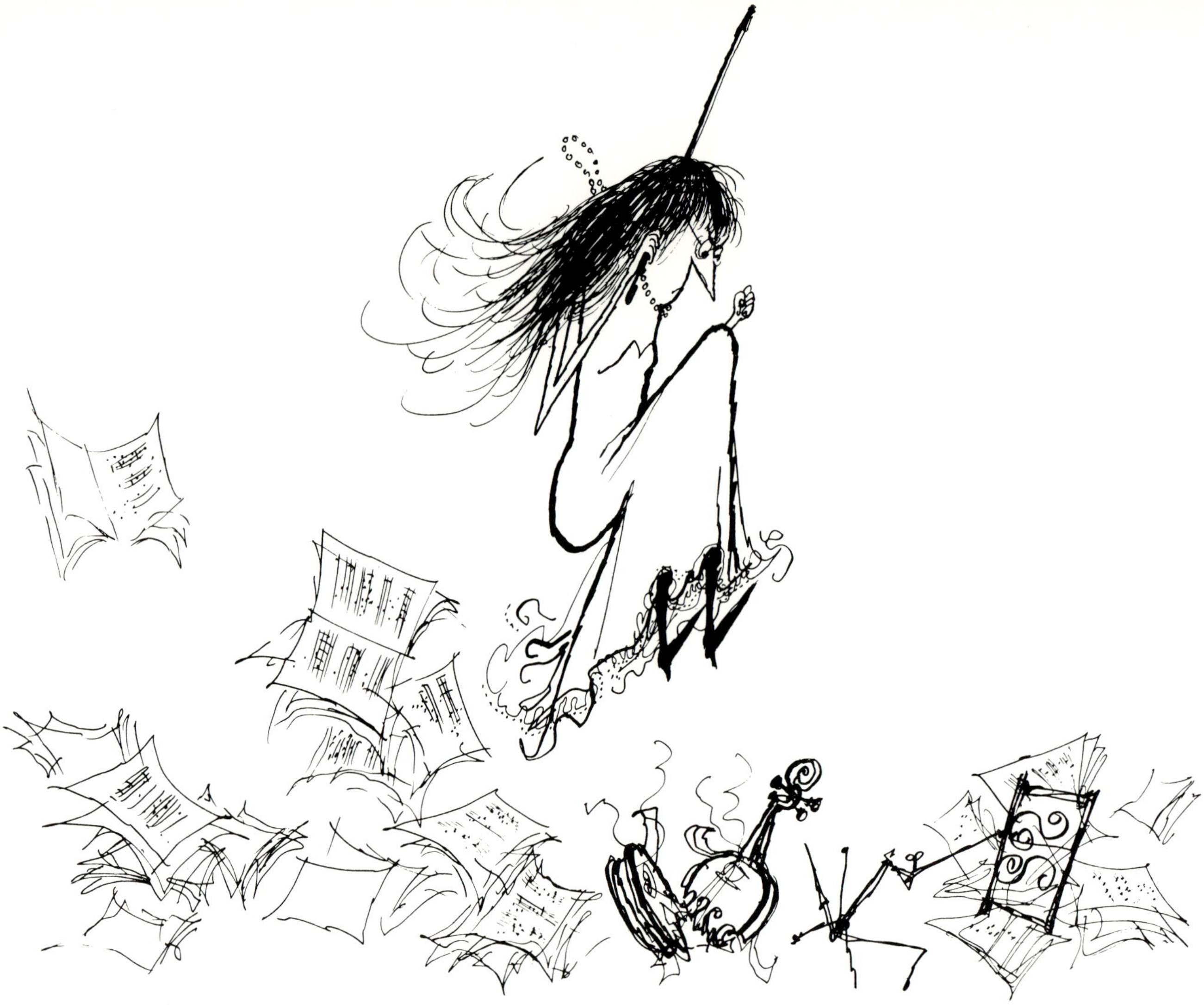

'Shitty Stockhausen!'

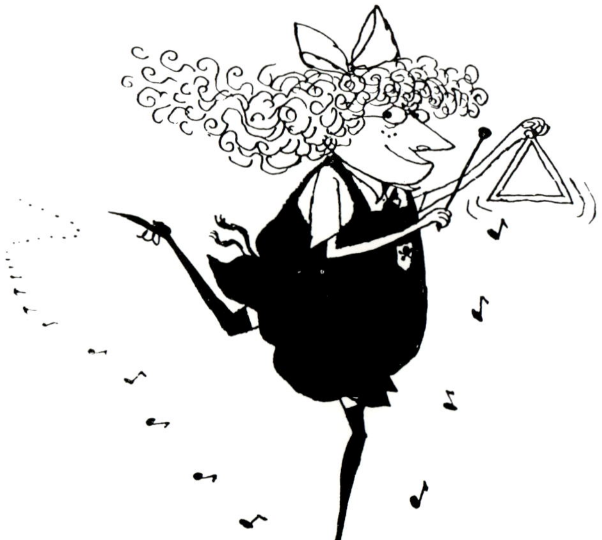

[1953]

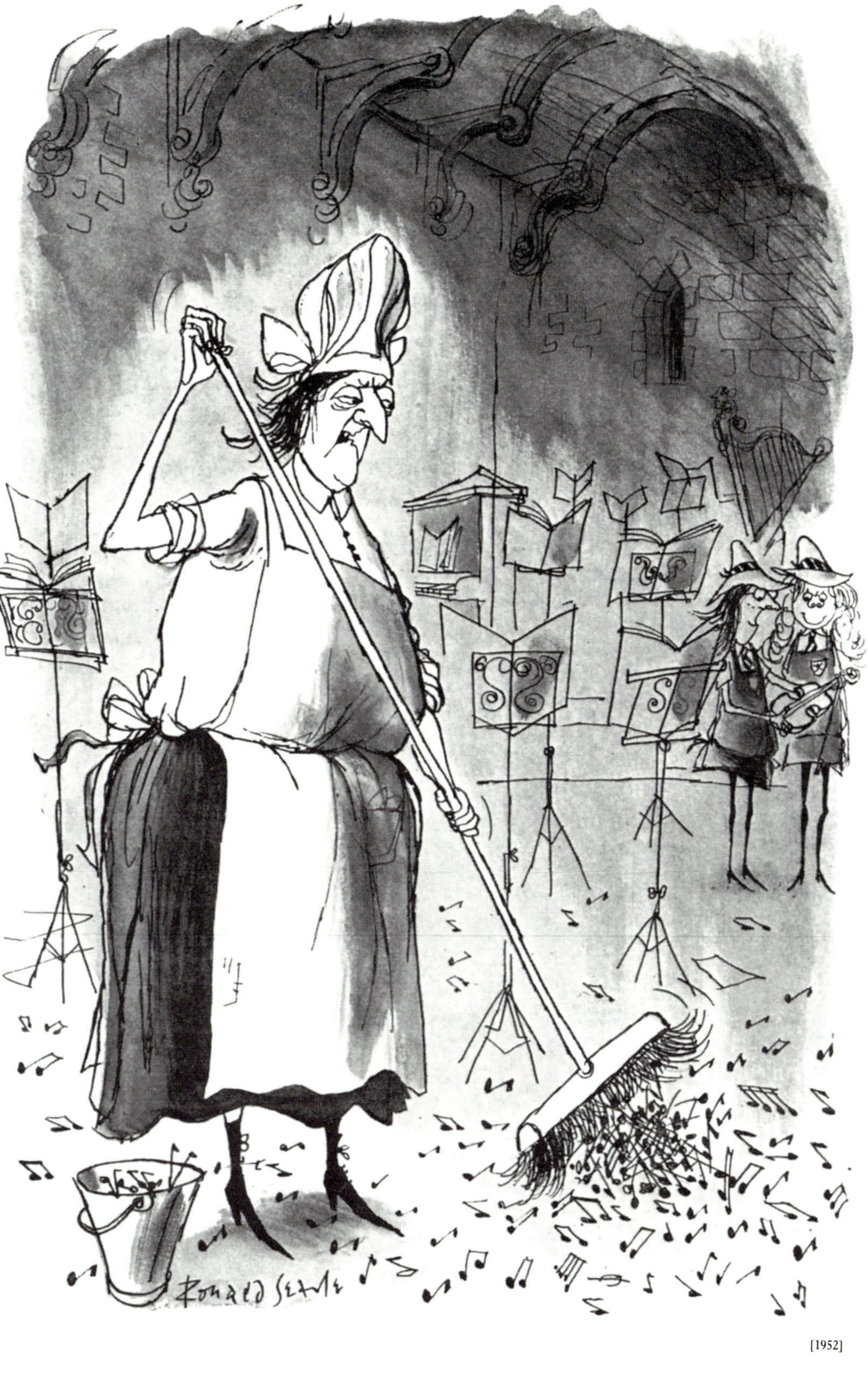
RONALD SEARLE

[1952]

'Ruddy music lessons...'

'Playing with lethal weapons, a boy of your age…'

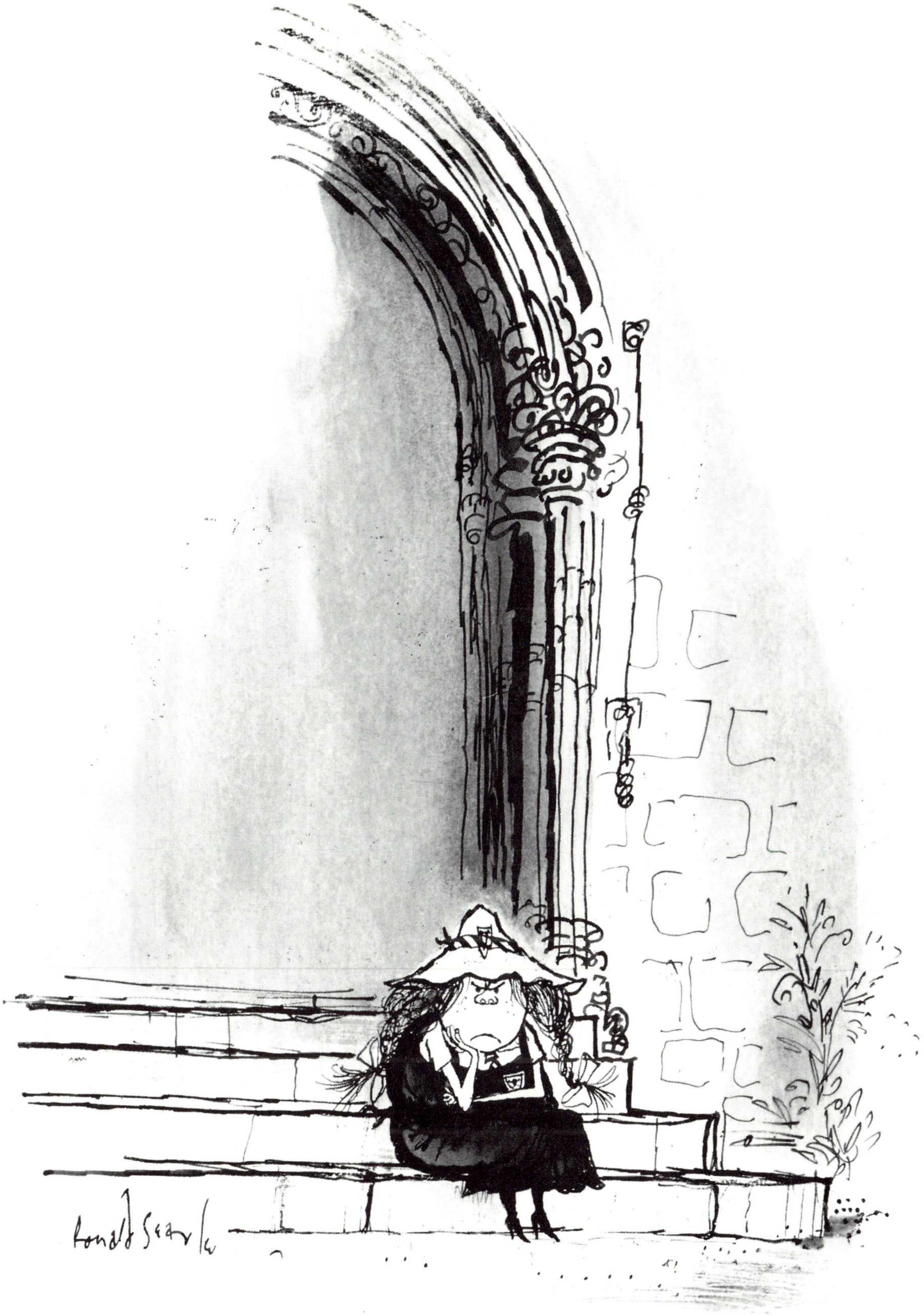

[1947]

'I'll just die and then you'll be sorry.'

[1953]

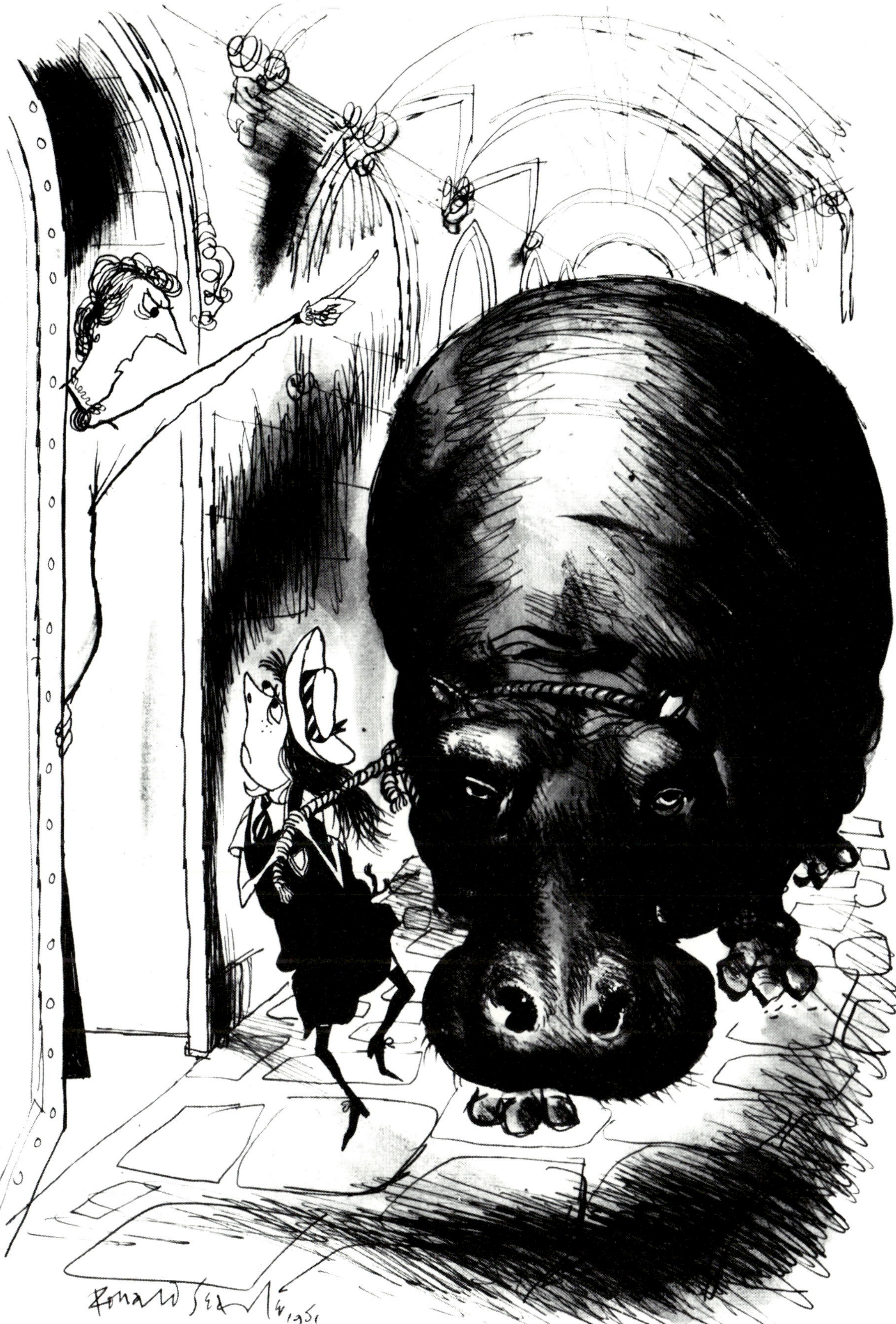

'Elspeth! Put that back AT ONCE.'

[1953]

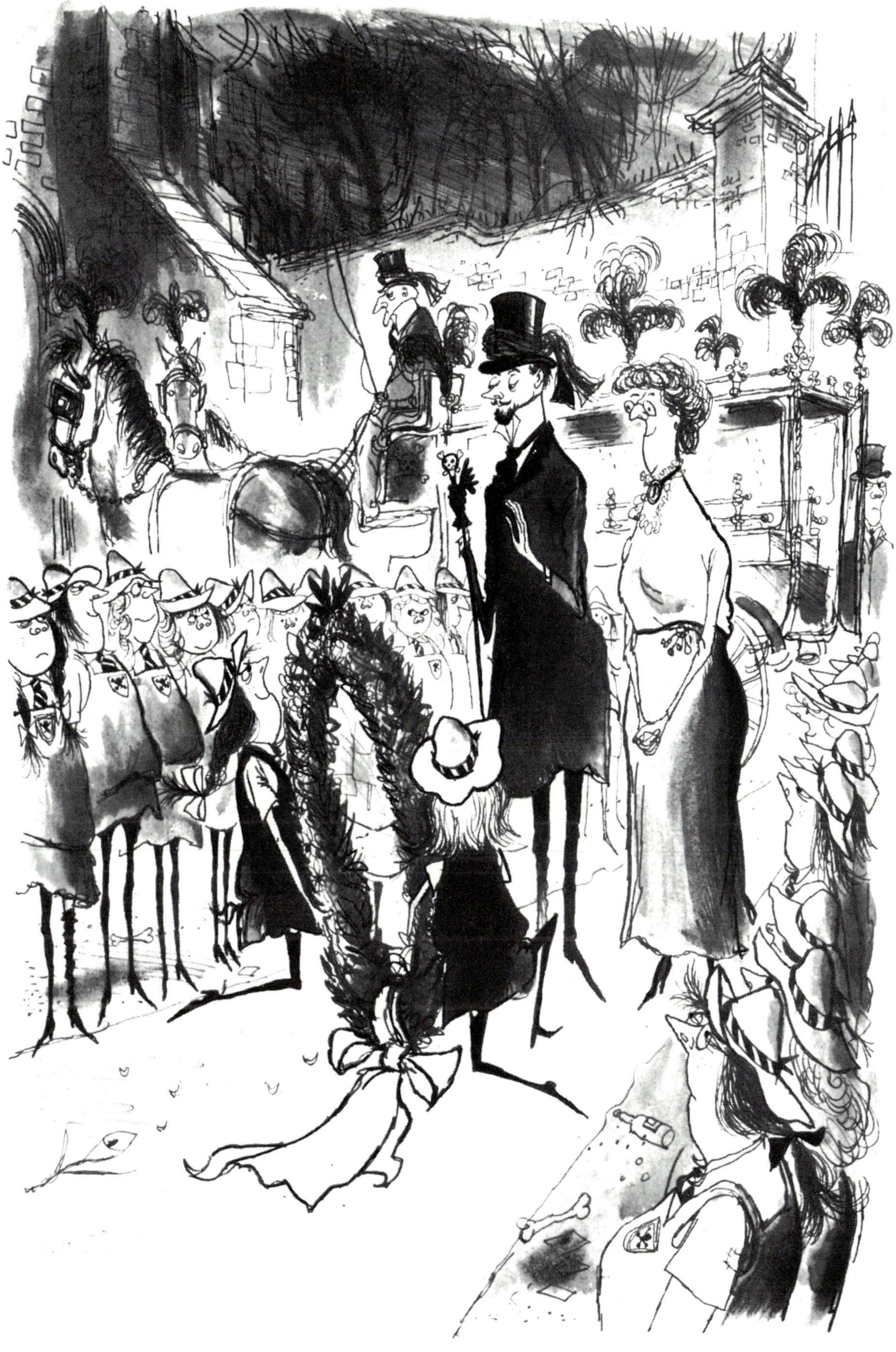

[1952]

Founder's Day

[1953]

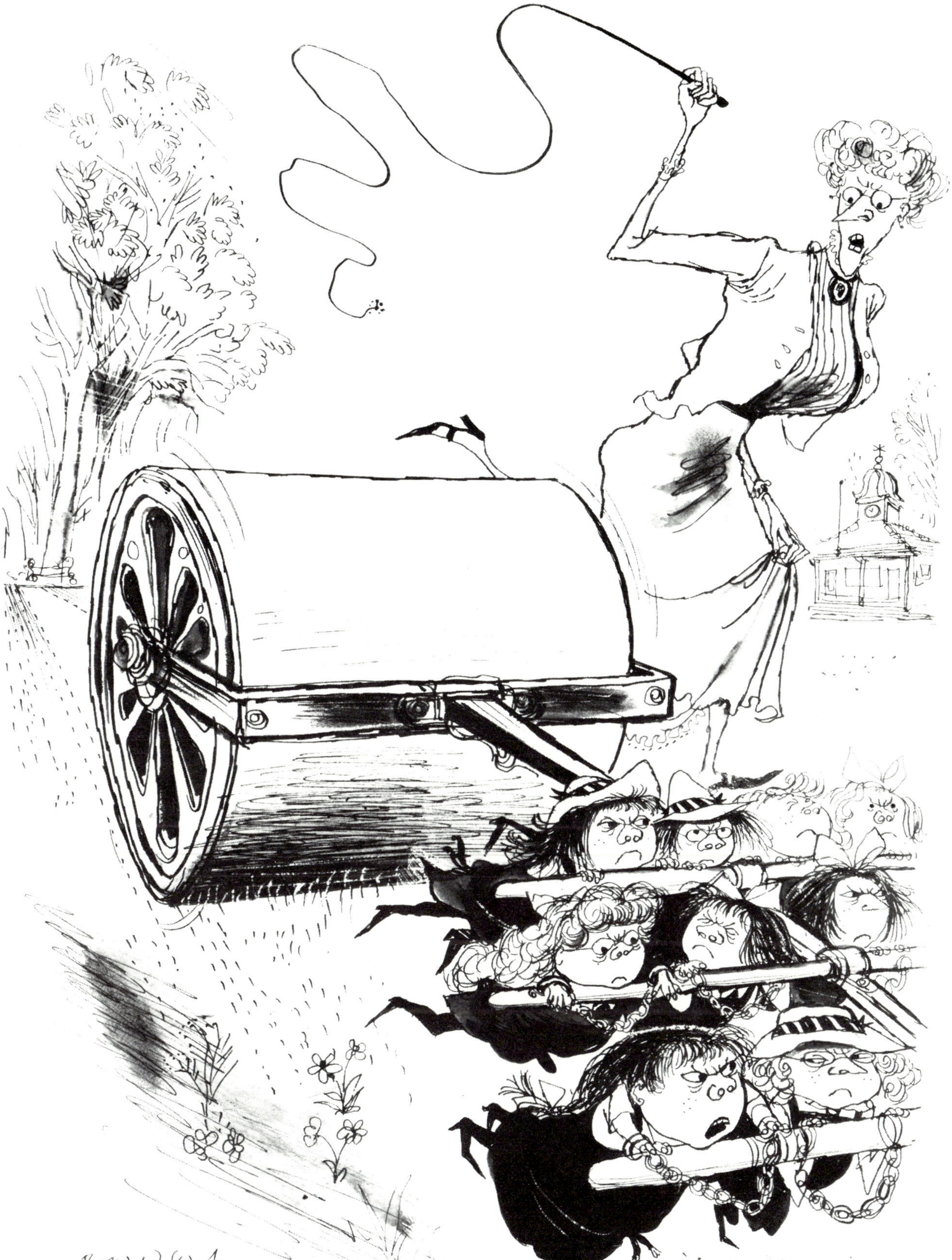
Ronald Searle

[1952]

'Bloody sportsdays...'

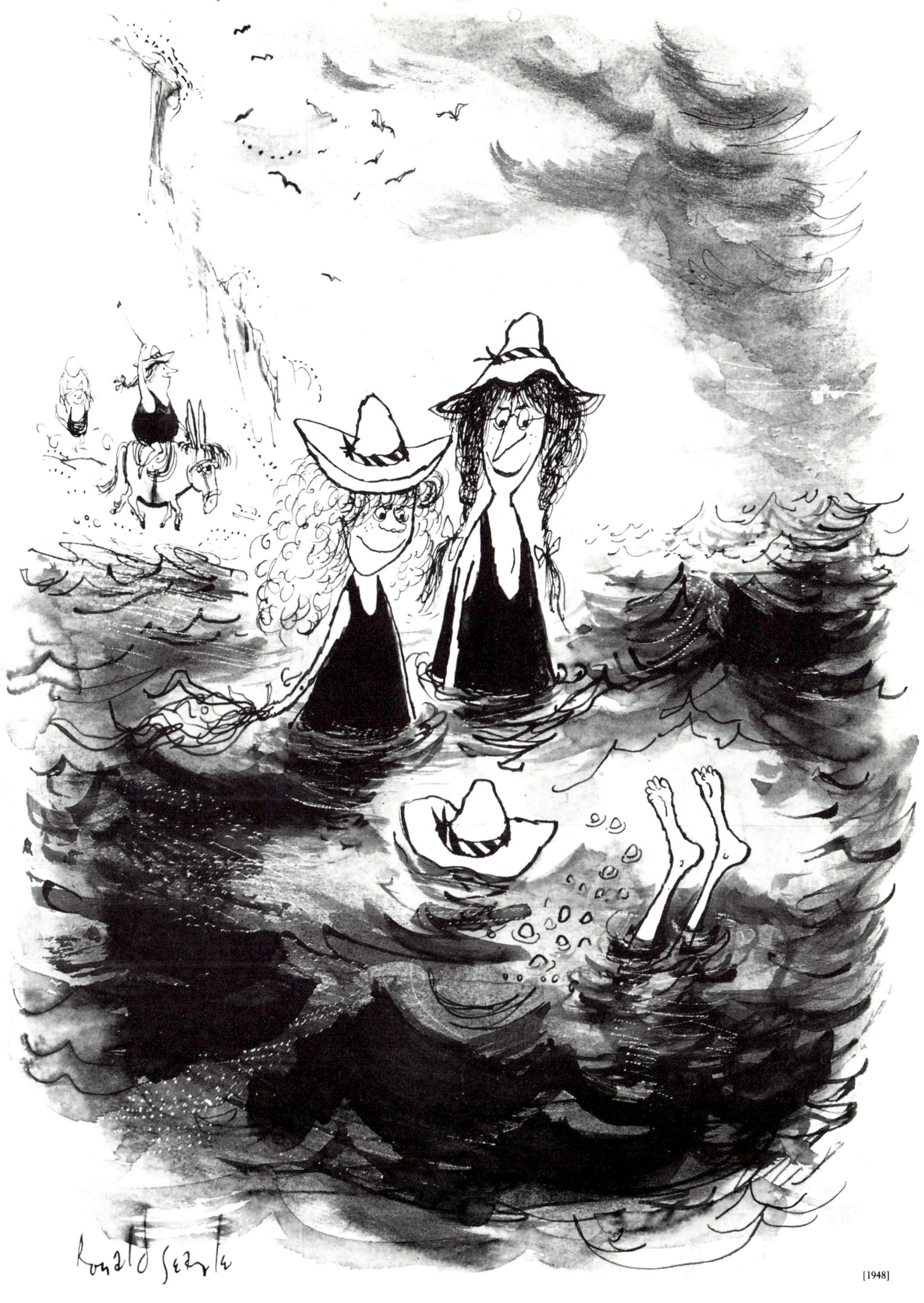
Ronald Searle

[1948]

'I didn't realise it took so long.'

PS

[1981] Some corner of a foreign field that is for ever England...

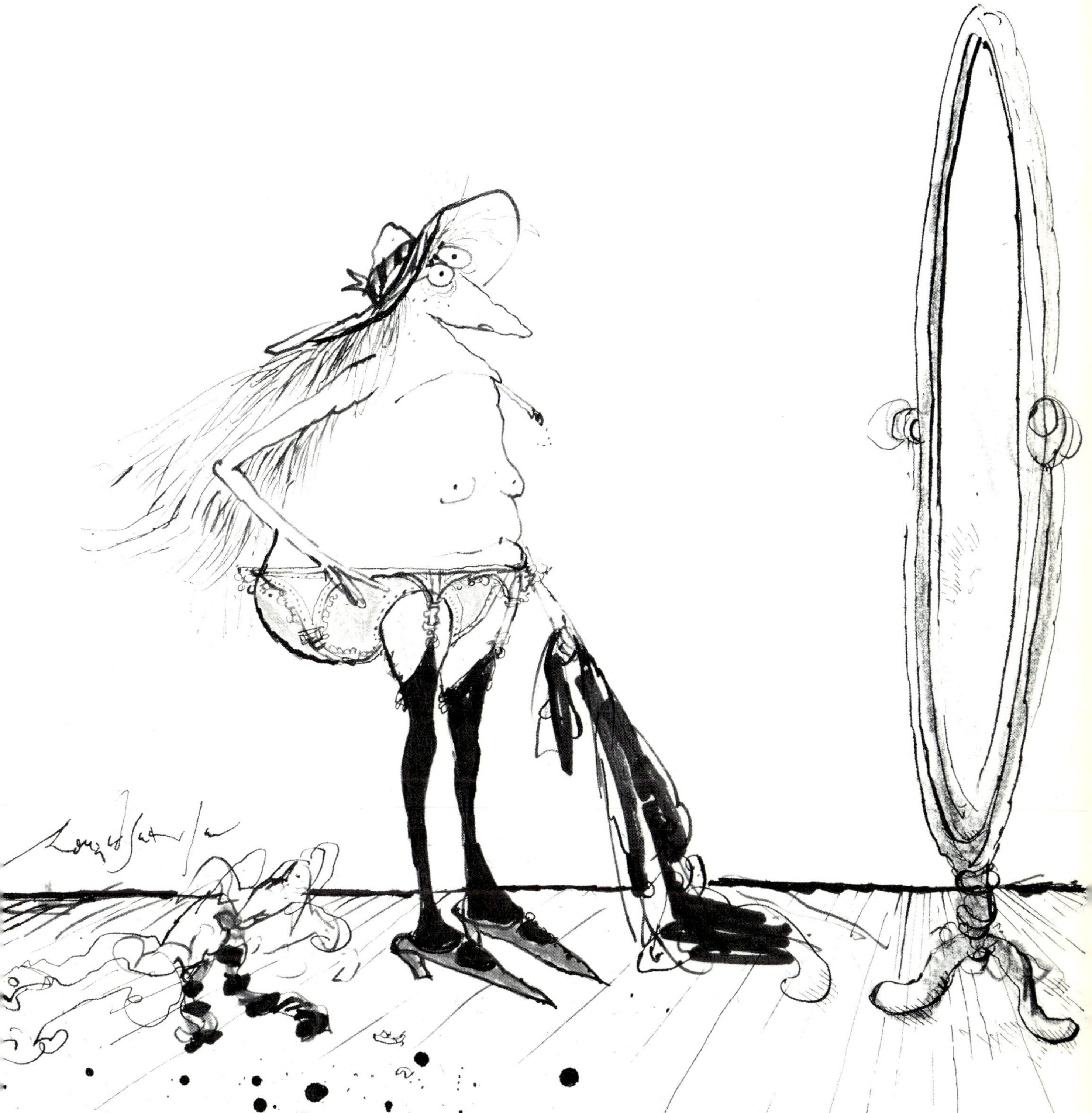

[Telescopic photo, taken through the window of the ladies' room of a well-known Port Said hostelry.]

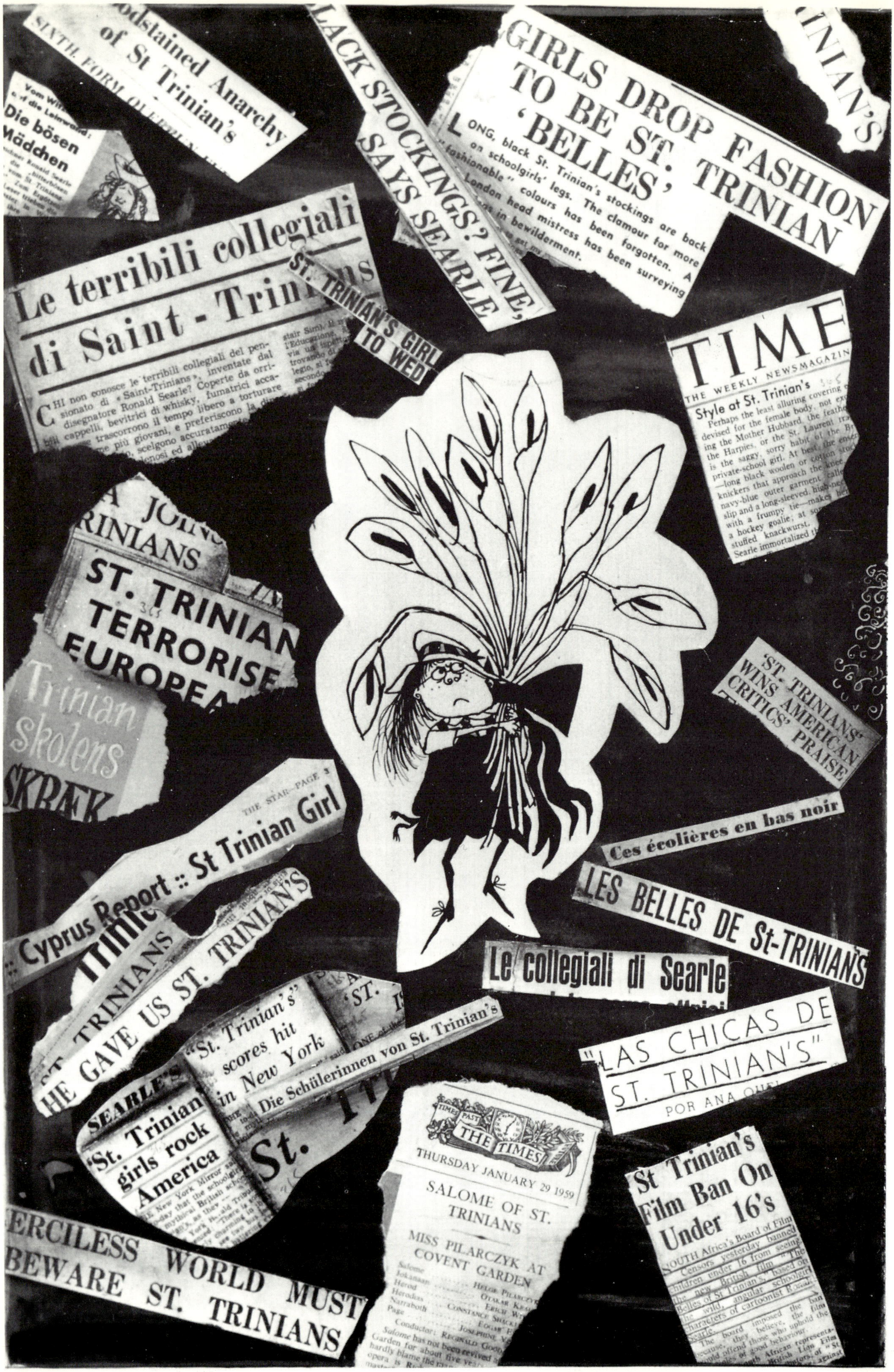
of St Trinian's
GIRLS DROP FASHION TO BE ST. TRINIAN 'BELLES'
Die bösen Mädchen
Le terribili collegiali di Saint-Trinians
ST. TRINIAN'S GIRL TO WED
TIME
THE WEEKLY NEWSMAGAZINE
Style at St. Trinian's
RINIANS
ST. TRINIAN TERRORISE EUROPEA
Trinian skolens SKRÆK
'ST. TRINIANS' WINS AMERICAN CRITICS' PRAISE
THE STAR—PAGE 3
St Trinian Girl
Ces écolières en bas noir
Cyprus Report :: St Trinian's
LES BELLES DE St-TRINIAN'S
TRINIANS
HE GAVE US ST. TRINIAN'S
Le collegiali di Searle
"St. Trinian's" scores hit in New York
Die Schülerinnen von St. Trinian's
"LAS CHICAS DE ST. TRINIAN'S"
SEARLE'S
'St. Trinian girls rock America
THE TIMES
THURSDAY JANUARY 29 1959
SALOME OF ST. TRINIANS
MISS PILARCZYK AT COVENT GARDEN
St Trinian's Film Ban On Under 16's
MERCILESS WORLD MUST BEWARE ST. TRINIANS

SOURCES

[1952]

Endpapers-illustrated magazine, 22 December 1951. Page 1-1953, for Souls in Torment. 2-1960, for Which Way Did He Go? 4-1956, for Merry England, etc. 5-1953, for Souls in Torment. 7-1955, for Merry England, etc. 8-(top) Lilliput, October 1941; (bottom) 1945, first published The Female Approach. 9-Lilliput, October 1941. 10-(top) drawn Changi Gaol 1944, first published in Les Lettres Françaises, 20 December 1946; (bottom) Les Lettres Françaises, 13 December 1946. 11-Drawn Changi Gaol 1945, first published Lilliput, January 1946. 12-(top) Lilliput, February 1947; (bottom) Drawn Changi Gaol 1944, first published The Tatler, 9 January 1946. 13-(top) Drawn Changi Gaol, 1944, first published The Female Approach; (bottom) First version published Punch, 5 March 1947. 14-(top) Drawn Changi Gaol 1944, published London Opinion, August 1946; (bottom) First version published Lilliput, April 1942. 15-Drawn Changi Gaol 1944, published Lilliput, August 1946. 16-Summer Pie, 1948. 17-(top) Drawn Changi Gaol 1944, published London Opinion, September 1947; (bottom) Les Lettres Françaises, 1946. 18-(top) Lilliput 194(7); (middle) Lilliput 194(7); (bottom) Lilliput, December 1947. 19-(top) Lilliput, December 1947; (bottom left) Lilliput, 194(7); (bottom right) Christmas Pie, December 1948. 20-Pie, 194(?). 21-1949. Another version used as Lilliput cover, September 1950. 22-The Tribune, 15 June 1951. 23-Drawn Changi Gaol 1945, published Souls in Torment. 24-Punch, 14 December 1955. 25-The Sketch, 6 December 1950. 26-News Chronicle, 12 June 1954. 27-News Chronicle, 10 July 1954. 28-1952, for Souls in Torment. 29-News Chronicle, 28 August 1954. 30-News Chronicle, 22 May 1954. 31-News Chronicle, 25 September 1954. 32-33-1952, for Souls in Torment. 34-1952, for Souls in Torment. 35-Punch, 2 October 1957. 36-37-1952, for Souls in Torment. 38-News Chronicle, 30 October 1954. 39-Punch, 9 June 1954. 40-44-Punch, 10 April 1957. 45-1952, for Souls in Torment. 46-1952, for Perpetua Books. 47-Greetings card 195(3). 48-Punch, 14 March 1956. 49-(top) 1952, for Souls in Torment; (bottom) 1952, for Souls in Torment. 50-Punch, 14 March 1956. 51-(top) 1955 for Merry England, etc.; (bottom) News Chronicle, 21 August 1954. 52-53-Punch, 14 March 1956. 54-1952, for Souls in Torment. 55-1952, for Souls in Torment. 56-News Chronicle, 16 July 1954. 57-News Chronicle, 26 June 1954. 58-Punch, 15 February 1956. 59-61 (top) Punch, 21 December 1955; 61-(bottom) News Chronicle, 16 October 1954. 62-Time & Tide, 19 February 1954. 63-Punch, 2 January 1957. 64-News Chronicle, 14 August 1954. 65-News Chronicle, 2 October 1954. 66-1952, for Souls in Torment. 67-68-69 (top)-70-71-1952, for Tony Godwin & Better Books advertising; 69-(bottom) 1951 W.H.Smith's Trade Circular. 72-1952, for Souls in Torment. 73-(top) 1952, for Souls in Torment (bottom) Punch, 4 January 1956. 74-78-Punch, 29 February 1956. 79-(top) Punch, 28 June 1961; (middle) Holiday Magazine, USA, July 1960; (bottom) Punch, 28 June 1961. 80-Punch, 8 May 1957. 81-Punch, 20 August 1958. 82-1952, for Souls in Torment. 83-1953, for Souls in Torment. 84-1952, for The Terror of St Trinian's. 85-1959 for The St Trinian's Story. 86-(top) 1959, for The St Trinian's Story; (bottom) Greetings card design 195(?). 87-1953, for Souls in Torment. 88-Drawn in Changi Gaol 1944, published Lilliput, April 1946. 89-(top) Lilliput, July 1946; (bottom) Lilliput, October 1947. 90-Lilliput, May 1947. 91-(top) Lilliput, September 1948; (bottom) Lilliput, May 1948. 92-Lilliput, January 1951. 93-Lilliput, April 1948. 94-Lilliput 1950. 95-Lilliput 1950. 96-(top) Lilliput, January 1949; (bottom) Lilliput, September 1949. 97-Lilliput, March 1952. 98-Lilliput, September 1949. 99-Lilliput 1951. 100-Lilliput 1951. 101-Lilliput, October 1950. 102-Lilliput, January 1951. 103-Lilliput, August 1950. 104-(top) 1959 for The St Trinian's Story; (bottom) Greetings card design, 195(?). 105-(top) Lilliput, May 1949; (bottom) Greetings card design, 195(?). 106-Lilliput, October 1950. 107-Lilliput, 195(1). 108-Lilliput, July 1951. 109-Lilliput, October 1950. 110-1959, for The St Trinian's Story. 111-(top) Lilliput, November 1950; (bottom) 1953 for Souls in Torment. 112-1953 for Souls in Torment. 113-Lilliput, January 1952. 114-(top) Lilliput, April 1951; (bottom) France Dimanche, 28 May 1950. 115-Lilliput, April 1951. 116-Lilliput, October 1950. 117-Lilliput, 1951. Original Victoria & Albert Museum, London, (E.5492-1958). 118-1953, for Souls in Torment. 119-Lilliput, October 1951. 120-(top) Lilliput, March 1951; (bottom) Lilliput, April 1951. 121-Lilliput, March 1951. 122-(top) 1959, for The St Trinian's Story; (middle) Greetings card design 195(?); (bottom) 1953, for Souls in Torment. 123-Lilliput, April 1952. Original Victoria & Albert Museum, London, (e.5491-1958). 124-1953, for Souls in Torment. 125-Lilliput, November 1951. 126-Design for an ashtray, Copenhagen, 1957. 127-Lilliput, September 1951. 128-(top) Greetings card design 195(?); (bottom) 1953, for Souls in Torment. 129-Lilliput, February 1952.

130-Lilliput, April 1950. 131-Lilliput, December 1947. 132-1953, for Souls in Torment. 133-Lilliput, August 1951. 134-1953, for Souls in Torment. 135-Lilliput, December 1951. 136-1953, for Souls in Torment. 137-Lilliput, May 1952. 138-1953, for Souls in Torment. 139-Lilliput, August 1948. 141-1981. First published Ronald Searle in Perspective, 1984. 142-1953, collage for Souls in Torment. 143-144-illustration for The Terror of St Trinian's, 1952.

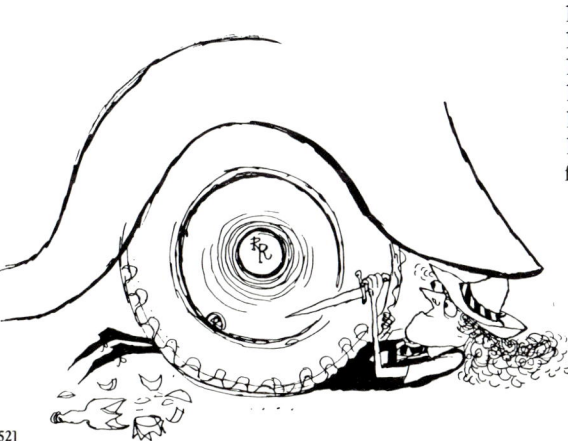

[1952]

[1952]

'Cynthia, you really *are* The End.'

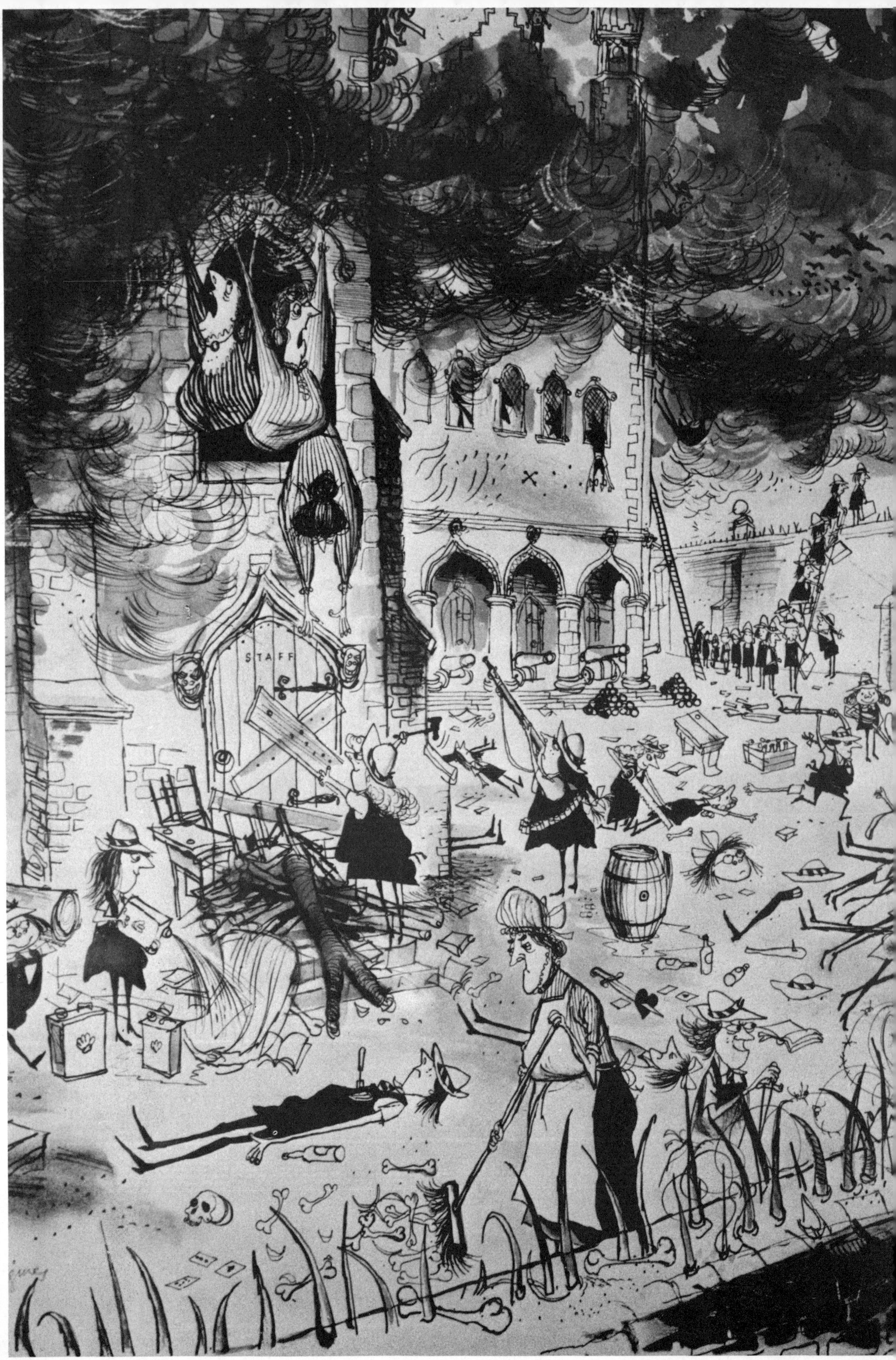
STAFF